Understanding and Treating Depression

**Recent Titles in
Abnormal Psychology**

Mental Disorders of the New Millennium, Volumes 1–3
Thomas G. Plante, editor

Bleeding to Ease the Pain: Cutting, Self-Injury, and the Adolescent
Lori G. Plante

UNDERSTANDING AND TREATING DEPRESSION

Ways to Find Hope and Help

Rudy Nydegger

Abnormal Psychology
Thomas G. Plante, Series Editor

PRAEGER

**Westport, Connecticut
London**

Library of Congress Cataloging-in-Publication Data

Nydegger, Rudy V., 1943–
  Understanding and treating depression : ways to find hope and
help / Rudy Nydegger.
        p. ; cm. — (Abnormal psychology, ISSN 1554–2238)
  Includes bibliographical references and index.
  ISBN-13: 978–0–275–99856–1 (alk. paper)
  1. Depression, Mental. 2. Depression, Mental—Treatment.
[DNLM: 1. Depressive Disorder. WM 171 N993u 2008] I. Title.
II. Abnormal psychology (Westport, Conn.)
  RC537.N93 2008
  616.85′27—dc22   2008017594

British Library Cataloguing in Publication Data is available.

Library of Congress Catalog Card Number: 2008017594

ISBN: 978–0–275–99856–1
ISSN: 1554–2238

First published in 2008

Praeger Publishers, 88 Post Road West, Westport, CT 06881
An imprint of Greenwood Publishing Group, Inc.
www.praeger.com

Printed in the United States of America

The paper used in this book complies with the
Permanent Paper Standard issued by the National
Information Standards Organization (Z39.48–1984).

10 9 8 7 6 5 4 3 2 1

This book is dedicated to the millions of people who suffer from mood disorders on a daily basis and who find the courage to battle this formidable adversary, even when it feels hopeless.

Contents

Series Foreword

Depression touches the lives of everyone. In addition to those who suffer from this challenging mental health condition, there are many who live or work closely with those who experience the symptoms of depression. It is a disorder that can be deadly and has been closely linked to numerous life-threatening conditions such as suicide, homicide, alcoholism, cardiovascular disease, and accidents, to name just a few. Although depression impacts all of us in one way or another, there are many myths and misconceptions about it that continue to be widely accepted by the general public as well as among many health care professionals. Furthermore, it is remarkable that, unlike much of the world, our society is fortunate to enjoy a generally very high standard of living, many modern conveniences, and outstanding state-of-the-art diagnosis and treatment of medical and psychological conditions, yet, depression is not only prevalent in our privileged community but is on the rise. It is especially disturbing that depression is so common among young people including children and teens.

In this book, Dr. Rudy Nydegger well articulates what is known about depression and what we can do about it. We all could benefit from Dr. Nydegger's thoughtful, scholarly, and engaging book in order to not only better understand this challenging condition but perhaps be better able to help ourselves if we suffer from depression, or to help others with whom we live or work. Dr. Nydegger is the right person, with many years of experience, to offer this book on depression at the right time when it is so critical that we all better understand this problem. Hopefully, many will benefit from this important work. The book can contribute to saving and preserving lives, and I am grateful that it is now available to the public and professionals alike.

Thomas G. Plante, Ph.D., ABPP
Santa Clara University and
Stanford University School of Medicine
Praeger Series Editor, Abnormal Psychology series
April 2008

Preface

It is a positive and active anguish, a sort of psychical neuralgia wholly unknown to normal life.
                                                              —William James

I am now the most miserable man living. If what I feel were equally distributed to the whole human family, there would not be a cheerful face on earth.
                                                              —Abraham Lincoln

Depression has very likely been part of human experience since the beginning of history. Interestingly, depression is one of those emotional states that is common to all people to a greater or lesser degree; yet, not all people suffer from what we call *clinical depression*. Because all of us have experienced being depressed about something, or just simply have been in a miserable mood, we might feel that we understand what it is to be truly depressed. Often we hear people refer to clinical depression, but it is not always clear what they mean. *Clinical depression* refers to any depressive state that reaches the threshold meeting the diagnostic criteria used to make a clinical diagnosis. We discuss these criteria in depth in Chapter 4 of this book, but basically, clinical depression is more than being in a bad mood or having a "down period" in our lives. When depression interferes with our ability to carry on our personal, social, and work lives and prevents us from enjoying the things in life that usually bring us pleasure, then we start to be concerned that we may be dealing with a clinical depression.

While many people think of depression as a unitary type of disorder, in reality, it is a type of mood disorder that exists on a continuum from mild to very severe. Depression is also represented in qualitatively different types of mood disorders and may be a part of other psychological and medical conditions as well.

When listening to a person who is suffering from a serious mood disorder, such as depression, it is clear they are dealing with something quite different from the experience of someone who is burdened by a less serious type of mood disruption. Some have referred to depression as "the common cold of mental health." However, depression is not as mild or as time-limited as a cold. Sometimes depression will disrupt—even destroy—the lives of those who suffer from it.

Many people, including numerous public figures, have helped us to understand depression and other serious mood disorders by sharing their own experiences. For example, some people who suffer from serious depression or other mood disorders include:

Buzz Aldrin: American astronaut and the second man to walk on the moon
Woody Allen: American film director/actor/comedian
Terry Bradshaw: American Hall of Fame Football player, TV sports commentator, and actor
Jim Carrey: Canadian actor/comedian
Winston Churchill: British Prime Minister during World War II
Kurt Cobain: American musician
Joseph Conrad: American writer
Sheryl Crow: American musician
Charles Darwin: British biologist
Charles Dickens: British writer
Thomas Eagleton: former American Senator and Vice-Presidential candidate
Carrie Fisher: American actress
Paul Gauguin: French painter
Vincent Van Gogh: Dutch painter
Tipper Gore: wife of former Senator and Presidential candidate Al Gore
Earnest Hemingway: American writer
William James: American philosopher and psychologist
Ashley Judd: American actress
Søren Kierkegaard: Danish philosopher
Abraham Lincoln: former American President
Martin Luther: German priest and philosopher
Herman Melville: American writer
Michaelangelo: Italian painter and sculptor
Kate Millett: feminist theorist, literary critic, essayist, and sculptress
Wolfgang Amadeus Mozart: Austrian composer
Isaac Newton: British physicist
Friedrich Nietzche: German philosopher

Edgar Allan Poe: American writer
Brook Shields: American actress
Rod Steiger: American actor
William Styron: American writer
James Taylor: American composer and musician
Leo Tolstoy: Russian writer
Mark Twain: American writer and humorist
Mike Wallace: American journalist and host of *60 Minutes*
Virginia Woolf: American writer, literary and social critic[1]

Although the list is long, and assuredly incomplete, it gives you an idea of the breadth and significance of depression while demonstrating how people with a serious mood disorder can transcend it and become successful. Tragically, this list also includes some exceptional talents whose lives were cut short by suicide, a result of their mood disorder. This list also suggests a relationship between creativity and "madness," and many believe that creativity and genius often coexist with mental disorders; a belief fostered by the many artists and creative people who have suffered from mental illness. However, there is no evidence that creative people are more at risk than others, or that psychological disturbance is a requirement for creativity. In fact, it is true that mild disturbance is more likely to be related to creativity than severe disorders.[2]

When we examine the impact of depression on the lives of those who have experienced it, it is clear that the real human cost is staggering and is one of the most important health concerns in the world today. According to the World Health Organization (WHO),[3] unipolar depression is predicted to become the second leading cause of global disability burden by the year 2020. As we discuss later, depression is twice as common in women as men, and the WHO expects this trend to continue. Presently, major depression is the leading cause of disease burden among females over the age of five worldwide,[4] and in the United States alone, depression directly and indirectly costs tens of billions of dollars every year.[5]

There is no doubt that depression is a costly and intrusive disorder—or rather, a family of disorders—that impacts many people, families, organizations, and societies around the world on a daily basis. In fact, because much of mental illness, including depression, goes unreported and untreated, we are only seeing the tip of the iceberg in our studies and statistics. Kessler et al.[6] estimate that less than 22% of people with depression receive adequate treatment, and that is in the United States alone. What we are finding is that depression is a problem all over the world, within all cultures, and in developed and developing nations alike. As one might expect, the reporting of disease and other conditions is less reliable in developing countries, and it is difficult to accurately estimate the magnitude of this problem in these areas, but new and better studies are starting to emerge.

This book examines depression in a way that clarifies this complex and difficult problem, and it examines various perspectives and models as well as different groups and demographic categories. Beginning with a definition, we then move into the direct and indirect costs of depression as they relate to families and communities.

We also explore a description of the history and experiences of four persons who have chosen to share their experiences of living with depression. These courageous people offer us hope that others, too, can emerge from the pit of depression to live a full and meaningful life. When one is in the depths of despair, it is difficult to imagine that you will ever feel normal again, but the countless people who have been successfully treated for serious mood disorders are testimony to the hope that exists today for the treatment of these conditions.

The next part of the book examines who is likely to develop depression and how the rates of depression are distributed among people in the United States and around the world. We examine the differing rates of depression between these groups and try to understand why some of these differences exist. Hopefully, by looking at the distribution of depression, we will gain a better understanding of the condition, its treatment, and its prevention. In addition to looking at the rates of depression, we also examine various types of depression and how they differ from one another.

Next, we examine the different theories and models of depression, including psychological, biological, and sociological/cultural models; modern thinking about depression concludes that all of these factors are important. This book does not intend to prove which of the models is correct but rather to show which parts of the different models are supported by research and which are not. It is hoped that you, the reader, will be able to construct your own "theory" of depression that makes sense to you. As such, this is not a doctrinaire "point of view" book that is trying to sell a particular model but rather a compilation of the best information from many sources and perspectives to shed some light on the mysteries of depression.

We then look at special patient characteristics including gender, age, race and ethnicity, and sexual orientation and how they interact with depression. We know that anyone can be susceptible to depression, but we see that there are also some interesting differences between groups.

The next part of the book examines the traditional forms of psychological and medical treatments and what the research evidence tells us about their effectiveness and utility. We go into the different types of psychotherapeutic approaches as well as a variety of medical treatments for depression. We examine the medications that are available, which ones are used most frequently and why, as well as other forms of medical treatment including: electroconvulsive therapy, vagus nerve stimulation, magnetic therapies, surgery, and other new and experimental techniques. We also look at topics that have been introduced into the nutritional and food additive areas and what kinds of treatments or supplemental therapies have come from them. One important area in the understanding of depression is how it tends to accompany other psychological and medical disorders and how these conditions interact and affect one another, and we examine this as well.

The last part of the book discusses some of the controversies surrounding the different treatments and how research and practice has begun to understand and settle on strategies that appear to be the most effective in treating depression. The advantages and disadvantages of different types of treatments are discussed along with the considerations to be examined when selecting a treatment modality. Finally, we look at the "common sense" things that people can do to help themselves in dealing with depression. Of course, these suggestions are not intended to replace professional treatment but are expected to give individuals an active role in their own recovery.

Information derived from the current professional literature is also presented in order to enable the reader to critically evaluate different ideas and approaches to the understanding of depression. Following the last chapter, there is a complete set of recommended readings and Web sites that can help you learn more about depression, its nature, and its treatment. Whether you are endeavoring to learn more about this important topic or are looking for information to help yourself or someone else, we hope that you find this book a valuable resource.

Acknowledgments

Of course, any work as time-consuming and involved as a book is never the product of a single person. I would particularly like to thank several people whose ideas and suggestions significantly improved this book. First, my wife, Karen, is a painstakingly thorough proofreader and copy editor who made sure that I remembered the audience I was trying to reach and who was always able to find ways to clarify my language and improve the delivery. This work is far better because of her help.

My kids all contributed something as well. Ashley's artistic genius provided some insights and suggestions for themes and graphic designs that were truly inspiring. Morgen—always a source of encouragement and support—was there with a pat on the back and even a kick in the pants when needed. Colby thoroughly, accurately, and intelligently provided clerical support and was always a cheerleader for my efforts. Liesl asked the right questions, provided clerical support, and always kept me on my toes with questions and ideas. Austin, my only child still at home, continually reminded me of all that is truly important and kept me grounded on a daily basis. I must also mention the two guys in my life that are the future of our family—my grandsons, Lucas and Sammy; they, too, always remind me of what matters most.

Finally, my editor, Debbie Carvalko, is someone I sincerely appreciate and respect. She asked the questions that need asking, provided ideas and information when requested, guided gently but meaningfully, and never intruded—what a gift. To all of you, "Thanks."

Abbreviations

In the book we refer to many different diagnoses, organizations, and technical terms. To make it somewhat easier to read, we rely on abbreviations. In every case, the abbreviation is not used before the term is introduced, and then the abbreviation is introduced. However, if you are reading and you come across an abbreviation that you don't recognize or remember, we thought that it would be helpful to have one central spot where you could check the meaning of any single abbreviation. We hope this is helpful.

AA   Alcoholics Anonymous
ABFT   attachment-based family therapy
AD   atypical depression
ADD   attention deficit disorder
ADDM   adjustment disorder with depressed mood
ADHD   attention–deficit/hyperactivity disorder
ApA   American Pyschiatric Association
APA   American Psychological Association
BA   behavioral activation
BATD   brief behavioral activation treatment for depression
BPD   bipolar disorder
BPDI   bipolar I disorder
BPDII   bipolar II disorder
CBT   cognitive-behavioral therapy
CNS   central nervous system
CTD   cyclothymic disorder
DBSA   Depression and Bipolar Support Alliance
DD   dysthymic disorder
DHA   ducosahexanoic acid
DPD   depressive personality disorder

DRI   dopamine reuptake inhibitor
EAP   Employee Assistance Program
ECT   electroconvulsive therapy
ED   erectile dysfunction
EPA   eicosapentanoic acid
FDA   Food and Drug Administration
HMO   Health Maintenance Organization
IPT   Interpersonal Psychotherapy
LGB   lesbian, gay, and bisexual
MAO   monoamine oxidase
MAOI   monoamine oxidase inhibitor
MDD   major depressive disorder
NIH   National Institutes of Health
NIMH   National Institute of Mental Health
NP   nurse practitioner
PA   physician's assistant
PCP   primary care physician
PMDD   premenstrual dysphoric disorder
PMS   premenstrual syndrome
PPD   postpartum depression
PPP   postpartum psychosis
PTSD   post-traumatic stress disorder
REM   rapid eye movement
rTMS   rapid transcranial magnetic stimulation
SAD   seasonal affective disorder
SAM-e   S-adenosylmethionine
SES   socioeconomic status
SJW   St. John's Wort
SNRI   serotonin and norepinephrine reuptake inhibitor
SSRI   selective serotonin reuptake inhibitor
VNS   vagus nerve stimulation
WHO   World Health Organization

Chapter 1

What Is Depression?

When depression is stigmatized as illness and weakness, a double bind is cre-
ated: If we admit to depression, we will be stigmatized by others; if we feel
it but do not admit it, we stigmatize ourselves, internalizing the social judg-
ment . . . The only remaining choice may be truly sick behavior: to experience
no emotion at all.

       —Lesley Hazelton, former psychologist and writer

If depression is creeping up and must be faced, learn something about the na-
ture of the beast: You may escape without a mauling.

            —Dr. R. W. Shepard

Depression is an equal opportunity disorder—it can affect anyone of any group,
any background, any race, any gender, any age—anyone. It is the great leveler of all
groups and can take the greatest and the smallest of us all and reduce us to the pain
and nothingness that is depression.

  The experience of depression clearly has a profound impact on the lives
and health of millions of people all around the world. Of course, all of us have,
from time to time, experienced mood swings, and we may believe that we, too,
have experienced true depression, or that we understand what it feels like.
To have experienced a difficult or traumatic event, to have had a significant
disappointment, to have lost someone close to us through death, to have a
relationship fail—all of these things can impact us and lead to emotional reactions that certainly feel like and might actually develop into depression. As
discussed in this chapter, depression is more than just experiencing a difficult
day or event or being in a miserable mood. In fact, many times people seek
help as a result of problems that they experience and the emotional impact
these events produce. Whether or not the symptoms reach the threshold of

being a diagnosable clinical depression, it is irrelevant to the person who is experiencing them—they simply feel significantly depressed and want some help. From a treatment point of view, it is helpful to know precisely what led the person to seek help and what conditions preceded this decision. Having a complete and accurate picture of the disorder and what symptoms are being experienced will hopefully lead to a diagnosis that will help to understand and treat the patient.

It is important when evaluating a person for depression to appreciate the differences between true depression and those moods that resemble depression. For example, depressed mood is not the same thing as a depressive disorder. Depressed mood refers to a negative affective or emotional quality such as feeling sadness, melancholy, moroseness, and so forth for an unspecified time period. A depressive disorder refers to a list of potential symptoms that must be considered before making a diagnosis. When we get into the details of differential diagnosis for mood disorders, we clarify these distinctions further.

Some people feel that all mood problems belong on a continuum from very mild to very severe, and as logical as this sounds, it is not universally accepted as true. For example, depressed mood is common to many people and is qualitatively and quantitatively different from a diagnosable depressive condition. Thus, many practitioners and researchers feel that to place these two different types of problems on the same continuum is like comparing apples and oranges; both may be fruit, but they are not the same type. However, as the proponents of the single continuum perspective point out, if a person suffers from a depressed mood, they are at a higher risk to develop a depressive disorder later.[1] Thus, there may not be a simple answer to this question, but certainly most would agree that depressed mood and depressive disorder are not just variants of the same condition.

Interestingly, we think of depression as *a* disorder, when in fact there are many different types of depression, and even more confusing, there are additional types of disorders that also have a negative mood component. Even more complicating is the fact that frequently depression will accompany other medical or psychological conditions, clouding the diagnosis and complicating the treatment planning even further. When people are suffering from depression, they often will experience emotional, motivational, behavioral, cognitive, and physical symptoms. Emotionally, for example, patients may feel miserable, empty, sad, humiliated, and worthless. From a motivational standpoint, there may be a lack of desire for much of anything, a decreased interest in work and social activities, and little desire to do anything that used to be enjoyable. In terms of behaviors, depressed people show decreased activity levels, often isolate and stay in bed far longer than they need to for normal sleep and rest, and they may not seem to have much energy. We also see different types of think-ing patterns in depressed people, for example, a very negative view of self, their situation and future, and pessimistic thoughts. In addition, depressed persons often report that they are not functioning very well intellectually, and they also frequently have problems with short-term memory, attention, and concentra-tion. Finally, people suffering from depression often complain of many physi-cal symptoms that are sometimes rather vague and diffuse, such as headaches, indigestion, constipation, dizzy spells, general pain, and sexual dysfunction.[2]

SYMPTOMS OF DEPRESSION

Officially, the American Psychiatric Association's (ApA) *Diagnostic and Sta-tistical Manual of Mental Disorders*, fourth edition, text revision *(DSM–IV–TR)* has a set of symptoms that are used to diagnose depression, and we examine them in more detail in Chapter 4.[3] Two of the basic symptoms that are the core characteristics of depression are depressed (or dysphoric) mood and lack of interest or enjoyment in things formerly found to be enjoyable. In addition, depressed persons almost always have difficulty with sleep, either problems getting to sleep or staying asleep *(insomnia)* or over-sleeping and never seeming to get enough sleep *(hypersomnia)*. One of my friends in college got to the point where he was sleeping 18–20 hours per day. The assumption was that he was suffering from a physical illness, but getting him out of bed to go to the health service was not an easy task. When he did finally go, it was determined that he was suffering from depression, but this possibility never even occurred to any of his well-meaning friends.

Other symptoms of depression that are expressed in extremes are nutrition and activity level. When depressed, some people can't eat and have no appetite, and obviously, they usually lose weight. Others seem to feed depression, and often with poor nutritional choices such as sugars and other simple carbohy-drates. In this case, overeating, poor food choices, and lack of activity usually lead to weight gain. The other characteristic prone to extremes is activity level. Most people who are depressed have reduced energy and a very low activity level. However, there are some who are anxious or agitated, and this can be a characteristic of depression as well. This is not the same thing as a manic state in bipolar disorder, but we look at these differences in Chapter 4.

Negative feelings about themselves and general pessimism are almost always found in any type of depression. The depressed person has difficulty thinking positively about themselves or anything else. Not surprisingly, a person who feels like this may often think of death or suicide. Most patients explain that they don't want to die, but rather they don't see a compelling reason to continue living, and anything that might stop the pain and suffering of depression would be a welcome respite. It is also common that depressed people will describe a lack of cognitive and intellectual efficiency and feel that they are not thinking clearly.

The diagnosis of major depression is frequently missed or misdiagnosed, and it often goes untreated for long periods of time. One problem is that its symptoms are often indicative of other types of problems; also, many people don't seek help because of the stigma or because they believe that nothing will help. Many depressed people are so fatigued and discouraged that they can't make themselves go to an appointment. Others don't know they are depressed because it is how they feel most of the time, and it may seem almost "normal" to them; they may not even be aware of the fact that they are actually experiencing symptoms of depression. Clearly, depression is more than the "blues" or a down day, or even a bad week, and to qualify for the diagnosis of depression a person must experience significant symptoms most of the time on a daily basis for at least two weeks.

FUNCTIONAL IMPAIRMENT ASSOCIATED WITH DEPRESSION

To diagnose depression, we look for symptoms that obviously interfere with a person's ability to function and that they are not experiencing a "normal" emotional state. When a person describes a normal or good mood, we refer to this as *euthymia*. If a person reports a negative mood that so interferes with their life that it is creating problems, we call this *dysthymia*, and this suggests that they may be suffering from a clinical depression. The depressed person's symptoms are subjectively experienced as unpleasant, abnormal, or dysfunctional and are referred to as *ego-dystonic*. In other words, these are symptoms that the person experiences as unpleasant relative to their own normal emotional state.

Depressed people usually report low self-esteem and are very critical of and discouraged about themselves. They often believe that they don't *deserve* to feel good and feel that being depressed is a punishment for being so worthless. It follows then, that if one is feeling this badly about themselves, it is unlikely that the depressed person will show the same level of mastery in their jobs, in their relationships, and in other activities, thus making them feel even worse. One of the most difficult aspects of depression is that this cyclical feeling of worthlessness leads to eventually just giving up. In fact, depressed persons feel so fatigued and tired of performing poorly, that they choose not do anything at all rather than to keep failing. More precisely, depressed people will usually perceive themselves as failing even if those around them do not agree. When this downward spiral begins, it is difficult to stop, and before long, others will recognize the performance and behavioral problems.

It is interesting to listen to writers who are acute observers of their own experiences and who have the talent to describe their own feelings in subtle and fascinating (sometimes troubling) detail. For example, Andrew Solomon in his book *The Noonday Demon: An Atlas of Depression* wrote:

> Grief is depression in proportion to circumstance; depression is grief out of proportion to circumstance. It is tumbleweed distress that thrives on thin air, growing despite its detachment from the nourishing earth. It can be described only in metaphor and allegory . . . Grief is a humble angel who leaves you with strong, clear thoughts and a sense of your own depth. Depression is a demon who leaves you appalled.[4]

When you read this passage, it is easy to understand how profoundly depression can affect one's ability to deal with even the simplest of daily tasks. It is important to recognize that depression is not just feeling poorly but that it also impacts and disrupts virtually all aspects of the lives of depressed people. Sadly, even when there are positive things in a depressed person's life, it is still very likely that the person will view them in a negative way. Even the good things rarely feel good to the depressed person.

THE COSTS OF DEPRESSION

During any one-year period, about 9.5% of the population in the United States, or about 20.9 millions adults, suffer from some type of depression.[5] This is a huge number, and we are not sure how many go undetected. According to some,[6] major depressive disorder (MDD) is the leading cause of disability in the United States. They point out that MDD results in more days of disability, lost work days, and presenteeism (when a person shows up to work too sick, impaired, stressed out, or distracted to be productive) than many other medical conditions, creating a huge financial burden for employers. In terms of lost hours of work, medical costs, reduced effectiveness, and other related problems, depression is an enormous expense to every one of us. Not only are employers impacted, but so are other employees, customers, insurance carriers, family members, and friends. There are various estimates of how expensive depression is to the United States, but some suggest that the impact on well-being and national prosperity, if we include all of the direct and indirect costs, is in excess of $83 billion per year.[7]

What is difficult to determine is the extent to which people, in addition to the depressed patient, are actually impacted by the disorder. Glenn and Bergman suggest that depression is associated with excess disability, impaired health, lower quality of life, and lower well-being for patients *and* their significant others.[8] They report that depression may be the most serious emotional problem among disabled people, which suggests that, of all of the disabling conditions, the total impact of depression may actually exceed any other medical or psychological disability. It also points out that the true cost of depression must also include those around the depressed patient who are impacted and harmed, including the effect on their lives, jobs, relationships, and so forth. It is a very serious and expensive problem to say the least.

One factor that is often overlooked is the impact of depression upon other psychological and medical conditions. Physicians and other health professionals do not always recognize depression as a major health risk. One set of studies followed depressed men and women for several years to see how their health status was affected by depression. They found that, after controlling for confounding conditions (interfering factors), men with *minor* depression had a 1.80-fold higher risk of death on a follow-up four years later. Women with *minor* depression, on the other hand, did not have a significantly increased mortality risk. However, both men and women with *major* depression had a 1.83-fold increased risk for mortality in general.[9] Because this study didn't spell out specific types of depression, it means that people with any serious, diagnosed depression are almost twice as like to die in a four-year time span than the controls who were not depressed.

Suffice it to say depression is a serious, costly, and dangerous condition that negatively impacts patients; their families, employers, and friends; and society in general. Depression is clearly one of the most pressing public health issues in the United States today.[10]

MISSING THE DIAGNOSIS OF DEPRESSION

Because the symptoms of depression are so unpleasant and intrusive, it may seem odd that depression is frequently missed or misdiagnosed. Because it often interferes with work, relationships, pleasurable activities, and most other aspects of life, it seems that, even if the depressed person does not want help, family and friends would encourage them to get help. Although there are many effective treatments available today, depression is often untreated.[11]

Why would a person who feels so miserable resist available help? There are many reasons and circumstances that determine whether or not someone might seek treatment. We know that many people, and especially men, are reluctant to pursue professional help because of the stigma or because it seems "weak" to seek help for something as "simple" as depression. Many people still adhere to the "just get up and do it—you can take care of this yourself" school of thought. Tragically, many people are reluctant to seek treatment because they are embarrassed and fear the reaction of people they know. Still others have no knowledge at all about the symptoms of depression and assume that how they are feeling is normal, or at least not something that might require professional help.

Many people are not aware of the fact that help is easily available and have the misconception that you must be "crazy" to qualify for professional help. When a person finally reaches the point of seeking help, they usually begin by seeing their primary care physician (PCP), which is a very good place to start because there may be physical conditions that present similar symptoms to depression that need to be ruled out. The first line of treatment for depression is often medication, and often this medication is prescribed by a PCP rather than a psychiatrist or psychopharmacologist.[12] If a person is *only* receiving medication from a non–mental health professional and this is the only care that they are getting, they may not be receiving adequate treatment. A PCP is certainly qualified to prescribe psychotropic medications (drugs for psychiatric conditions), as it is sometimes difficult in some areas to find a psychiatrist who can see a new patient reasonably soon. Although some treatment is better than none, we see in later chapters of this book that treatment often needs to be multimodal and coordinated to be fully therapeutic.

In a related issue, depression is frequently misdiagnosed or missed altogether by health professionals and can be confused with other conditions. For example, it is common for persons to self-medicate depression (and other conditions) by using alcohol or nonprescription drugs. Using alcohol as a central nervous system (CNS) depressant can be problematic for two reasons: It can produce symptoms similar to depression, and it may mask symptoms of depression even if the physician is aware of the alcohol or drug abuse (frequently hidden or denied by patients). Another unfortunate reality of medical care today is that physicians are under pressure to see as many patients as possible and often don't have the time to listen carefully to detect the subtle indicators of depression. Some of the aches and pains that a patient presents may actually be related to depression, but in the absence of other indicators, the physician simply may not "see" the depression. Finally, some people believe that all depression is transitory and that if you just leave it alone it will go away by itself.[13] Fatigue and lack of motivation are very common symptoms of depression and often puts the patient in the difficult position of not wanting to or being able to do those things that may help them. In John Barth's book *End of the Road,*[14] the protagonist Jacob Horner clearly suffers from what today is called major depressive disorder. He describes his condition as being "paralyzed." When he is very depressed, he is emotionally, cognitively, and behaviorally incapable of doing anything—including anything to help himself. This is a masterful description of how serious depression feels to some people and states even more clearly why it is so difficult for depressed people to seek the help they need.

Finally, and tragically, many people do not receive the help they need for depression and for many other conditions because they simply don't have access to services due to economics, knowledge of treatment options, logistics, or location. Society is making choices about health care, and specifically mental health care, and these choices are preventing millions of people from receiving the help they deserve. This may seem a harsh statement, but the evidence clearly points to this conclusion.

SUICIDE

The most tragic result of depression is suicide—when a person feels so helpless and hopeless that he or she would rather die than continue to live feeling as they feel. There are many different reasons why a person ends their life, but we do know that depression, and especially major depression and bipolar disorder, are significant risk factors for suicide. Even among depressed persons there is rarely one specific reason for attempting or committing suicide, and they may say that they don't necessarily want to die but rather want to end the unremitting pain. However, from the view of a survivor or those who are trying to prevent a suicide, the motive is irrelevant. We may hear comments like, "They are just trying to get attention," or "It wasn't a serious attempt, and so don't worry about it." From the perspective of a mental health professional, trying to guess at the motives is not very helpful—it is more important to stabilize the situation, keep the person safe, and determine what type of treatment intervention can be utilized.

According to the Suicide and Crisis Center, suicide is the 11th leading cause of death among all ages in the United States.[15] Recent statistics report that about 30,000 people commit suicide in the United States each year, and while this number is unsettling, annually there are 730,000 persons who attempt suicide each year but who do not successfully complete the act. In fact, successful suicides outnumber homicides in the United States by 3 to 2, and over 90% of people who die by suicide suffer from either depression or some other mental or substance use disorder.

Some facts about suicide:

+ Suicide is a major complication of depression.
+ One in 16 people with depression die by suicide.
+ About two-thirds of people who die by suicide are depressed.
+ Highest risk factors include:

+ older white males
+ people who live alone
+ people who have had prior suicide attempts
+ those who refuse psychiatric evaluation
+ people who abuse alcohol and/or drugs
+ Women attempt suicide about three to four times more often than men.
+ Men are three to four times more likely to commit suicide.
+ Risks are particularly high in people with bipolar disorder—about 25–50% of patients with bipolar disorder attempt suicide at least once.[16]

In Sweden, one study found that people with a serious physical illness were more than six times more likely to commit suicide than those who were similar but didn't suffer from a serious illness.[17] It is understandable that someone facing a lingering illness would be more likely to commit suicide to escape from significant pain, increasing disability, being a burden to others, and so forth. However, the fact that it makes sense to a suffering patient does not mean that we should abandon our efforts to provide the most meaningful treatment for any person suffering from a serious depressive episode.

Suicide is also a significant problem for adolescents and young adults, and it is the third leading cause of death between the ages of 15–24. The Cross-National Collaborative Group reveals that clinical depression and suicide appear to have increased substantially in both men and women over the past century.[18] Some of the earliest statistical reports on suicide found that in the nineteenth century, the risk of suicide increased with age until reaching middle or old age.[19] Presently, we find that the suicide rate is lowest in the 5–14 age group, increases dramatically in the 15–24 age group, and then stays fairly level at about 16 per 100,000 persons until the 65–74 age group, where it starts increasing through the mid-80s.[20] Other interesting findings relate suicide to marital status. Out of 100,000 persons in the United States, 12.4 married people, 18.4 single people, 21.8 widowed persons, and 37.3 divorced persons commit suicide. Clearly, divorce is an important risk factor for suicide.

There is no single reason why someone chooses to take their life. While each case is unique in its own way, there are patterns that shed light on the different motives people have for considering suicide. According to Shneidman,[21] there are a number of patterns that describe circumstances under which someone may end their life:

+ Death seekers: These people intend to end their life, although they will usually wax and wane in this intention. If you think of suicide as a threshold phenomenon, when a person reaches their threshold, they will actively try to end their life. If, however, they dip below this threshold, they may not actually attempt it even if they are still contemplating suicide. From a prevention perspective, it is a very tenuous situation because this person can shift their intention from minute to minute. However, clinicians will help a person to develop coping skills to deal with the dangerous periods when they are above the threshold. The patient will hopefully continue treatment to keep them below their threshold.

+ Death initiators: These people also want to end their life, but they have very different reasons. They act upon the idea that their death is a virtual certainty in the near future, and they are simply helping it along. It is thought that Ernest Hemmingway was in this category, and one of the main reasons he committed suicide was that he felt his body and his health were failing him; his death was simply a matter of time. Rather than watch himself slide into ill health and incapacity, he sped up the process that was already in place.

+ Death ignorers: This is a very interesting and troubling pattern. People in this group actively and intentionally kill themselves. However, they do not believe that this act will end their existence, but rather, it will help them move to another, even better, level of existence. This pattern is often found among cult members who participate in mass suicide or in the suicide bombers who feel that their act will send them straight to heaven. If they are correct, of course, then the act is not self-destructive but rather self-actualizing. If they are wrong, then the act is a delusional self-deception with a tragic and often unnecessary outcome.

+ Death darers: These people seem to have ambivalent feelings about death and engage in very risky behavior that could possibly end their life. The behavior is intentional, but the outcome is uncertain. Often, when queried, these people say that risking death makes them feel even more alive. When questioned further about how they feel about the prospect of dying as a result of this behavior, they usually say something like, "Then it was meant to be," or "That is the way I would like to go." A good example is a person who plays "Russian Roulette"; they could easily die from the act, but they might survive it as well.

In addition to these patterns of intentional suicide, there is another pattern that Shneidman refers to as "sub intentional death."[22] In this type of situation, the person has an indirect, covert, partial, or subconscious role in their own suicide. Thus, their behavior may lead to their death, but the intention is not obvious. In cases where the person survives the attempt, they might even deny the intentionality. For example, a person who is terminally ill and who doesn't really intend to kill himself makes a mistake with the medication and "accidentally" overdoses, which leads to death. In reality, we might never know for sure if the person intended to commit suicide, but we must keep in mind that there are cases when the intention is not clear even if the outcome is.

A similar pattern was mentioned by Menninger who described what he called "chronic suicide."[23] This pattern refers to a person who behaves in life-endangering ways over extended periods of time, engaging in behavior that they know will probably result in their death. Because their death will occur in the future, they will often say something like, "Well, you can't live forever," or some such platitude. When I was working as a coach while a college student, I over-heard one of my young athletes lecturing a father who was waiting for his two boys after practice. It should also be mentioned that the two boys in question were a bit of a handful. Seeing him smoking, the young girl said, "Mr. X, don't you know that each cigarette you smoke takes eight minutes off of your life?" To which he responded, "When you've got kids like mine, you don't want to live forever." What Menninger is referring to are patterns such as smoking, drug or alcohol abuse, very risky occupations, or any form of consistent behavior that will likely result in death—eventually, at least.

In trying to understand the reasons and dynamics of suicide, many research-ers and clinicians have recently begun to focus on the cognitive aspects of suicide—that is, how a person's thoughts and perceptions are related to the attempt or commission of suicide. Aaron Beck was one of the first to study cognition as it relates to depression and suicide, and it was largely his work that spurred the interest in this approach.[24] Martin Seligman and his cowork-ers, too, did some of the seminal work looking at the relationship between feelings of helplessness and depression.[25] These early approaches to under-standing the cognitive elements of depression and suicide have significantly shaped the way in which these phenomena are understood and treated. For example, Beck found that feelings of hopelessness are better predictors of eventual suicide than the diagnosis of depression alone.[26] Further, Salkovskis reports that three prominent cognitive mechanisms found in patients who have made suicide attempts include:[27]

+ deficits in problem-solving skills and especially in social and interpersonal problem solving,
+ the retrieval of over-general memories, and
+ feelings of hopelessness.

Clearly, what these researchers and clinicians are telling us is that, at some level, the way people think, and not just their emotions, significantly contributes to the decision to attempt suicide.

It is important to learn about the many warning signs that may indicate that a person is contemplating suicide. We are not going to address the con-troversial issue as to whether or not a person has a right to choose the time of their own death, although it is an important issue. We will explore the clinical, empirical, and theoretical aspects of suicide in order to understand the dynamics of suicide for the purpose of providing patients with appropriate options for treatment. Evidence is clear that most persons who end their life are somewhat ambivalent about the act; for example, Swartz reports that about 75% of people who commit suicide had visited their PCP within one month prior to their suicide.[28] This is not intended to impugn the PCP's but rather to point out that, at some level, these patients were trying to find some type of assistance. This also suggests that it is important that all of us be aware of the typical warning signs of depression and suicidality and to be prepared to take appropriate action. Some of the warning signs we can look for include:

- social isolation (usually self-imposed)
- drastic mood swings or personality changes
- neglecting their home, financial responsibilities, or pets
- recent psychological trauma
- exaggerated complaints of aches and pains
- giving away special possessions
- "putting things in order"
- sudden calm or even cheerfulness after a period of depression
- frequent use of alcohol or drugs
- buying a gun
- verbal threats of suicide or desire to die
- family history of suicide or previous attempts

While being aware of these warning signs, it is important to keep them in perspective. Worrying about someone to the point of following them around, watching them constantly, calling 911 for the most minimal warning signs, and so forth will not likely help and might even make things worse. The best course of action is to talk to the person and offer to help but not play the role of a treating professional. A friend can't be their doctor, even if the person says they won't talk to a stranger; but a friend or relative can offer to help them find a professional and even go with them—their personal physician is a good place to start. Do not ever allow yourself to be put in the position of keeping someone alive. First, if they really want to kill themselves, they will likely find a way to do it regardless of what you do. Second, it will distort and disrupt the relationship that you do have with them, and third, you will be taking away from them something that they really do need—a friend. If a situation is acute and life-threatening, you must take emergency action—call 911, then their doctor or a relative. They may initially feel that you have betrayed them by "telling on them." That is when you need to make it clear that, if you are going to err, you are going to err on the side of keeping them safe.

There are few things in life more tragic, and that may appear to be senseless, than suicide. At times, a suicide may seem entirely understandable and rational (e.g., someone who is dying from a painful and lingering illness), but more often than not, a suicide seems like the last desperate act of someone who feels they have no alternative. The responsibility of a treating professional is to help them find and act on some alternatives. Clearly, the act of committing suicide eliminates any options that may have been available and that might have actually helped.

SUMMARY

This chapter has discussed what depression is and the signs and symptoms that indicate when depression is present. The differences between depression and normal variations in mood were discussed and examined, as well as some of the functional impairments associated with depression. We also discussed some of the reasons depression goes unnoticed by friends, family, and professionals and how the absence of an accurate diagnosis will delay, disrupt, or negate treatment that could have helped.

We discovered that the costs of depression are extraordinarily expensive to patients, families, employers, and society at large. Worldwide, depression is a major public health and societal issue that has enormous direct and indirect costs, but one of the biggest costs is the loss of life due to suicide. We discussed the warning signs of depression and how best to aid someone who may be contemplating suicide. In the next chapter, we look at the experience of depression and how it affects the people who suffer from it.

Chapter 2

Depression and the Depressed: What Does It Feel Like?

During depression the world disappears. Language itself. One has nothing to say. Nothing. No small talk, no anecdotes. Nothing can be risked on the board of talk. Because the inner voice is so urgent in its own discourse: How shall I live? How shall I manage the future? Why should I go on?
—Kate Millett, U.S. feminist theorist, literary, critic, essayist, autobiographer, sculptor

When you realize how hard it is to know the truth about yourself, you understand that even the most exhaustive and well-meaning autobiography, determined to tell the truth, represents, at best, a guess. There have been times in my life when I felt incredibly happy. Life was full. I seemed productive. Then I thought, "Am I really happy or am I merely masking a deep depression with frantic activity?" If I don't know such basic things about myself, who does?
—Phyllis Rose, U.S. biographer

THE PHENOMENOLOGY OF DEPRESSION

When a person describes his or her experience of depression, it is clear that it is a pervasive and invasive experience that dominates and dictates one's life. During the years I have worked as a psychologist, I have heard thousands of personal descriptions of depression, and while none of them are identical, there is uniformity and thematic similarities that are frequently found. It is clear that when one is depressed there is little else in a person's life that can be experienced as meaningful—depression seems to rob one of any semblance of normal life experiences.

After listening to someone describe how it felt to be depressed, I observed that the visual image that came to mind was being trapped at the bottom of a deep well—perhaps so deep that you couldn't see the opening at the top.

I imagined that the walls of this pit were slippery with grease or slime and that as I tried to climb I would work exhaustively only to slide back down to the bottom. After trying for hours, I finally gave up and accepted the reality that my life was to be lived and to end at the bottom of this pit. I described this image in somewhat less detail to a patient who seemed surprised that someone else understood how he felt. I assured him that millions of others have shared his experience and that we would work together to find a way out of the pit. In fact, using this metaphor, I told him that we would look at therapy as a way of making and using hand holds that would help him climb up and see the light of day once again. Fortunately, he did well in therapy and has been productive and depression free for many years.

This description is similar to the approach that Martin Seligman has developed as a way of understanding depression. While a graduate student, Seligman and some of his colleagues found an interesting phenomenon; some dogs in his research became so accepting of discomfort they seemed to "give up" and just accept it without resistance. Psychologically this doesn't seem to make any sense unless you assume that the dogs had learned to behave in a passive and dysfunctional manner. Eventually, Seligman referred to this phenomenon as "Learned Helplessness," and after having gained some more training in clinical areas, he decided that this phrase could explain some of the experiences that people have with depression.[1] Like being trapped at the bottom of the slippery well, some people come to learn that they are a helpless victim of their depression and that there is nothing they can do except suffer and accept it. This observation led to further research in order to understand the cognitive aspect of depression—usually thought of as a strictly emotional condition. It is hardly surprising that one of the people with whom Seligman worked was Aaron Beck who is frequently called the "father" of the cognitive approach to understanding depression.

In order to more fully understand the experience of depression, in this chapter you will read the experiences of four persons who have courageously volunteered to share their thoughts and feelings about the depression they have dealt with for much of their life. In order to stimulate their thinking, I gave them questionnaires to help them organize their ideas and to make it easier for them to recount their experiences. I then wrote their thoughts and ideas in a first-person, descriptive form to make it easier for you to understand the reality, pain, and complexity of depression. As you read these cases, you will see that there is nothing easy about remembering and writing down the pain and problems that one has lived with for many years. Hopefully, as each person unfolds their lives for you, it will help you to appreciate what it means to be depressed.

CASE 1: LONNIE, 61-YEAR-OLD MALE

The earliest I remember being depressed was in the third grade; my teacher said that I appeared to have a very lazy and negative attitude and decided to "help" me by punishing this "obviously" bad behavior. I had to agree that her observations of me were accurate, but her interpretation was not. At that moment, I realized that how I felt was different from the other kids and that to be safe and to avoid punishment I needed to "hide" inside myself and suffer alone.

In reality, I feel that I have been depressed since conception. For me, it seems an affliction I was born with, and the only blame I can lay is on faulty genes. I can report depression on both sides of my family; depression was a common and obvious companion to many. On my father's side there was my grandmother who "married out to America" (she had an arranged marriage to a man in America who she had never met), hated everything about it, and died of a "broken heart." My father, a charmer and a compulsive gambler who nobody but my mother (who never said a kind word about anything or anyone) spoke ill of, also had the "family curse" (depression). Probably the most upsetting of my depressed relatives was my Uncle John, who was always my favorite. He was engaging, supportive, a racecar driver who ate meat on Fridays, and a *bon vivant* who ended his life with a bloody suicide—I was crushed. Even the most religious member of my family, my Aunt Agnes—the mean aunt, the strident Catholic, the defrocked nun—suffered from depression.

On my mother's side, my great-grandfather, my grandfather, my great-aunt, and my mother all were depressive as well. Even today, both of my siblings suffer from depression, although my brilliant and talented sister has the worst of it. Both of them have full and enviable lives, but they have had to learn how to deal with depression as have many others in my family. The one that probably troubles me most is my daughter who, full of life as she is, has her bouts of depression as well.

In terms of my own depression, it is hard to specifically identify the ways in which it has affected my life, but it certainly has. Although, who knows what my life would have been without the depression—perhaps even worse. I do know that the depression has affected my productivity, caused some missed and lost opportunities, and has led to failed personal and professional relationships. On a daily basis, when depressed, I have chronic sleep deprivation, a lack of motivation, feelings of despair, a bizarre diet, social isolation, paranoid feelings, and, at the end of an episode, the "blackness"—nothing, a void. I can even say that depression worsens my physical problems. While depressed,

I suffer mysterious aches and pains, gastric problems, neglected hygiene, and the aggravation of chronic pain from earlier injuries.

As mentioned previously, depression has negatively impacted many of my relationships over the years. My indifference, irritability, and intolerance when depressed placed severe strain on my friends, family, and partners. As much as I love being around and enjoying people, I also find that I need long-term and purposeful seclusion. Lately, I have found that I am isolating more than usual, and I have been reluctant to succumb to new close attachments and even keep my old friends at arm's length. Is this depression? Fear of loss or rejection? Fear of commitment? Who knows? Actually, I feel happy now even though most would wonder why.

In trying to isolate the cause of my depression, I will stake my bets on defective DNA as the primary factor—certainly there are other things as well, but the family patterns as well as my own experiences make it seem clear to me that I didn't start with a clean slate—depression was there from the beginning. I did have one girlfriend who postulated that the problem was demonic possession, and I even entertained that idea for awhile. I do know that inadequate management skills and tools, including wrong medications and many misdiagnoses, have also been culprits. Unfortunately, societal ignorance and prejudice surrounding depression has been a major problem for me. I not only bought into these archaic and harmful myths, but they kept me from getting the help that I needed in a timely fashion.

My depression has certainly complicated my medical picture, but it is also true that my medical picture has complicated my depression. Heart disease, advanced atherosclerosis, and injuries have all played a part in my general physical and mental health. Probably the biggest problem that I faced in coping with my life was a descent into alcoholism that lasted from the ages of 17–40. Fortunately, and with a lot of work, I have been sober for over 20 years. No doubt I was depressed before I became an alcoholic, and in fact, it is very likely that I was self-medicating with the alcohol. That coupled with bad genes was a tragic combination for me, and even if alcohol seemed to help a little at first, it aggravated my condition and my life in general.

In terms of my management of depression today, it can best be described as a balancing act. I take medication, go to regular psychotherapy, go to my AA meetings, read enthusiastically, and work. I found early in therapy that my ability to work and the quality of what I produced was a very sensitive indicator of my depression. Professionally, I am a composer of classical music and need my mind and wits about me in the most complete manner possible. When depressed, the symptoms make it impossible for me to work, but when on medication, I find that after awhile I find my mental acuity and creativity blunted. Even though I can do some of the work I need to do, I cannot function at a high enough level to do the things that require the utmost level of functioning possible. Thus, the balancing act; what I find that I need to do is to catch the depression before it gets too bad and start on the medication. I then stay on the medication until I find that I can't work up to my needs, and then I taper off of the meds. Both my physician and my psychologist are aware of this and work with me to help maintain the balance that I need. Sometimes I miscalculate, and I pay a price for that. Recently, while working very productively and at a very high level, I stayed on my medication "holiday" for over four months, which turned out to be too long, and the depression came down upon me. It has taken about three months to get back to where I need to be, but I learned from this and will be more careful in my "balancing" in the future.

I suppose that my approach to dealing with depression involves many things. Medications are a necessity for me; but then so are my friends, support groups, therapy, and the ability to talk about and understand what I am dealing with. I am not one to give others advice, but for what it's worth, here are some thoughts that come from my own struggles, successes, and failures:

+ The most difficult thing about depression is that I must seek a solution while depressed—a decidedly unpleasant situation.
+ "Feeling bad" all of the time is neither normal nor healthy.
+ Without effective treatment, depression doesn't go away.
+ Feeling "a little better" is a poor substitute for "feeling good."
+ Sometimes my mind is not my friend.
+ I have accrued no benefit from courageous suffering.
+ If I think I'm depressed, I probably am. I am learning to listen to my mind and my body.
+ Professional treatment, especially medication, for me at least, is critical to the solution.
+ Folk remedies, including religion, often pursued out of desperation or on the advice of the well-meaning, have been of no help whatsoever and have often been extremely detrimental—the bringers of false hope and harbingers of doom.
+ Trying to cope with depression *alone* is a recipe for disaster—it is like being my own lawyer or surgeon.
+ Sugar, stimulants (even caffeine), and alcohol are best avoided.
+ On occasion, managing depression can be a dreadful and difficult full-time job.
+ "When your horse dies, get off." Sometimes the medications (or even the whole strategy) stop working, so I try a new approach.

CASE 2: LOTTE, 39-YEAR-OLD FEMALE

It never occurred to me that I was depressed until I awoke in the hospital after having my stomach pumped from having taken over 100 Motrin (600 mg tablets). I was in the 11th grade and was suddenly and acutely aware that I didn't want to die—just to get away from my house. My new goal was to drink, make sure I could always turn heads by dressing sexy, and being thin. I did get out of my house into the arms and home of the best man I could find, and I thought that I was happy. I pursued my new goal for about five years, and then I found that I was an anorexic/bulimic alcoholic, which had not actually been my intention.

Even though depression was not something I was aware of or knew anything about, I was quite aware of how unhappy I was as a youth. I was convinced that I should have been a boy and that God had either made a mistake or was punishing me. I would look in the mirror and sob at my plight and would at times turn around and find my mother watching me cry. Her smile of enjoyment confirmed my belief that my pain was part of the plight of being a woman—something I wanted no part of. My mother, who obviously had her own problems, was physically, sexually, and psychologically abusive of me throughout my childhood, and she typically brought Jesus and Satan into the picture for even more drama. She was such a rage-aholic that I truly felt that it was only a matter of time before she would really kill me. In fact, I often hoped that she would finally just do it—get it over with so I could get away from the pain and humiliation that she seemed to enjoy visiting upon me; my life, my body, my mind were not my own. The ever-present anxiety and worry over some impending and unexpected rage that would be the end of it all was my constant companion. I finally accepted the fact that life was not something that was to be valued but tolerated and escaped from whenever possible.

As you might guess, my mother's side of the family was filled with mental illness. Her own father was physically and sexually abusive, and her mother was a fierce woman who delighted in manipulating and pitting the children against one another. There are histories of physical, sexual, and psychological abuse throughout that side of the family. There are many who are so mentally ill that they cannot function outside of the dysfunctional family system at all, and it seems like the only healthy ones found some way to escape. I do remember my mother and her siblings sitting on our front porch talking and crying and trying to unwind the sick webs that my grandmother had woven.

My own siblings are marked with the family's stamp, but fortunately, most of us have managed, to greater or lesser degrees, to achieve some semblance of a life. I am the eldest and, in many ways, bore the brunt of much of my mother's rage and pathology. I have battled eating disorders, depression, and alcoholism for most of my life—a battle that I continue to wage, but it has certainly been a struggle at times. My sister who is next in line was always my mother's favorite, and this was painfully clear to the rest of us. She has been diagnosed with bipolar disorder, but I think a better description would be borderline personality disorder. She is the one that announced in writing to the whole family that my father had raped us. This, of course, was not now or ever true—there was certainly enough sickness to go around, but this was not part of it. Her telling of this lie is, however, an even better example of how the family dynamics play out in sick and hurtful ways. Sadly, too, all of her children have serious psychological and mental conditions.

My next sister also battles anxiety and depression and has received treatment in the form of medication and psychotherapy over the years. She also has a son, and thankfully, he is a lovely young man who shows no signs of serious psychological problems. The youngest sibling in our family is my brother—the only son and the only male other than my father. Like me, he is an over-achiever who has a manic side but who believes that his willpower has kept it in check. He also has a strong tendency toward alcoholism, but this has yet to fully surface. A good example of how my family history has affected him is that he will not (cannot?) hold my only daughter who is three. He is very afraid that someone might think that he is doing something inappropriate.

My depression, as well as my other problems, has frequently and insistently interfered with my life, plans, and prospects. For example, through most of school I was a straight-A student who lettered in three sports and who had impressive submissions to two different science fairs. I was even taking college courses during my senior year of high school, but I did not graduate from high school. One course in which I had an A average was the main problem for me. Due to excessive absences, I failed this required course and couldn't graduate with my class.

My senior year in high school was somewhat unusual to say the least. Following my suicide attempt, my parents decided that I should live with another family. In fact, I was seeing a psychiatrist who wanted to see the whole family, and the conclusion widely agreed upon was that I was the crazy one, and I was responsible for the family's woes. Thus, my being exiled was seen as the best decision to preserve this otherwise "normal" family. As it turned out, I spent my senior year living not with another family but in another town with a 37-year-old man who provided me with all of the pot and booze that I wanted. At the time, I thought that he was my savior who was taking care of me and letting me do what I wanted. In retrospect, however, it is clear that he was a criminal who was sexually exploiting a 16-year-old girl and illegally providing her with drugs and alcohol.

Finally, I did finish high school, but I did not go directly to college as was expected. I was far too depressed to accept the softball scholarship to an excellent local college, nor could I work. I quit or was fired from dozens of jobs because I just couldn't get out of bed to go to work. After moving around trying to find where I belonged, I did go back to college, but I was drinking and finally dropped out of that, too. Even though part of my family was a wonderful source of support, mainly my father's side, I decided to escape from all of them when my sister accused my father of raping us—although I knew this to be untrue. At the time, however, I didn't have the psychic energy necessary to confront her and her tall tales, and so I withdrew. After strewing this poison throughout the family, she finally disclosed that she was a victim of "false memory syndrome" and that there was no truth to the rape allegations. Of course, she did not broadcast this as widely as she had the allegations. I have re-established relationships with my family, but that sister is still estranged from all of her siblings and most of the rest of the family.

After having dropped out of college, my alcoholism, depression, and eating disorders finally took over, and I spent the next few years of my life in and out of alcohol rehabs, crisis clinics, inpatient private mental hospitals, and other facilities. Finally, I spent six weeks in a state mental hospital, and this experience helped me enormously. Without much fanfare or enthusiasm, I decided to apply to another high-quality private college that I was fairly sure I would get into. I only applied to one college because the task of applying to more than one was too much for me, and I knew that I would never be able to fill out all of those other applications. Fortunately, I was accepted and actually took the education seriously. Although few from my "crazy" days would believe me, I graduated summa cum laude, Phi Beta Kappa, with departmental honors and the highest grade average in all of the Humanities—will miracles never cease?

Coping with and recovering from everything that I deal with is a full-time job every day and without respite—but I do it knowing that I can and have to. My body has suffered from all of the abuse it has been through, including alcohol and binging and purging with food, and I also frequently physically hit and hurt myself. In addition to recovering from alcoholism and being treated for it as well as the depression, I suffer from fibromyalgia and post-traumatic stress disorder. The things that I have to continually keep coping with and working on include symptoms of depression, dissociation, nightmares, restless sleep, losing track of time, hearing things, hitting myself, fits of rage, and just going numb. Getting through the normal functions of daily living is sometimes a challenge, and pushing myself to shower and to put on clean clothes is even more than I can muster on some days. Sleep has never been something I could count on. Between insomnia and fibromyalgia (let alone the depression), it is rare that I feel rested and well. Particularly when I am tired, I have trouble focusing, paying attention, and remembering even the simplest things. I am very good at covering up and faking it—that, too, is often a struggle, but I do it. I should also mention the nightmares—only recently has there been a respite from these. For years I was tormented with the most awful, graphic, and terrifying nightmares and rarely had the luxury of a night without them. Being married, feeling more secure and safe, and taking the proper medications has given me a break from the awful curse of the nightmares. For years I couldn't even imagine how damaged I must be to have things like that rolling around in my head. While I don't often have them now, I never entirely forget them.

Presently, I have a more complete life than I ever thought possible for someone like me. I am married and have a beautiful daughter—two feats far beyond what I ever pretended to hope for. They are two of the reasons why I continue to struggle and to work so hard to get better. There is no doubt in my mind that I am where I am today because of the time and energy I have invested in therapy as well as patiently working with my physicians to find the medications that are most helpful to me. Every day I awaken ready for my life, and this is true even if it is a bad day. I am volunteering at organizations that seem to need my help, and I enjoy doing this, although I feel guilty for not using my education, my brain, and my abilities to do more. It is hard enough to focus, to do the work, and to even show up—so for now, this is what I do.

When I reflect on the things that have allowed me to actually have a life beyond the depression and alcoholism that has scarred me, I know it has been a lot of work, but it has also involved the efforts and support of others as well. On my own, I take medication, go to therapy, write daily in my journal, stay active with my family, tell the truth, stay sober, believe that I will continue to get better, and try to put good suggestions into action. I do know that two six-week stays in a psychiatric hospital (10 years apart) were enormously helpful, as was the acknowledgment from my father, during a family session at the hospital, that he understood the craziness and tried to do something about it. Even though he couldn't fully appreciate what we went through, the fact that he even acknowledged that it was there was affirming and reassuring.

My advice to people who are suffering from depression is to tell someone. Tell your doctor—that is a good place to start. Don't hide it or from it; tell the truth completely and unashamedly. You can't get help if people don't know what you are dealing with. Look at therapy and medication as something to be grateful for rather than something to resent or avoid. Be thankful that effective treatments are available, and use them; previous generations and many others today don't have these options. Throw the excuses away, be honest, ask for help, and take it. One thing I am somewhat hesitant to add, but I feel that I should, is how my "demographics" contributed to my treatment and continuing recovery. I do feel that my trip "through the system" was helped by the facts that I am a white, thin, relatively attractive female who had a father with a good job and good insurance. Treatment was available, people wanted to help me, and I had the resources to provide the assistance I needed. I saw others have a far more difficult time getting and accepting the help than I did. This is one of the unfortunate realities of life today, but if we can't fix the system, we can at least try to fix ourselves, and if the help is there, take it gratefully, and use it.

CASE 3: RALPH, 66-YEAR-OLD MALE

I was probably 50 years old before I actually knew that I was depressed, although I had been in treatment for psychological issues well before that. At age 33, I was having difficulty committing to marriage and went into counseling for that for about one and a half years, ultimately marrying the woman in question, to whom I am happily married today. This earlier counseling focused only on relationships and family issues, and the idea of depression never came up. However, at age 50, I knew that I needed to talk to someone about the way I felt—hopelessness, anxiety, and fear were always with me. Although I didn't recognize these feelings as depression, I did know that I was tired of feeling the way I was. I spoke with my family physician, a man I respect and whose opinion I value, and he referred me to a clinical psychologist who recommended medication and psychotherapy. This was where the actual treatment of my depression began.

When I look back, I can see that even as a child of eight or nine I had trouble focusing in school, I had fears and anxiety, was very insecure about myself, and was frightened about the stability of my family. My parents frequently argued about many things, and these arguments were often loud and frightening. It is probably true that I have been depressed to one degree or another for most of my life, and it took 50 years for someone to accurately diagnose what I was dealing with and to prescribe the appropriate treatments. I am not blaming anyone who I saw earlier; they didn't know what I was dealing with because I didn't tell them—nor did I even know myself.

I do think that my depression is probably a familial characteristic. Many of my relatives were clearly depressed, and others may have been as well, although perhaps not as obviously so. Apparently, my maternal grandmother was critical of her children and made life very difficult for them. One of my aunts was mentally ill and spent the last 20 years of her life in a mental hospital, although

I am unsure of her diagnosis. Certainly, my mother had some of the symptoms of depression; she was often "down" and teary. She appeared to enjoy very little and had few if any close personal relationships. I also have a sister who has had chronic, untreated depression since her late teens. Presently, because of obesity and other physical problems, she is unable to care for herself and is in a supervised living situation. One of my other sisters also suffers from some depressive symptoms but has a supportive and involved family; she is extroverted and outgoing and is very active and involved in life. Thus, she manages well and seems to keep the depression at bay most of the time. My third sister seems to have missed the family disease, but I see her rarely, and so my knowledge is incomplete. If she has some problems with depression, I have never seen evidence of it, and she seems happy and secure in her life.

At my age, it is tempting to look back over my life and wonder about the "what ifs." I do think that depression has taken its toll on me. It seems clear to me that the difficulties focusing and concentrating in my formative years in school made it more difficult for me later to achieve in college and postgraduate work. I feel that I could have, perhaps should have, accomplished more. Yes, I graduated from college; and yes, I received a Master's Degree; and yes, I worked as a professional person for many years, retiring just a few years ago. Yet, I feel that I should have done more. I loved my job; I think I was good at it, and people respected me for my competence. I do not think that my inability to be promoted beyond my last position was due to my competence but to my lack of confidence and my fear that I couldn't manage more responsibility than I already had. This is pretty good evidence of what a life of being depressed will do to you.

Personally, I know the depression kept me from accomplishing more in all areas of my life. My lack of confidence intruded on all of my activities, relationships, and professional life. I sometimes fear that my inability to make decisions, my lack of confidence, my continual questioning of myself, and my uncertainties about almost everything must have affected my children's behaviors and choices in life. I should point out that they are both college educated, one with a graduate degree, and both have very impressive professional careers. Still, I question myself and what I may have done to them.

As I think about my life, I truly feel that if my depression had been caught and treated before I was 50 years old, it might have made a difference. By the time I was in treatment, the depression was well-entrenched and the illogical thought patterns were a part of who I was. These deeply ingrained patterns and emotions made treatment more extensive and involved. Finding a physician who recognized what I needed and who referred me to the person who really saw what I was dealing with and getting help from a psychiatrist who listened to me and provided medications that were helpful and minimally intrusive were all important. Having professionals who respect one another as well as their patient and who are willing to work together and compare notes is very important. In my case, a clinical psychologist who could see the whole picture, put it together, and make the right suggestions for treatment was the key. I would advise any patient to try to find such a person.

I also would tell a depressed person to establish a good support system of professionals, family, and friends who all can help in different ways. By having good and competent professionals, you don't need to use your family and friends to lean on as much, and you can then enjoy those relationships as a fulfilling part of your life. It may seem frustrating to try to put all of this together, but keep trying; it is worth the struggle. Find the people who can help, listen to them, do what they suggest, and start to work. Take it from one who has been in the trenches for many years—it's worth the struggle!

CASE 4: CHARLES, 40-YEAR-OLD MALE

I will start my journey through depression with the acknowledgment that it has been through the help of many dedicated mental health professionals that I have outlived my depression. I didn't have a clue that what I was experiencing was more than a "down time" until I experienced a totally debilitating major depression that lasted for six months, four of which were spent in a mental hospital. This was a pretty clear indication that what I was experiencing was more than just a "bad day."

Until this depressive episode at age 29, I hadn't really started putting the puzzle pieces together. I had been diagnosed with some form of depression at age 20, but those symptoms paled in comparison with what I was to experience 10 years later. My earlier depression was mild enough that, in my mind, depression wasn't that big of a deal; I felt differently later. In retrospect, I suspect that I had episodes of depression at earlier ages, too, but I didn't know what it was, nor did I know that I could, or should, do something about it. A vivid memory still remains of me lying in bed at 3 P.M. on a sunny, warm afternoon just looking at the wall. As much as I liked being outdoors with my friends and doing things for fun, I just laid there, inert. I even remember thinking, "I am not sick, there is nothing wrong, I feel OK; why am I doing this?" I didn't have an answer, and so I stayed there looking at the wall.

By the time I was 15 or 16, I was getting some more signals. I had started thinking about and entertaining notions of suicide, which, at the time, didn't seem as strange to me as staring at the wall had been. Ending my life appeared to be a logical act; lying in bed staring at the wall seemed aberrant. One of the interesting things that I noticed was that the more depressed I got, the more comforting the whole idea of suicide became. That doesn't necessarily mean that I was going to actively attempt to kill myself because that would have required more energy than I could muster at the time; however, as I started coming out of the depression and was more energized, the suicide might have been more of a risk. As I started thinking more clearly and began regaining my cognitive acuity, I found that when I began considering suicide I could shoo the thoughts away like an annoying fly. The knowledge that I can think suicidal thoughts and push them away so easily certainly gives me a confidence and comfort that I never had before.

My family has certainly had its share of mental illness. Presently, I have two siblings who are being treated for depression and another sibling who is diagnosed as being schizophrenic. He is now in custodial care and is generally doing well. I have found that when his schizophrenic symptoms lessen, he starts to become depressed because he realizes how impaired he is, how much of his life he has missed and that he will continue to live a marginal, albeit comfortable existence. It is a somewhat sad but accurate reality that our family struggles with mental problems of many and varied kinds, including depression, schizophrenia, and alcoholism. These problems, of course, touch everyone in the family either directly or indirectly, and I am quite sure that my depression has not only affected me but also the others who care about me, have to deal with me, and who worry about me.

Certainly, depression has impacted my life in many ways. In fact, it is hard to think about any part of my life that hasn't been affected by my depression. For example, even physically the depression has taken a toll. During the two major depressive episodes that I have experienced, I lost 30 to 40 pounds each time. The complete lack of physical energy was beyond description. If you have not experienced this complete mental and emotional exhaustion, you cannot imagine what it is like. One of my well-meaning friends almost dragged me out of my apartment during a depressive episode to get me outdoors to do something. He took me to the park, and we actually tried to take a walk. Ordinarily, I am a vigorous and physical person. On this day, I could not walk more than 20 paces without having to sit down and rest. At one point in what must have sounded like utter desperation, I pleaded with him to let me lie down on the grass and rest—I simply could not move another inch. If this sounds like an exaggeration, let me assure you that it is not—I couldn't have moved under threat of death, which actually would have sounded pretty good at the moment. Probably the most obvious symptoms of depression that others would have seen were the physical ones. Almost every aspect of my physical, mental, and emotional being was completely devastated. The physical things were the easiest to see, but they were not the only suffering I experienced. To describe depression as the most profoundly painful condition I have ever experienced is a start in the direction of explaining it, but even that doesn't come close. Depression has exacted heavy tolls on my life financially, vocationally, socially, and in every other area of my life.

When I remember how depression affected my life generally and specifically, probably the best description is that while depressed I didn't have a life. There was no life—period. There was only the inescapable mental, emotional, and physical anguish of the interminable moment—that first moment for me lasted six months—it never occurred to me that it might actually end. Of course, with treatment it did end, only to reappear seven and a half years later, and this one lasted for 22 months. Interestingly, I recently found myself slipping into another depression, but with new medication strategies and firm direction from my psychologist, it appears that I may have dodged the bullet this time—we'll see.

One thing that happens to me when I come out of a depressive episode is that I find interest and comfort in the normally mundane aspects of life that seemed so impossible to me while depressed. Grooming myself, cleaning my apartment, going to the store, and actually enjoying taking my time to find the things that I need without running out of the store in tears because it is too much for me; these were things I found comfort in. Even being able to open my mail on a daily basis and take care of my bills and my correspondence is something that I now enjoy and appreciate. Does depression give me a heightened appreciation of the simple things in life? Not really, but I certainly don't take them for granted anymore.

The one area of my life that has been permanently ruined by depression is my social and family life. I once had a "true love" that was lost during the first depressive episode, and at first I thought that the depression was a fluke, and I should get back into the scene ASAP. Following the second depression, I now no longer care or even want to try again. The knowledge that I will never be married, never have kids, or never play with my grandkids really hurts and makes me very sad. However, having a wife and children that I couldn't support and care for because of a recurrence of my depression is more than I can risk—that would destroy me. I cannot nor will not take that chance.

I have a decent life, and I am working on making it even more full and more interesting. My depression cost me a career that I liked and was good at. I was a licensed special education teacher, and without depression, I would have been a credit to the profession I am sure. However, there is no way that I can do that again; I know that it would be too much for me. I am trying to get off of disability, but even that is frightening. I want to do something new and meaningful, but the fear of failure and the fear of having the depression descend on me again makes it very scary—with help and therapy I am going to do something new and productive, but as simple as it may sound, this will be one of the most difficult things I have ever attempted.

Looking back at my life and my depression, it seems clear to me that there was not a simple cause but a complex of many important things that contributed to this awful condition. Genetically, I am sure that I was predisposed—there are too many in my family who are tainted for it to be a random phenomenon. Trauma? Yes, I had my share, including an alcoholic father who stopped drinking when I was three years old but who continued with the erratic, frightening, abusive, and terrifying behavior of a "dry drunk" over the next 20 years. As a very sensitive youngster, I was traumatized by many things, including my home life. I learned to escape mentally from these terrors, and this type of escape, as I have learned, is what set the stage for the dissociations I have experienced over the years as well. There are times when I can't tell what is real or what is not, nor can I even be sure who I am. This is not the complete failure of the ability to perceive reality that the schizophrenic experiences, but rather the mental puzzlement of someone who is in touch with reality while feeling they are an outsider who is only visiting.

The treatment, or more precisely, *treatments* that have helped me battle the depression, the dissociations, and all of the rest of it are part of an armamentarium of tools, strategies, and tactics for managing a life that is bruised and battered but certainly improved and improving. I can't really say that one form of treatment is more important than any other. However, I would say that, for me at least, the medication is crucial. Of course, it doesn't really "cure" anything, but without the medication, I can't function, I can't take advantage of psychotherapy, and I can't even take care of myself. From my perspective, asking for help, taking advantage of what is offered, being honest with the providers, listening to them, following their advice, and working on what they suggest all contributes to what certainly begins to feel something like hope—at least as I remember it.

My advice to anyone who is depressed, or who thinks that they might be, is to get it checked out. If you are getting depressed, it is certainly easier to deal with if you catch it before you get where I was at the worst of my depressive episodes. If you are now depressed, nobody will know how you feel or what you are experiencing. You are in excruciating mental, physical, and emotional pain, and no matter how much you cry, pray, or curse the universe, there seems to be no way out of this moment-to-moment torment other than killing yourself. When suicide seems like the right solution, then you know that you are truly sick, and you must do something. If you kill yourself, all bets are off, and the depression wins again. So what to do? Hang on for one more miserable, awful, painful day. That's right! Hang on. "For what?" you say, which is what I, too, would have said: *for a new life* when the depression breaks, which it will. With treatment, it will break sooner, but it will break. Remember smiling? Remember someone smiling at you? Remember closing with satisfaction the book that you just finished and really enjoyed? Remember gazing up at the stars in amazement? Remember when you hugged someone out of pure love? These memories are only a glimpse of what life still holds for you when (you notice I said *when*) the depression breaks. This is why you must hang on.

SUMMARY

These stories are powerful examples of how completely and profoundly depression can impact the life of a person who, in many respects, may be like many of us. The personal and family costs are enormous and cannot be underestimated. These brave, sensitive, and obviously very insightful people have chosen to share their journeys to help you understand a life with depression. As Williamson points out, depressive symptoms are associated with high levels of functional disability and pain, and that is certainly clear in these case studies.[2]

One thing that stands out as I read each case is how much personal strength these people must have to battle something so overpoweringly debilitating. However, I don't see even one of them gratuitously blaming themselves for having this illness. Researchers have found that depressed individuals don't usually blame themselves for their condition and actually see themselves as being worthy.[3] If you don't view yourself as worthy, how could you possibly work as hard as these people have to get well?

Another observation in these four cases is that depression is rarely a solitary condition; it is almost always complicated by other physical and mental or emotional problems. Professionals refer to this as *comorbidity*, when a condition is accompanied by other problems. You read that some people suffer from anxiety as well as depression—two conditions frequently found in the same patient. Substance abuse and alcoholism were mentioned in the case studies, specifically, and it is certainly understandable why a depressed person would "self-medicate" with drugs or alcohol to ease the pain. Awareness of the complexities and the problems that accompany depression is a step in the direction of understanding how to approach the treatment and care of depressed individuals—it is never a simple issue.

Chapter 3

The Epidemiology and Etiology of Depression: Who Gets It, and Why?

The term clinical depression finds its way into too many conversations these days. One has a sense that a catastrophe has occurred in the psychic landscape.
—Leonard Cohen, Canadian singer, poet, novelist

If we admit our depression openly and freely, those around us get from it an experience of freedom rather than the depression itself.
—Rollo May, U.S. psychologist

Epidemiology is the study of the incidence, distribution, and control of disease. By understanding who gets a particular disease, it is sometimes possible to develop better methods to control, treat, and prevent a particular condition. Because depression is widely experienced around the world, it is important to establish patterns that might help manage this costly and difficult disorder. *Etiology* refers to the causal factors related to depression. This chapter examines things that have been causally linked with depression as well as some ideas that may explain why certain people suffer from depression and others do not.

Nearly 19 million Americans suffer from depression, which leads to significant costs for victims of depression and their families, friends, work colleagues, organizations in which they work and function, and even society as a whole.[1] In fact, in any one year, depression affects about 12% of American women (more than 12 million persons) and 7% of all American men (more than 6 million persons).[2] Blazer et al. reported that the lifetime prevalence rate for men with depression is 12.7%, and for women it is 21.3%.[3] They also report that, when asked if they had suffered from depression in the last 30 days, 5% of men and women stated that they had been treated for or experienced significant depression. Relatives of persons with depression are at a higher risk for the disorder, and in fact, 20% of the relatives of depressed persons suffer from depression as opposed to 10% of the general population.[4]

These statistics are impressive given the large number of people who are impacted by mood disorders in general and depression specifically. In addition to the obvious harm these disorders do to a person's life, there are many other indirect costs. For example, we find that older persons with depression use our health care systems at a higher rate than the general public, which includes increased use of medications, more frequent emergency room visits, and more office visits to their medical providers.[5] Although there are a few estimates, it is difficult to calculate the total cost of depression within our health care budget for two reasons. First, depression is not always recognized by a doctor or other health professional; these cases may never be recorded, nor the cost or impact realized. Second, because many (probably most) people experience depression with coexisting or comorbid medical or psychological conditions, they may be receiving treatment for a different disorder even if the depression could be identified as the primary problem. In cases such as these, the depression may not be considered an independent condition and will probably not be recorded as such. Consequently, all of the statistics that we have about the incidence and impact of depression are very likely low estimates.

In one very creative study, they looked at the frequency of depression among elderly people within a community who were not being treated for depression. That is, just regular people who were drawn randomly from a community population. This study also looked at patients from the same community who had been identified in their primary care setting as having some symptoms of depression, but they were not being treated for that condition. They found that patients who did not reach the threshold for major depressive disorder (MDD) but who did display symptoms severe enough to significantly impinge upon their life's activities, ranged from 10–25% in both the community and primary care samples. This indicates that about a quarter of the population may be experiencing significant depressive symptoms even though they are not severe enough to warrant the diagnosis of MDD.[6]

It is clear that depression impacts many people personally and professionally; it dramatically reduces the quality and quantity of creative and productive work, often ruining people's careers.[7] It is impossible to determine the lost potential of persons who have suffered depressive disorders, but as we will see later in this book, whatever has been lost in the past may be unrecoverable. However, with new and more effective treatments, there is real hope that less will be lost in the future and hopefully much to gain.

GENDER, AGE, AND DEPRESSION

Historically, it has been reported that mood disorders usually emerge between the ages of 20 and 30, but they can occur at virtually any age.[8] There is very compelling evidence that depression is occurring earlier in life than in past decades.[9] One study demonstrated that people born after World War II have higher rates of depression, get depressed at younger ages, and are more likely to commit suicide than people of earlier generations.[10] As was discussed previously, women are more likely to be diagnosed with depression than men. It is difficult to explain these facts, and the answers are rarely simple. Are we merely detecting depression more accurately today, or are these new rates indicative of changing patterns of depression? Hopefully, as we examine these issues in more depth some explanations for these questions will start to emerge.

As a way of summarizing the epidemiologic information on depression, the following table indicates recent data that displays some interesting patterns related to the distribution of depression. We will examine one-year prevalence—that is the percentage of people in a given year who will suffer from depression—and will also look at the female–male ratio and at the typical age of onset. Further, there is information about the prevalence among first-degree relatives (immediate family) and the percentage of patients who actually receive treatment, and statistics on mood disorders in addition to depression are included for comparison purposes. I will discuss all of these mood disorders in detail in Chapter 4 of this book.

Table 3.1 presents some interesting patterns: In column one, looking at one year prevalence, depression is far more common than bipolar disorder (BPD) or cyclothymic disorder (CTD). This suggests that at any time less than 1% of the population will have BPD or CTD, and in terms of MDD or dysthymic disorder (DD), about 2.5–10% of the population will be affected. Interestingly, the female–male ratio is around 2:1 for depressive disorders in general (although some studies find 3:2 rates for DD), but there are no sex differences for BPD and CTD. In terms of age of onset, DD is likely to be diagnosed much earlier than MDD, and the age range for BPD I and II is much broader. This indicates that this disorder can and does appear earlier than MDD, but it can also emerge well into adulthood. Cyclothymic disorder appears at about the same younger age as BPD, but it typically does not emerge after young adulthood. It is also clear that the very serious disorders (MDD and BPD) are more likely to be treated and that almost 60% of people with BPD and almost half of those with MDD are receiving treatment.

Another impressive study looked at 6,694 patients from California and New York between the ages of 18–96 who suffered from depression. They found a

Table 3.1.
Mood Disorders Profile

	One-Year Prevalence (%)	Female–Male Ratio	Typical Age at Onset (years)	Prevalence among First-Degree Relatives	Percentage Receiving Treatment
Major Depressive Disorder	5–10%	2:1	24–29	Elevated	49%
Dysthymic Disorder	2.5–5.4%	Between 3:2 and 2:1	10–25	Elevated	37.8%
Bipolar I Disorder	0.7%	1:1	15–44	Elevated	58.9%
Bipolar II Disorder	0.5%	1:1	15–44	Elevated	58.9%
Cyclothymic Disorder	0.4%	1:1	15–25	Elevated	Unknown

R. J. Comer. (2004). *Abnormal psychology* (5th ed.). New York: Worth.

prevalence rate for MDD of 5.2% and found the rate to be higher in middle-aged, white, non-Hispanic women. Other factors producing a higher risk for MDD were obesity, poor health status, and smoking. As reported in Table 3.1, these researchers also found that the more severe the problem, the more likely the patient was to receive treatment. As positive as this appears for a limited segment of society, the elderly and nonwhite people were less likely to receive the appropriate care for their depression.[11]

Depression can and does appear in children and adolescents, and they are frequently seen in treatment. Events in childhood can contribute to an increased susceptibility to depression in adulthood, and DeMarco reports that trauma experienced as a child, as well as early childhood experiences involving parental substance abuse and/or mental health problems, are significant predictors of adult MDD.[12] While similar assumptions go back to Freud or even earlier, DeMarco's modern, data-based study substantiates what we have known all along: that events in childhood can impact the mental health of the adults who were victims of these early problems. This is a risk factor that is culturally relative and is more common in specific social groups, cultures, and subcultures. There is a gender factor as well because women are more frequently victims of these types of problems than are men.

SOCIAL CLASS AND DEPRESSION

Certainly, there are cultural and subcultural factors that impact the incidence and distribution of depression within a population. Social status has been examined as a risk factor, but as one would expect, it is not a simple relationship. Several studies have demonstrated that the frequency of mental disorders, including depression, is inversely related to socioeconomic status (SES). However, apparent in the aggregate of findings is that the relationship is only a slight one and differs for various conditions. Measures such as education and income do have a direct impact on depression, but socioeconomic status in general only explains a small portion of the variance in depression.[13]

Even when relating SES to depression, there are additional factors that enter into the picture. Education is the strongest predictor of depression in women (the more educated a woman is the less likely she is to be depressed). This particular component of SES is a better predictor of depression than SES itself— at least for women. Family income is the best predictor for men (the higher the family income, the less likely a man is to be depressed). Note that this is family income rather than personal income. So, while SES is a relevant predictor of depression for both men and women, specific components of SES (education for women and family income for men) are the best single predictors for those two groups. Paradoxically, SES variables have the strongest predictive power for unemployed housewives.[14] The lower the SES, the greater the likelihood an unemployed woman will become depressed. This relationship is stronger for unemployed housewives than any other single group of men or women. Ross and Mirowsky also reported that distress, which includes depression, is inversely related to SES, but they, too, found that the salient variables for SES are income and education.[15] MacLean and Hauser did an extensive study and found, unlike other studies, that there were no gender differences with respect to SES and depression.[16] However, they did find, in a sample of high school graduates and their siblings, that net worth was the most powerful explanatory SES variable with respect to depression, and this was true for both men and women. This finding suggests that the higher a person's net worth, the less likely they are to be depressed. This certainly doesn't mean that wealthy people can't get depressed, but it does suggest that wealthy people are *less* likely to get depressed than poor people.

DEPRESSION AROUND THE WORLD

Depression is found in all cultures, and no country or people are safe from experiencing depression. As mentioned before, depression is becoming a major public health issue around the world. In 1990, unipolar MDD was ranked fourth in the world as a cause of disease burden behind respiratory infections, diarrheal diseases, and perinatal diseases. Depression is projected to become second in disease burden in the world behind ischemic heart disease by 2020.[17]

In looking at symptoms of depression, some interesting patterns emerge. For example, in non-Western countries, depressed people are more likely to be troubled by and seek treatment for the physical symptoms of depression, while in Western countries, depressed patients are more likely to complain of the affective (emotional) and cognitive symptoms of depression. One fascinating finding is that as emerging nations become more Westernized, the symptoms of depression also start to change and to look more like the patterns found in Western societies; namely, they start to present with more affective and cognitive symptoms and fewer physical ones.[18]

In general (around the world), rates of depression tend to show women with a greater frequency of depression than men. In the United States, the gender ratio, as shown in Table 3.1, tends to be around 2:1; in most studies, women are reported with depression at about twice the rate of men. However, in Santiago, Chile, the rate difference is 4.7:1, again with women far outnumbering men in the frequency of being diagnosed with depression. Completely reversing this trend, data from Ibadan, Nigeria, shows that 5.3% of the men and 3.8% of the women are diagnosed with depression. This is a gender ratio of 0.7:1 with men being more likely to have depression.[19] While this finding is unusual, these highly variable ratios suggest that simple biological models of depression cannot explain all of what we find.

When looking at some of the secondary and indirect effects of depression, it becomes obvious that this disorder places enormous burdens on the families of depressed patients and certainly increases the stress under which caregivers must function. Because we know that increased stress increases the susceptibility to depression and other psychological disorders, this is a serious issue. Women are more likely to be the caregivers for mentally ill family members, and they often have access to fewer resources. This means that women will experience a disproportionate amount of the secondary stress from caring for a depressed person.[20] One study suggests that of the more than 100 million or so people around the world who are depressed, there are at least three times that number who are affected negatively by the patient's illness.[21]

Violence is one of the factors that contributes to people suffering from disorders such as depression, and this is relative to the location and culture in which a person lives. In fact, among the most disabling effects of violence are the long-lasting mental health effects. For example, people victimized by violence are more susceptible to depression and are more likely to attempt and commit suicide than the general population.[22] Because these factors are culturally relative, one would expect more negative mental health problems, including depression, in cultures where violence is more common. Unfortunately, in most cultures, women are more likely to be victimized by domestic violence and educational and occupational discrimination, which puts them at higher risk for depression. In fact, it seems surprising that there aren't even more women who are depressed than there actually are.[23]

To carry this beyond violence and domestic violence, being denied educational and occupational opportunities are factors that also negatively impact one's mental health, and these outcomes are also more likely to affect women than men in most cultures. There is a demonstrable link between disorders such as depression and economic deprivation resulting from such things as unemployment, being in debt, or belonging to a lower socioeconomic class in society. Thus, people who are already vulnerable in a society are at risk for developing another condition that will likely disable them further. Once again, this particular burden disproportionately affects women, and this is true all over the world.[24]

According to the WHO, about 80% of the 50 million people negatively affected by violent crime, civil war, disasters, and displacement around the world are women and children making them more vulnerable to depression.[25] Even among those who are at a higher risk for depression, there are some measurable differences between peoples in differing cultures. One interesting study looked at women in Harau, Zimbabwe, and compared them to women in Camberwell (a region in London, England). In both of these samples, the women were from low-income urban settings. In Harau, about 18% of women were depressed as compared with 9% in Camberwell. It was also true that in Harau, 54% of the women had experienced severe life events, while only 31% of the women in Camberwell had.[26] These numbers are actually very high for both groups of women, but they show that even among the disenfranchised, there are differences between cultures that suggest additional factors contributing to depression.

Studies regarding patients from other countries were also very interesting in terms of their implications. While studying depressive disorders in Europe, Ayaso-Mateos and Vázquez-Barquero found that depressive disorders are highly prevalent on that continent.[27] By studying many different sites, they found there was an overall prevalence rate of 8.56% of persons diagnosed with some type of depressive disorder. They also found that among men the prevalence rate was 6.61%, while in women the rate was 10.05%, a finding consistent with much of the rest of the world. Among the sites they studied, the highest rates were found in urban Ireland and the lowest in urban Spain, with the rest of the sites falling in the medium prevalence range.

Another study looked at depressed patients in Austria and Pakistan and examined the different types of symptoms that were expressed. Specifically, they looked at "ethical anxiety" and "delusional guilt." By ethical anxiety, they refer to feelings patients reported when they feel as if they did something wrong and feel badly about it. Delusional guilt refers to faulty beliefs held by patients regarding the feeling that they are guilty of something that they could not have actually caused. They found that in both cultures, patients experienced and were troubled by feelings of ethical anxiety, but only in Austria did patients express feelings of delusional guilt.[28] Thus, while the rate of depression may have been similar in the two groups, the expression of the symptoms was clearly culturally relative.

WHAT ARE THE IMPLICATIONS OF EPIDEMIOLOGICAL FINDINGS?

As we look at the various epidemiological findings regarding depression, it becomes obvious that there is no simple causal pattern. Factors such as gender, age, culture, SES, disease and physical condition, stress, childhood trauma, and abuse are all related to adult depression, and we will discuss all of these in more detail in subsequent chapters; however, where does this myriad of information leave us?

First, is depression a genetically linked disorder? One of the strongest statements in this particular area comes from Sullivan et al. who state that, "Depression is a familial disease and this is mostly or entirely due to genetics."[29] However, they go on to state that environmental factors are causally important for individuals. Thus, MDD is a complex disorder that depends on both environment and genetic factors. Even as a familial disorder, MacLean & Hauser found that, among siblings, depression levels were only moderately correlated.[30] Thus, let's go back to the original question: "Is depression a genetically linked disorder?" The answer is clearly, "Yes, but . . ."

We have also seen that depression is related to gender, and while there may be a genetic link related to this finding, there are clearly other factors including psychological, social, and cultural issues that play a part in depression as well. MacLean and Hauser conclude that the underlying structure of depression is the same for men and women but that the way the disorder is expressed is different for men and women.[31] In other words, the disorder itself is not different for men and women—it is the same disorder. However, depression manifests itself differently in men and women and at different rates.

The complex relationship between gender and depression at different ages, as MacLean and Hauser suggest, is most likely a curvilinear function.[32] Think of a graph with a horizontal axis representing age and the vertical axis representing incidence of depression. If we plot the relationship for women and for men there will be two different lines, and they will not be simple straight lines but will curve showing a complex and different relationship. A simple linear relationship would indicate that depression rates are either positively or negatively related to age, or that the rates are the same for all ages. Because none of these conditions are true, it is clear that the relationship between age, gender, and depression is complicated by additional factors. While childhood trauma and abuse are related to adult depression, they are not prominent causes. Most children who are abused in various ways do not grow up to be depressed. Cultural and social factors play a significant role in depression, but these variables alone do not explain it, or everyone in a particular culture or social setting would be depressed.

ETIOLOGICAL (CAUSAL) FACTORS IN DEPRESSION

People have tried to make sense of depression since the beginning of medical and scientific history, with explanations ranging from the mundane to the fantastic. I will present some of the more widely researched and accepted theories of depression from a variety of different sources. At the end of the chapter, I will present a model that ties together all of the factors related to depression and its causes, as well as those that may have a positive impact on the expression of the disorder.

When addressing the multiplicity of potential causal factors in depression we must begin with an appreciation for the breadth of this topic, including psychological, environmental, and biological factors. Psychological factors that have been linked to depression include such things as:

+ Unresolved issues from childhood or early life that are manifested later
+ A history of depression
+ Damage to the body (injury, illness, surgery, etc.)
+ Fear of death
+ Frustration with bodily/psychological changes like memory
+ Difficulties coping with stress and change
+ Substance abuse
+ Low self-esteem
+ Extreme dependency
+ Chronic pessimism

Environmental factors that are related to depression include:

+ Loneliness/isolation
+ Retirement

- Being unmarried (especially if widowed)
- Recently bereaved
- Lack of a good support system
- Decreased mobility/independence

Biological/physical factors that are related to depression:

- Genetics (inherited predisposition to depression)
- Comorbidities (other physical or psychological conditions)
- Vascular changes in the brain
- Vitamin B-12 deficiency (there is some question as to whether this is a cause or an effect)
- Chronic, severe pain
- Drugs and certain medications[33]

The NIMH mentions that certain illnesses (stroke, heart attack, cancer, Parkinson's, hormonal disorders) as well as other physical factors can lead to depression.[34] They also suggest that a serious loss, relationship problems, financial difficulties, and major life changes are frequently related to the development of depression, supporting the theory that depression is usually the result of a combination of many factors and not just one or two.

Biological Factors

There are a huge number of different approaches to trying to uncover the biological basis for depression. In addition to genetics, which I will discuss separately, some look at the endocrine glands, others look at the hypothalamic-pituitary-adrenal axis, and others have focused primarily on the neurotransmitters such as serotonin, norepinephrine, dopamine, acetylcholine, and gamma-aminobutyric acid. With improvements in neuro-imaging techniques, other researchers have looked for structural changes in the brain as well as functional analyses examining changes in brain activity. Some are even looking at cellular activity in the brain to see to what extent this might be related to depressive conditions.[35] As we examine the biological bases for depression we should also remember that some forms of depression are more likely to have biological causes than others and that one single biological model will never suffice to explain everything that depression has come to mean.

Several researchers are convinced that in some medical conditions there is a biological connection between the illness and depression, and it is not just that the person is depressed because they are ill.[36] For example, neurological conditions such as multiple sclerosis, stroke, vascular brain changes, different types of dementia, brain trauma, and others are frequently associated with depression. Other conditions such as hypothyroidism, fibromyalgia, and chronic fatigue syndrome are often associated with depression.

Drugs of all kinds can also lead to depressive symptoms. Prescription drugs and recreational or "street" drugs can precipitate a depressive episode, as can some CNS depressants; for example, alcohol, marijuana, and "downer drugs," such as barbiturates, narcotics, tranquilizers, pain pills, and antipsychotic medications, are often sold "on the street" to people who are either addicted or dependent upon them or who are using them recreationally. Interestingly, the "energizing" drugs, such as amphetamines, cocaine, phencyclidine (angel dust), and others, can also lead to depression, but through a different pathway. Historically, some of these energizing types of drugs, such as dextroamphetamine, were used to treat depression because it was thought that they could help someone who was lethargic and lacked energy due to depression. What typically resulted was that the patient was still depressed but was now in a state called "agitated depression." An additional risk is that when this type of drug starts to wear off, one of the symptoms is likely to be a depressive state, and in a person who is high risk for depression, the withdrawal from this type of drug can actually lead to a serious depressive reaction.[37]

Some researchers and theorists have postulated that hormones can be related to depression. Holsboer points out that people with unipolar depression have abnormally high levels of cortisol, which is one of the hormones released by the adrenal glands when a person is under stress.[38] This connection is not entirely clear but certainly suggests that depression and hormones are related. Another approach to hormonal impact on depression involves studying the relationship between gonadal functioning and depression. Some men with low serum testosterone (the level of testosterone in the blood) will have depression.[39] However, this finding is not always consistent, and there are probably other factors involved as well. It has also been discovered that testosterone gel may produce antidepressant effects in the large and probably under-recognized populations of men with low testosterone levels.[40] Another article by Schweiger found the relationship between depression and gonadal functioning has had mixed findings.[41] However, this study did show that there was a decreased testosterone secretion in men with major depression, and particularly in men under the age of 55. Interestingly, they also found a negative correlation between cortisol (the stress hormone) and testosterone. Thus, the lower the testosterone levels, the higher the cortisol levels.

As you recall from an earlier description of depressive symptoms, very frequently people with depression report problems sleeping. They find that their sleep schedule, appetite, and other aspects of their life just seem to be dysregulated—that is, the normal bodily rhythms seem to be "out of whack." Bunney and Bunney conclude that depression is often the result of an imbalance between the circadian rhythms of the body and the normal or typical rhythms of the environment.[42] Similarly, Thase et al. report that the sleep cycle in depressed people is apparently reversed; this means that they often stay up at night and sleep during the day.[43] Depressed individuals never seem to have their sleep regulated in a way that is consistent with other people or with the way they were prior to being depressed. We do know that depressed people move into rapid eye movement (REM) sleep, when most dreaming occurs, sooner than nondepressed people. They tend to have longer REM cycles early in their sleep and fewer later in the sleep cycle. They also seem to have more eye movements during the REM periods than normal people, and they spend less time in the deeper stages of sleep.[44]

Probably the area of biological inquiry that has stimulated the most interest in recent years is the study of the relationship between neurotransmitters and depression. Neurotransmitters are the chemical messengers that send information from one nerve cell to another. For many years we have known that low levels of norepinephrine and serotonin are linked to depression, and it used to be thought that low levels of either of these could cause depression. Today, we realize that it is much more complex than this.[45] More recently, it has been established that people who are depressed have an overall imbalance of serotonin, norepinephrine, dopamine, and acetylcholine. Some researchers seem to think that while all of these neurotransmitters are important, serotonin apparently regulates the levels of the others.[46] It does appear that low levels of serotonin and norepinephrine lead to depression, while low serotonin and high levels of norepinephrine lead to mania.[47] This, too, is over-simplistic, but it does suggest the relative importance of these chemicals in brain functioning. Much of this work is based on the therapeutic effects of antidepressant medications, and as we learn more and more about these medications, we are also learning more about brain function and the various roles of these neurotransmitters in conditions such as depression. In sum, it seems clear that the four neurotransmitter substances named previously do have some role in depression, but there is still much to discover. We do know that, with the discovery of the importance of neurotransmitters in depression, we have seen a virtual explosion in the availability, quality, and efficacy of medications for the treatment of depression and related conditions. One of the negative side effects of these drugs is that they are probably overused and misused by many who are looking for a quick and easy solution to the treatment of a very complex disorder. As we will see later in the book, medication certainly has a prominent role in the treatment of depression, but it is rarely curative by itself.

Genetics

Another area in the biological realm of depression is the field of genetics. Because there is so much research on this biological topic alone, I will discuss this separately. For a very long time we have known that depression tends to run in families, but there has been considerable speculation as to the extent to which this might be due to heredity or to environmental influences. Of course, today the conclusion is that both have a role in depression, but it is important to continue to address this issue so that we can have a more accurate perspective on the causal factors. There is no question but that genetics plays some role and even if it is not always the main factor related to the cause of depression. For example, if one monozygotic (identical) twin has depression, the other twin has a 50% likelihood of developing depression as well. However, in dizygotic (fraternal) twins the same ratio is only 20%. I must point out that if depression were a simple genetic disorder, monozygotic twins should have 100% concordance—that is, if one of the twins was depressed, then the other would always be as well because they are genetically equal. But, because the concordance rate for monozygotic twins is substantially higher than for dizygotic twins, who also have very much the same environment, then there must be an important contribution from genetic factors. Other studies have demonstrated that adopted children who had a biological parent with depression were three times more likely to develop depression than the biological children of the same parents.[48] A different study found that the relationship between the biological parents of adoptive children was more pronounced for severe depression than for mild. This has led some people to speculate that severe depression is more likely to be genetically linked than the milder forms of depression.[49] Another interesting finding is that patients will do better on the antidepressant medication that was effective for a first-degree relative (parents, children, siblings), and this, too, is suggestive of a genetic link.[50]

Bipolar disorder also seems to have a high genetic risk. Some studies find that while the likelihood of two people in the general population both having BPD is about 1%, this rate is in the 5–10% range for first-degree relatives but up to 40% in monozygotic twins.[51] It is clear that there are environmental factors at work in BPD as well, and while there is a strong genetic component for this disorder, environmental factors also have to be part of the picture.[52] Many researchers around the world have tried to find specific genetic markers for depression, but the results have been mixed and confusing. At this point, the evidence leads to the conclusion that depression and BPD are not simple genetic problems. Some have looked at the sex specific rate differential in depression, which shows, in general, that women are much more prone to depression than are men, and some see this as evidence for a genetic link. However, one study showed that relatives of male and female depressives were equally likely to get depressed. Thus, it can't be a simple sex-linked gene.[53] Bebbinton, in reviewing the studies on the sex-linked potential for liability to depression, finds that the sex ratios in depression cannot be due only to genetic factors—it must involve some extra-familial influences; thus genetics cannot be the sole cause of the sex ratio.[54] He concludes that the even sex ratio in depression is a very complex issue and will not be explained with a simple model.

Social, Family, and Environmental Factors

In addition to genetics, depression has been linked to a number of social and family processes; for example, Kennard et al. support a longitudinal model of depression where there are various factors occurring over a period of time that lead to depression.[55] They found that the best predictor of future depression is concurrent depressive symptoms and stressful events. If these factors are accompanied by cognitive errors or distortions, then this strongly links the person to future episodes of depression.

Interestingly, Lindeman et al. report that depression is more marked in married than never married groups.[56] However, among the married group, unsupported mothers are especially at risk.[57] Others who are particularly subject to depression are caregivers. These are the people who are caring for others who are disabled or suffering from conditions that necessitate their being cared for by another person or persons. Caregivers are far more likely to succumb to many disorders, including depression, and have higher mortality rates in serious diseases such as cardiovascular disease, diabetes, and cancer. Caring for someone, particularly if one has little help, can be very stressful. Social isolation, financial strain, worry, and being cut off from activities that are rewarding can often lead to depression.[58] In addition to caregiver issues, such things as family size, parental age, marital disruption, and remarriage are all related to the development of depression.[59,60]

Social and environmental factors such as financial strain, decreased feelings of control and self-worth often lead to symptoms of depression.[61] Decreased satisfaction with social contact, lower levels of perceived social support, and more disruptions in social relationships lead to depression as well.[62] Interestingly, Myers points out that Americans today spend less time visiting family and friends and less time in community service and related activities than in the past.[63] Today's children are more likely to come from families of divorce and are less likely to live near extended families. Materialism is more important to children and adolescents today, and students entering college today rate "living well" as more important than "developing a meaningful life philosophy," the opposite of what was found 30 years ago.[64] Contrast these findings with research that demonstrates lower rates of depression among people in Mediterranean countries, rural New Zealand, and British Orthodox Jews;[65,66,67] cultures that place high value on the home-making role and tend to be more family-centered. What may be happening is that the possible "protective effect" of a supportive family/social system is not as prevalent in today's culture (at least in the United States) as it was in the past, and this, too, might be related to higher rates of depression.

We know that depression, like other mental disorders, is also inversely related to social class.[68] People in the lower social strata tend to deal with more stressful and difficult situations than those in more advantaged levels of society. As a result, many have concluded that depression is primarily situational—it is a state rather than a trait. As discussed previously, regardless of gender, people with more accumulated wealth tend to have lower levels of depression.[69] However, there is a very complex relationship between social milieu and emotional functioning.[70] The availability of social support also seems to influence the likelihood of depression.[71] Thus, we must keep in mind that when a person is high risk for depression, the extent to which they have meaningful and available social support will certainly help mitigate and even perhaps prevent its onset.

Psychological Factors

The oldest of the psychological approaches to understanding depression is psychoanalysis as originally developed by Sigmund Freud. This approach typically looks for the source of a person's difficulties in their subconscious, and problems in this realm of psychic functioning can lead to a pathological condition such as depression. Psychoanalysts tend to search for the source of an adult's difficulties in the person's history and childhood, and the rationale for this approach is that as a person develops through life's stages, certain events occur (trauma, for example) that can disrupt development leading to later problems. Psychoanalytic psychotherapy is used to correct the deviations in development that laid the foundation for these problems, including depression.

Freud wrote about melancholia, which is like what we would call depression today. Of course, he was not the first to write about this condition, and in fact, we can find references to depression or melancholia throughout recorded history. However, Freud was the first modern writer to address depression from a purely psychological perspective. Freud believed that melancholia basically meant that the person had internalized either anger or loss or both. The implication was that the person suffering from depression does not know the true nature of their condition and that they cannot fully understand or relieve it without appropriate treatment—in this case, psychoanalytic therapy. Freud, and one of his followers, Karl Abraham, wrote extensively on melancholia and were among the first of the psychological theorists to systematically address depression. They both saw the similarities between depression and grief, which led them to the belief that depression is a regressive response to loss. They also believed that the loss in question may be a real loss or a symbolic loss but that either could lay the groundwork for depression.

There are now several newer psychoanalytic or psychodynamic approaches to depression, and all rely on the perspectives of intrapsychic factors (inside the person's mind) and developmental aberrations. The more modern theories typically address issues other than unconscious instincts and conflicts, looking more at the conscious process and contemporaneous events and issues. A good example of a modern psychodynamic theory is Object Relations Theory as typified by the writings of Kernberg.[72,73] He looks at the relationship people have with various love objects and examines how this relationship can lead to problems. For example, he would say that, when relationships leave a person feeling unsafe and insecure, this can lead to depression.

In addition to Kernberg, several similar approaches look at depression as a real or symbolic loss that occurs during childhood. While there is considerable literature regarding the newer and more traditional psychoanalytic approaches, little systematic research exists, and with respect to the empirical and theoretical work that has been done, the evidence supporting this approach is sparse and mixed at best. However, it is a compelling and interesting approach that continues to be a significant force in the field.

A more recent psychological tactic for understanding depression is the cognitive approach. Beginning with the early work of Aaron Beck, this approach demonstrates very good explanatory power, good empirical support, and has been a significant stimulus to the development of effective and well-supported therapeutic advances.[74] The main idea in the cognitive theories is that depression is a function, at least in part, of how people think. Even though depression is a disorder of mood, it may be caused or exacerbated by how people think about and perceive things. Beck feels that there were typical types of thinking that lead to depression;[75] for example, some people have maladaptive attitudes that lead to depression. If someone has an attitude that they are only worthwhile if everyone loves them, you can see how the person has set themselves up for stress, disappointment, rejection, and ultimately, depression. A person can also exhibit errors in thinking that might become problematic, such as a patient seeing themselves as responsible for something bad that has happened to them (e.g., getting a disease) even when she/he couldn't have possibly caused the event; if the person continues to blame themselves in spite of efforts to convince them otherwise, this is an error in thinking that can very likely lead to depression.

Others experience automatic thoughts that pop up during certain circum-stances. If they are related to negative thinking, then this, too, can lead to depression. For example, anytime a person notices that someone else isn't pay-ing attention to them, they automatically assume that person doesn't like him or her. Obviously, there are many people who don't notice us during a given day, and this certainly doesn't mean that they don't like us; chances are they haven't even noticed us. However, if the automatic thought is, "they don't like me," we can then spend a lot of time counting people who we think dislike us—clearly a path to depression.

Beck and others also talk about the "Cognitive Triad": three ways of think-ing that are very commonly found in depressed people:

+ Negative feelings about their experiences
+ Negative feelings about themselves
+ Negative feelings about the future[76]

Unlike the psychodynamic approaches that look into the person's history and development to find the roots of depression, the cognitive approach is more direct. It addresses how the person is thinking now, how that is related to depression, and how the person can be helped to think differently.

For some people the relationship between how we think and how we feel is not that simple, and just learning to think differently may not be the only way to treat an emotional disorder such as depression. As Beck and others point out, cognition acts as a mediator between events in our lives and our mood.[77] In other words, things happen to us, we find ways to understand and think about them, and then some of these thinking patterns may lead to the devel-opment of different emotional states, including depression. It is important to remember that cognitive predispositions to depression are more complicated than simply looking at specific thought patterns. One study found that the cog-nitive predisposition to depression seemed only to predict depression for the more serious cases and not for the milder variants.[78] The cognitive approach has clearly changed the way we think about depression, and as we will see later, it has had a significant impact on the treatment of depression as well.

Another of the psychological approaches to depression that has been around for many decades is the behavioral approach. The work of Peter Lewinsohn in this area explains that depression is a reaction to the things that people experi-ence, and therefore, the environment is an important part of understanding the cause and the treatment of depression. As Lewinsohn et al. point out, depres-sion is due to changes in the rewards and the punishments people receive, and for some, a decrease in positive rewards leads people to perform fewer con-structive acts, therefore receiving fewer rewards.[79] This continues until people receive very few rewards at all, and we know that the absence of social rewards is very important in depression.[80] On the other hand, if people continue to receive significant punishments, this, too, will lead to depression. Certainly, it is easy to believe that the more positive experiences there are in one's life, the more they will produce more positive feelings. Seligman also recognizes the importance of reinforcements, but he looks at it from a cognitive perspective.[81] He explains that when people feel that they no longer have control over their reinforcements, they are likely to feel helpless, possibly leading to depression.

Some of the behavioral theorists also focus on the relationship between environmental influences, such as stress, and its impact on depression. Although she is not a behavioral theorist, Swartz points out that many believe that dysthymia (a milder form of depression) may be caused by severe stress.[82] We do know that stress frequently precedes depression, but what the behavioral approach doesn't explain well is why there are individual differences.[83] That is, if several people are exposed to the same stress, then why don't all of them become depressed?

The behavioral approach has been very helpful in understanding the relationship between environmental events and depression and has also led to some helpful treatment approaches. However, many feel this approach is somewhat limited by itself. Today, a major trend in the study and treatment of depression has been the merging of the cognitive and behavioral approaches. This model, called, appropriately enough, the Cognitive-Behavioral Model, is very influential and is well supported in the empirical literature. In a later chapter, I discuss treatment approaches and how this model has dramatically influenced how depression is treated today.

AN INTEGRATIVE APPROACH

Throughout this book, I have frequently discussed how complex depression is and how many factors might be involved in the understanding of mood disorders in general. I believe that all of the previously discussed approaches have something valid to offer to help understand depression; however, how they all fit together is not so obvious. Rather than performing a microscopic analysis of each factor, I would like to present a model that is a more general and conceptual model and will help us understand how these factors fit together. I assume there are some things that predispose people to depression and that these may lead to factors in a person's life that may interact with one another to produce depressive symptoms. However, at the same time, there are other factors that are more positive in their influence that may help prevent or mitigate the situation and have a positive impact on depressive symptoms. It is my view that all of these things continually interacting with one another have a dynamic and cumulative effect on people that determines when or if they will become depressed. This also explains individual differences and why some people will develop depression when others in similar situations, or from the same backgrounds and gene pool, will not get depressed.

The following model, presented in Figure 3.1, is adapted from work by Power and includes all of the factors that we have discussed in our review of epidemiological and etiological factors.[84] The assumption is that depressive symptoms will emerge through an interaction of risk factors and "relieving factors"; next, we will discuss the various factors and their interactions.

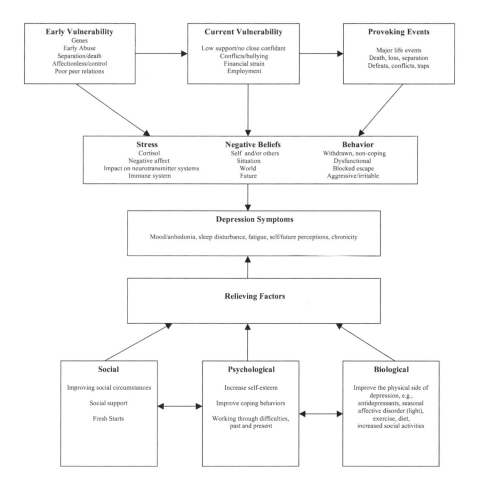

FIGURE 3.1: Biopsychosocial interactions in depression.
From M. Power (Ed.). (2004). *Mood disorders: A handbook of science and practice.* Chichester, UK: John Wiley.

We know that there are people who are predisposed to depression or who suffered abuse or trauma during their early development. However, current factors can also make people more vulnerable to depression; for example, having poor social support or no close relationships, having significant conflicts in life, or being unemployed or underemployed. In addition, major life events that are traumatic or stressful, including the death of a loved one, various losses and separations, as well as defeats, conflicts, and feeling trapped may also contribute to depression.

Stress can lead more directly to depressive symptoms, including some psychophysiological changes that can occur in response to stressful situations. Under stress, the body produces hormones that will change bodily and emotional functioning and also alter the functioning of the neural transmitter systems in the brain. Further, stress impacts the immune system and its ability to deal with various pathogens, as well as causing changes in mental processes. Cognitive factors such as negative beliefs about self, the world in general, and the future will certainly impact whether or not a person becomes depressed. Finally, behavior such as social withdrawal, inability to cope effectively, and feeling trapped will also influence their susceptibility to depression.

While all of these factors will either create a predisposition for depression or have an immediate effect on depression emerging, "relieving factors" will also impact depressive symptoms but in the opposite way, by lessening the probability that depression will emerge. For example, improving one's social circumstances, receiving good social support, and having the opportunity for a fresh start can all help a vulnerable person fight depression. Psychological factors such as improved self-esteem, better coping skills, and working through problems are also examples of relieving factors that will help the person avoid depression. Finally, biological factors can also be improved and help with the physical side of depression. Taking appropriate medications, sleeping well, receiving enough light (especially for seasonal affective disorder), exercising, and getting appropriate nutrition will help a person avoid or improve a depressive state.

Probably the best way to think about this model is to use a "threshold" metaphor. When a person's negative mood level reaches a specific threshold, depression will result. Now, imagine several factors at work that increase vulnerability, add a few stressful events or situations, some negative beliefs, and nonhelpful behaviors, and you can see how their interaction could push the negative mood to a certain level, which might result in depression. At the same time, however, the relieving factors interact to actually shift the threshold higher (or push the mood level lower) making it less likely that depression will emerge. If, in the interaction of all of these, positive and negative factors result in a negative mood level above threshold, then the person will manifest depressive symptoms. Then, the relieving factors, including psychological and medical treatments and improved lifestyle, will hopefully push the threshold higher or suppress some of the negative influences, and then the depression will either be improved, become subclinical (not manifesting symptoms), or will be relieved or "cured."

As we have seen from our examination of the epidemiological and causal factors in depression, there are many things that may impact depression, and there is not one single variable or even a fixed set of variables that will routinely and reliably produce depression in all or even most people. There are too many factors involved to have a simple model, but hopefully, the model provided will help you understand how depression emerges and some of the factors that are involved in the complex processes that underlie it. Appreciating this will also help understand why treatment is rarely simple either and is often multifaceted, using several different therapies simultaneously.

While discussing depression relative to the different approaches and theories, we must always remember that, even with the same disorder, no two patients are exactly alike. We can certainly learn and apply ideas from one patient to another, but each patient is always unique. Models and theories can help guide our thinking to make it easier to conceptualize specific cases, but we must avoid the "cookie-cutter" approach that tries to fit a patient into a specific category without appreciating their individuality, or assume that the same treatment approach will always work the same way with all patients—it just doesn't happen that way.

Chapter 4

The Different Types and Manifestations of Depression

Geez, if I could get through to you, kiddo, that depression is not sobbing and cry-ing and giving vent, it is plain and simple reduction in feeling. Reduction, see? Of all feeling. People who keep stiff upper lips find that it is damn hard to smile.
—Judith Guest, U.S. author

My dear Kafka,
When you've had five years of it, not five months, five years of an irresistible force meeting an immoveable object right in your belly, then you'll know about depression.
—Philip Larkin, British poet

When we think of depression, most of us have a fairly clear idea of what it means to us, but is it the same thing that it means to others? Although there are common themes and symptoms, the experience of depression is as individ-ual and unique as the person who suffers from it. This individual experience of depression is also complicated by the fact that there are different types of depression with different causes, different courses or patterns, different out-comes, and even different types of treatments.

Basically, there are a few specific diagnostic categories for depression. We examine different types of mood disorders that involve depression, different psychological problems of which depression is a component, and different medical problems that involve depressive symptoms. It is tempting to think of the different forms of depression as "quantitatively" different—that is, some are worse, and some are not so bad. There are, however, various types of depression that differ *qualitatively*; that means that the form and content of the depression as well as the causes and course of the disorder are different—sometimes sub-tly and sometimes more extremely, but different nonetheless.

All of the forms of depression do share at least some of the symptoms that comprise the common characteristics that inflict themselves upon those who suffer from it. It is common for many who suffer depression to have a persistent sad, anxious, or "empty" mood, although sometimes this is difficult to describe while one is experiencing it. People who are battling depression are victims in the sense that something bad is happening to them. They feel as though there is nothing they could have done to prevent it, and they often feel guilty without knowing what they are feeling guilty about. Sometimes they will have a distorted sense of things they may have done wrong for either real or imagined transgressions.

Another prominent symptom of depression is *anhedonia*, which means the absence of pleasure in things that had previously been enjoyable. We often see a loss of interest in hobbies or recreational activities, feeling so fatigued and "empty" they can't muster the energy to do much of anything. Even things such as recreation, social activities, and sex are not experienced as pleasurable. This is often very frustrating to those who are trying to be supportive to a depressed person; efforts to get a person moving and involved will not only likely fail, but the depressed person will probably resent anyone who tries to force them to be active.

In addition to being physically "slowed down," the depressed person will frequently complain of feeling mentally slowed down as well. Difficulty concentrating, remembering, making decisions, and even thinking are very common. This type of cognitive inefficiency sometimes leads depressed people to feel they are "losing their minds" and that they will never be "normal" again. This is perhaps one of the most frightening aspects about depression—a fear that it will never go away—ever.

Invariably, people with depression report having problems sleeping; this can take a number of different forms. The most typical type of insomnia is when a person takes a long time to fall asleep or awakens frequently during the night never achieving a consistently restful sleep. Some depressed persons will find they waken earlier than usual (by several hours) and can't get back to sleep. Others have hypersomnia where they sleep more than they need to. Even if they sleep 10–12 hours or more, they will awaken still feeling exhausted. Whether they sleep too much or too little, they are always tired and have no energy or motivation to do anything. This is sometimes a very perplexing diagnostic issue because one of the more common symptoms of sleep deprivation is an alteration of normal mood states—including feeling depressed. Thus, we often face a "chicken or the egg" problem when looking at both sleep problems and depression. When doing a clinical interview with someone who reports both depressive and sleep problems, we try to determine, though the history and intake, which of these conditions started first.

Problems with food and weight are similar to sleep problems found in depression because they also can take several different forms. Patients report that they either have no appetite, don't want to eat and thus lose weight, or they eat compulsively or binge and gain weight. When a person is depressed and overeating, they usually don't choose food items wisely and will often overdo the simple carbohydrates and sugars. If you combine fatigue, reduced motivation, lowered levels of physical activity, poor food choices, and overeating you will most assuredly gain weight. We sometimes refer to this as "self-medicating" with food. As mentioned previously, however, some people seem to lose their appetite entirely and neither want to eat nor do they push themselves very hard to eat. They might choke down a few morsels but then feel stuffed and unable to eat more.

Similarly, when people are depressed they are more likely to drink alcohol abusively; particularly men. This, too, is called self-medicating. Once again, we have a "chicken or the egg" problem, because while depression might lead to alcohol or drug abuse, it is also true that alcohol and drug abuse might lead to depression. Obtaining a clear clinical history and a good timeline as to when problems or symptoms emerged is very important to the understanding of the nature of the problems that are presented.

Additional symptoms that are common in depression are morbid and persistent (sometimes obsessive) thoughts of death, dying, or suicide. Certainly, a depressed person is higher risk for suicide attempts or commission, and when evaluating a person for depression it is necessary to assess the suicidal risk the person is presenting. Behaviorally, when depressed people withdraw and become socially isolated, their activity level will decrease as will their social involvement. They are often restless and irritable and are rarely pleasant to be around. The worse they feel the more others may initially try to help, but when nothing seems to work, others start avoiding them, which, of course, plays into the person's feelings that they are worthless and no one cares about them.

Perhaps the symptoms of depression that will most likely lead a person to seek help are persistent and often vague physical symptoms that do not respond to conventional medical treatment. It is not usually depression that brings the person in for an appointment with their physician but rather one or more of an extensive list of persistent physical symptoms, such as headaches, digestive disorders, chronic pain, sexual dysfunction, muscular–skeletal problems, sleep problems, and many other physical complaints. That doesn't mean that the physical symptoms are necessarily the first to emerge, but they are often the first that are seen by a health professional.

As discussed in Chapter 1, depression can affect people of any age and at any time. For many patients the first episode of depression occurs in childhood or adolescence, and for many people it becomes a life-long episodic disorder with multiple occurrences. In fact, 20–25% of people with major depressive disorder (MDD) experience a chronic and unremitting course, and 72% have double depression, MDD plus dysthymic disorder (DD). Further, 65% of people with recurrent depression have some chronic symptoms.[1,2,3]

DIFFERENT TYPES OF DEPRESSION

Unipolar Depression

When we talk about unipolar depression we are referring to depression that is only manifest in one direction—negative mood states. We will discuss bipolar disorder (BPD), a different type of problem, later in this chapter. Unipolar depression refers to depression that does not vacillate between the lows of depression and the highs of mania. When a person suffers from unipolar depression that means the depression is the primary type of symptom pattern. Of course, that doesn't mean the person cannot exhibit other conditions, but in terms of mood disorders, depression is the main problem.

Major Depressive Disorder

To begin with, you have to determine whether or not a person has experienced a major depressive episode. To qualify for this, the person must experience at least five of the following symptoms, and they *must* have either depressed mood or loss of interest or pleasure or both. In addition, the symptoms must not be due to a medical condition. They must be present during the same two-week period and be a change from the way the person was functioning prior to the onset of symptoms. These symptoms can be based on self-report or the observation of others.

Symptoms of major depressive episode include (most of the day and on most days):

1. Depressed mood (in children or teens, this could be an irritable mood)
2. Diminished pleasure or interest
3. Significant weight loss when not dieting, weight gain (more than 5% change in weight in a month), or a decrease in appetite (in children this could be a failure to gain weight normally)
4. Insomnia or hypersomnia
5. Psychomotor retardation or agitation (this must also be observable by others and not just subjective feelings)
6. Fatigue or decreased energy
7. Feelings of worthlessness or excessive guilt (which may be inappropriate or even delusional)
8. Decreased ability to think, concentrate, and make decisions
9. Recurrent ideas about death and suicide, although this may not be experienced every day[4]

To be considered to be depression it is important to note that these symptoms cannot be part of a mixed episode with depressive and manic features and that the symptoms must cause significant distress in the social, occupational, recreational, and "normal" areas of a person's life. These symptoms cannot be due to substances or medications or directly due to a medical condition. Finally, the symptoms cannot be due to simple and uncomplicated bereavement, although bereavement can occasionally lead to MDD.

When MDD is diagnosed, there are a number of different considerations that need to be determined. Is this a single episode, or is it recurrent? How severe is the episode (mild, moderate, or severe), and are there psychotic features? Psychotic features usually take the form of unusual and sometimes bizarre beliefs (delusions). This also means the depressive disorder needs to be differentiated from other psychotic disorders. It is not depression if it is part of a schizoaffective disorder or if it is imposed upon another type of schizophrenic disorder, delusional disorder, or other unspecified form of psychotic disorder. Also, it cannot be diagnosed as unipolar depression if there has ever been a manic or hypomanic episode in the patient's past.

When the diagnosis of MDD is made, there are additional qualifiers to consider. For example, if catatonic features (an almost vegetative state) are present this needs to be noted as well as melancholic or atypical features. It needs to be specified whether or not this is a chronic condition or if the condition is in full or partial remission. Finally, special note is made if the MDD has a postpartum onset or if there is a seasonal pattern to the depression. As you can see, the diagnosis of an MDD is not a simple matter. As we consider other forms of depression and other mood disorders, the picture becomes even more complex.

Dysthymic Disorder

MDD has symptoms that interfere with the ability to work, study, sleep, eat, and enjoy previously pleasurable activities. It may occur only once, or it can occur a number of times in a person's lifetime. On the other hand, DD is a long-term, chronic disorder in which the symptoms do not disable but do keep one from functioning optimally or feeling good. Some people who have DD can experience episodes of MDD, and when they occur together this is referred to as double depression.[5]

In order to be diagnosed with DD, a person must feel depressed most of the day, and on most days, and this must have continued for at least two years. The diagnosis may be made based on the person's subjective report or by the observations of others. Interestingly, people with DD frequently do not even realize they are depressed because they have felt like this for so long it feels normal to them. Frequently, when they receive treatment and start to improve, they realize it has been a very long time since they have actually felt truly normal—that is to say appropriately happy or sad depending on the circumstances.

In addition to the symptom of feeling depressed most of the time, to receive the diagnosis of DD the person must also exhibit at least two of the following symptoms:

1. Poor appetite or overeating
2. Hypersomnia or insomnia
3. Decreased energy or fatigue
4. Diminished self-esteem
5. Poor concentration and difficulty in decision making
6. Feelings of hopelessness

In addition to these considerations, the person must have experienced these symptoms for at least two years (one year for children and adolescents) and must not have been without the symptoms for more than two months at a time. It is also important to note that the symptoms could not be better explained with another diagnosis.[6]

Atypical Depression

Atypical depression (AD) is found in about 30–40% of depressed patients, and they share many of the usual symptoms of depression, although there are some differences. For example, they may have pleasurable experiences in certain specific and key areas of their life. Also, they usually don't have sleep problems or loss of appetite. In fact, these may be some of the patients who tend to overeat and oversleep. Some of the common symptoms of AD include:

+ General sadness that can be broken with pleasurable activities
+ Feelings of rejection—usually very strong
+ A sensation of heaviness; especially in the arms
+ Strong preference for carbohydrates, which, by the way, may be linked to increased serotonin levels

The symptoms of AD are very debilitating even though they may not seem as severe as those in MDD. It is usually true that the episodes of AD are shorter but more frequent than those of MDD.[7]

Adjustment Disorder with Depressed Mood

This disorder is not actually grouped with the mood disorders but is in a different category—the adjustment disorders. An adjustment disorder is when there are emotional or behavioral symptoms that emerge as a response to an identifiable stressor that has occurred within three months prior to the onset of the symptoms. These symptoms are clinically significant insofar as they produce marked distress and are in excess of what might be expected as a normal response to the stressors in question. There also needs to be significant impairment in normal social, occupational (academic) functioning. In the case of adjustment disorder with depressed mood (ADDM) the significant symptoms are the same as we would see in other depressive disorders. However, in this case, the symptoms are clearly in response to a specific stressor, and the depressive symptoms are not due to another depressive disorder. Adjustment disorders can be acute or chronic as well. A chronic adjustment disorder would be a situation where the stressor does not go away, and the person continues to be exposed to it and continues to react to it with depression.

While this is not actually a unipolar depressive disorder, it is certainly similar, and I will group it here just to demonstrate how these disorders are alike and yet importantly different. Two different disorders might appear to be exactly the same, but a careful history and clinical interview will demonstrate that they are in fact different.

Depressive Personality Disorder

Depressive personality disorder (DPD) shows a pervasive pattern of depressive cognitions that began at least by early adulthood and usually well before that. The person with this problem will show at least five of the following symptoms:

1. The typical mood for this person is dominated by feelings of dejection, gloominess, cheerlessness, joylessness, and unhappiness.
2. Their self-concept centers on beliefs of inadequacy, worthlessness, and low self-esteem.
3. They are critical, blaming, and derogatory toward themselves.
4. They are brooding and tend to worry.
5. They are negativistic, critical, and judgmental toward others.
6. They are pessimistic.
7. They are prone to feeling guilty or remorseful.[8]

It is important to note that this diagnosis is not assigned if the symptoms can be explained more effectively with the diagnosis of MDD or DD. What is very tricky with this diagnostic category is that it may look very much like early onset DD, and in fact, some would say that there is not a meaningful distinction between these two disorders.[9] However, others feel that the chronic attitudes of pessimism, negativism, hopelessness, and dejection that are found consistently over time in persons with DPD cannot be adequately explained by the dysregulation of mood as would be the case in DD.[10] While these distinctions seem miniscule and perhaps insignificant, think about the potential strategic therapeutic issues that would arise in deciding how to treat three very similar appearing disorders: DD, ADDM, or DPD. With DD, a therapist tries to help the person with activities or medication to regulate their mood more effectively and to learn how to cope with their issues, including the history that is involved with the disorder. With ADDM, the main issue is that the person is reacting with clinical significance to a specific stressor. The focus of the treatment involves trying to regulate the mood while focusing on coping with the specific stressor and developing strategies for handling similar situations in the future. Finally, with DPD, a therapist acknowledges that the patterns involved with this disorder have existed for many years. They probably do not even feel like symptoms to the patient because this is normal for them. Mood regulation is not as important as addressing the maladaptive ways of thinking and perceiving. Clearly, this approach to therapy is somewhat longer and more historically based than treatment for the other conditions—at least in most situations. As you can see, an accurate differential diagnosis can be very important in determining appropriate treatment for the type of depressive condition that the patient presents.

Other Forms of Depressive Disorders

As discussed previously, the accurate diagnosis and understanding of a specific depression in an individual patient is very important in determining how best to treat a person appropriately and reasonably quickly. Unfortunately, in today's health care reimbursement climate those lucky enough to have mental health coverage often have a limited number of visits available to them. This makes it very important to work quickly and efficiently and to identify the correct diagnosis so that time is not wasted on treating the wrong condition. Therefore, it is most important for a clinician to conduct a thorough clinical interview to gather an appropriate history of the disorder and of the person in general. An experienced practitioner can do this efficiently and completely, but it takes many years of training and experience to do it well.

Seasonal Affective Disorder

The acronym for this condition is SAD, which is a good way to think of this disorder. People with SAD begin experiencing mood problems when the days get shorter and there is less light, and they tend to show improvement in the spring when days start to get brighter and longer. As you might expect, this condition is more common in the extreme northern and southern latitudes where there is more of a difference in the number of hours of daylight throughout the year. It is suggested that the hormone *melatonin* plays a role here. Secreted by the pineal gland, melatonin is only produced when it is dark, and there are some people who are apparently so sensitive to the winter's higher levels of melatonin that it is difficult for them to function normally. When this change takes the form of depression every winter then it is called SAD.[11] There are a number of effective treatments for SAD including psychotherapy, medication, and increased light. Many treatment providers will strongly recommend that their SAD patients take a walk or find other outdoor activities as weather permits.

One of my daughters lived in Alaska for a few years, and she found that staying active during the dark and cold winter days, and especially while caring for a new baby, was quite challenging. Several suggestions I made included closing the blinds during the dark days and turning on all the lights in the house to provide more light, planning get-togethers with friends, and exercising and being more physically active. For any patient with SAD (in Alaska or elsewhere), we always recommend increased physical and social activities and increased exposure to light. In addition to these suggestions, some patients also need medication or psychotherapy to help cope with this condition.

Premenstrual Dysphoric Disorder

Premenstrual syndrome (PMS) has been discussed for decades in the professional literature and even longer among women. People joke about it, dismiss it as nonsense, or simply ignore it, but it is very real to the 80% of women who report at least mild premenstrual symptoms and the 20–50% of women who report moderate to severe symptoms.[12] The symptoms can include dysphoric (depressed) mood, irritability, sleep disturbances, labile (changeable) mood, and others. The symptoms usually appear a week or so before the woman's period, and they usually subside about a week later. In most women it is more of an annoyance than a problem, but for some it can be very severe. About 5% of women will have symptoms so severe that for at least several days during each cycle they will experience significant difficulty with normal roles and social functioning. If this condition remits as menstruation commences and ends, and if there is no other diagnosis that more appropriately fits the symptom patterns, then we refer to this more severe type as premenstrual dysphoric disorder (PMDD). To qualify for this diagnosis a woman must have the symptoms for most of their periods over the past year and must have at least five of the more serious symptoms of depression. This is a highly treatable problem, but often women will not seek treatment because it always goes away by itself (although it typically returns), it might be embarrassing to discuss, or they are not aware that treatment is available.

Postpartum Depression

Some women experience severe mood changes following the birth of a child. It is estimated that at least 40% of live births in this country are complicated by postpartum mood disorders. These can be very mild and pass in a few hours or days; this is usually referred to as the "Baby Blues," and while this is not an official diagnosis, most mothers and physicians know exactly what it is. A small percentage of women will experience a very severe condition known as postpartum psychosis and may require hospitalization. A slightly larger group (about 10–15% of women) will experience what we call postpartum depression (PPD).[13] This is a debilitating condition that not only affects the mother but also impacts others in the family, including the new baby. Postpartum depression is a highly treatable condition that responds well to appropriate care, such as medication or psychotherapy. In spite of feeble attempts by high-profile personalities to dismiss this condition as imaginary, women and their families and friends need to be educated about the symptoms and treatments for PPD that are readily available. Later in this book, we will discuss PPD in more detail.

Depressive Disorders Accompanying Other Conditions

The word *comorbidity* refers to when a person suffers from more than one disorder at the same time. They can be either psychological or medical conditions or both, and as you might imagine, they can complicate diagnosis and treatment. There are many medical and psychological problems that will make a person higher risk for depression as well as situations where depression can result from medical conditions or from medications.

Psychological Comorbid Conditions

Depression can and often does accompany a number of different mental disorders. For example, depression is very common in alcohol and substance abuse disorders and in many anxiety disorders, including panic disorder, phobias, general anxiety disorder, posttraumatic stress disorder, and obsessive-compulsive disorder. It is also common in somatization disorder, eating disorders, personality disorders, and grief and bereavement.[14] While the relationship between comorbid conditions is not simple, it is easy to imagine that a person suffering from substance abuse disorder might also be depressed—and they often are.[15] Determining which came first, the depression or the substance abuse, can be very complicated. Is the person self-medicating the depression, or is the person depressed as a result of years of substance abuse and seeing their life destroyed? There might also be a common physical or genetic basis to the disorders that made them more likely to coexist. It is not always easy to tease out the subtleties.

One of the most common comorbid conditions for depression is anxiety.[16] There are many different types of anxiety disorders, but anxiety in general can be a serious problem for people with depression. It is estimated that fully one-half of people with MDD also have an anxiety disorder.[17] Looking at it from the other side, people with anxiety disorders have higher rates of depression than the rest of the population.[18]

Adults who suffer from both severe anxiety and severe depression usually develop (on average) the anxiety symptoms at about the age of 16, and they develop depression at about age 23.[19] Does this mean that the anxiety "causes" the depression to emerge, or that the person gets depressed because they have such a difficult time dealing with their anxiety? Distinguishing between anxiety and depression is more difficult than it might seem.[20] For example, sometimes anxiety and depression exhibit common features such as worry, withdrawal, and demoralization. Sometimes the same types of treatments (cognitive behavioral psychotherapy or even antidepressant medications) work well on both conditions. Certainly, it is far more complex and disabling to have both anxiety and depression at the same time than it is to have either alone,[21] and the symptoms of depression last longer in persons who also suffer an anxiety disorder.[22]

Why are anxiety and depression so similar? There has been considerable speculation, but there is no agreed upon conclusion. It is true that anxiety and depression have some common physical bases such as the increased production of the stress hormone cortisol and decreased activity of the neurotransmitter serotonin.[23] However, it could also be that intense anxiety leads to depression, or that the factors that cause anxiety (or depression) make the person more vulnerable to the factors that cause the other condition. At some point we will have better answers to these questions, but for the time being we will need to accept what we know, which is that:

+ Depression and anxiety to seem to coexist in many people.
+ The co-occurrence of these two conditions complicates diagnosis and treatment of both.
+ We have many good treatments that seem to help with both of these conditions.

One of the other disorders that is often found with depression is attention–deficit/hyperactivity disorder (ADHD) and attention deficit disorder (ADD).

This is true for children, adolescents, and adults as well. Typically, it is thought that the frustrations, continuing failures, and stigma of ADD and ADHD probably lead people to be depressed. However, one study found that ADHD and MDD had independent and distinct courses, indicating that ADHD-associated MDD reflects a depressive disorder and not merely demoralization from the ADHD.[24] Certainly having depression and an attentional/hyperactivity disorder at the same time would complicate treatment considerably. Once again, making sure that the clinician knows precisely what they are dealing with in a patient will make treatment much more successful.

We need not go into all of the various psychiatric disorders that might accompany depression, but the fact is that depression can be a complicating factor in *any* psychiatric or mental disorder; from schizophrenia to minor adjustment disorders, depression can be a factor. The important thing to remember is that when depression is present it should be one of the foci of treatment—even if it is only a secondary condition, and the primary condition is something even more disabling.

MEDICAL FACTORS IN DEPRESSION

Medical Conditions and Depression

There are some medical conditions that are frequently comorbid with depression, and the treatment of these conditions depends in part on the treatment of the depression that accompanies it. Some of the medical conditions that frequently involve depression are: stroke, Alzheimer's disease, Parkinson's disease, diabetes, coronary artery disease, cancer, fibromyalgia, and chronic fatigue syndrome,[25] and one study demonstrates that depression can worsen asthma symptoms.[26] It has been found that 50% of stroke victims, 17% of heart attack patients, 30% of cancer patients, and 18% of diabetes patients will suffer from depression directly because of their illness.[27] One interesting study looked at how soon after diagnosis patients developed depression. They looked at three diseases and found that depression emerged the earliest with cancer patients, next with chronic lung disease, and last (2–4 years post-diagnosis) for arthritis.[28] The reasons why depression emerges are:

+ Psychological reactions to the diagnosis
+ Debilitating chronic pain and impairment
+ Direct or indirect effect of their illness on the brain
+ Depression may be triggered by certain medications used to treat the illness[29]

Other conditions that frequently lead to depression are Huntington's disease and hormonal disorders such as hypothyroidism, which actually manifests with symptoms similar to depression. Cushing's disease may also lead to depression because it affects the adrenal glands, which leads to the increased production of cortisol in turn leading to symptoms of depression.[30] Any person who has one of these conditions is higher risk for depression than someone in the general population. In fact, any physical health problems that result in functional disability are a major risk factor for depression.[31] Likewise, depression is found at higher rates in people with any serious illness.[32] Not only do physical conditions increase the likelihood of depression, this mood disorder itself will impact the medical condition. It has been demonstrated that comorbid depressive symptoms will exacerbate the physical symptoms and even complicate recovery and response to treatment of medical conditions.[33] In persons who have major chronic impediments, such as polio or cerebral palsy, depression is found to be the most common and disabling secondary condition.[34] It is also true that some obese people are more prone to depression and anxiety, but for some reasons that are not entirely clear, this relationship seems to hold primarily for white individuals who are also college educated.[35]

Depression also increases the mortality risk for serious illnesses, such as cardiovascular disease and other potentially fatal conditions.[36] In fact, the more severe the depression, the higher the mortality risk, and this risk was also found to be higher in men.[37] In persons with diabetes and accompanying depression the mortality risk is higher when both are present than for either condition individually.[38]

Unfortunately, when depression accompanies medical conditions and disabilities, it is often overlooked because some of the symptoms of depression are also similar to the symptoms of the medical condition.[39] It is also true that many times medical professionals will view the emotional reaction to a medical illness as being a normal reaction (which it often is), but they will not think of the depression as a separate condition that should be treated. If depression is a comorbid condition with any other illness it should also be a focus of treatment to help the person feel better and to decrease one of the major complicating factors in many illnesses.

Two conditions that are frequently linked to depression are cancer and cardiovascular disease. As far back as the 1950s it was demonstrated that patients with rapidly progressing cancer experience more problems with depression and anxiety.[40] It was also found that cancer patients with the most severe illnesses and with the shortest life expectancy were characterized by the highest levels of depressive symptoms.[41] Another study found that cancer patients who just "give up" have a worse prognosis than those who kept "fighting."[42] Similarly, Klopfer concluded that patients who were highly defensive and not very emotionally open did not have the capacity to fight off cancer as well as other patients.[43]

Research has demonstrated strong relationships between how people respond to cancer and cancer treatment and their emotional state. One study found that patients with malignant melanoma who had access to early, structured psychiatric intervention had decreased recurrence rates and increased survival rates.[44] Speigel et al. also demonstrated that patients suffering from metastatic breast cancer who received oncological care and participated in a support group survived for 36.6 months, while patients who were just provided with oncological care only survived for 18.9 months.[45] One finding from Schrifte's work demonstrated that cancer patients in remission were more receptive to influences from the environment.[46] She concluded that their ability to take things in from the environment gave the patients needed support, coping mechanisms, or perhaps something else that provided an advantage in their treatment.

As might be anticipated, not all of the research on the relationship between cancer and emotional factors produced such clear findings. One very significant study involved a 12-year follow-up of cancer patients who had been cancer free for 2–4 years at the beginning of the study. They were able to demonstrate only a slight relationship between depression and the recurrence of cancer, but there seemed to be a much stronger effect if the patients had smoked cigarettes.[47] This effect was not due just to the smoking but rather to the combination of depression with smoking, which was particularly dangerous from a recurrence-risk standpoint. Other studies that looked at thousands of patients over time found *no* relationship between cancer and depression,[48,49] although one study did identify a relationship between depression and noncancer deaths. The relationship between cancer and depression is not a simple one and has yet to be fully explored. Clearly, depression has a negative impact on the cancer patients who are dealing with both disorders simultaneously; not only does it impact their quality of life, but it may increase the mortality risk of their disease as well.

In terms of coronary heart disease, there are numerous studies that demonstrate that depression negatively affects patients following a heart attack. Frasure-Smith et al. found that, in both men and women, the presence of depression following a heart attack increased their mortality risk significantly.[50] Further, if a person has symptomatic depression, they are more likely to contract coronary heart disease.[51] This sounds as if the cardiac patient cannot be allowed to become depressed because it may kill them. Realistically, being depressed following a major reversal in one's health status is quite normal. The key is that when a patient with a serious disease such as cancer or cardiovascular illness becomes depressed, the depression as well as the primary illness must be treated. In fact, it is assumed that if the depressive condition is being treated, the increased risks are neutralized.

Medications and Depression

It is important to be aware that many medications can actually cause the development of or worsen depressive symptoms. This does not mean that these drugs should be avoided but that it is important to be aware that mood changes that occur while on these drugs may actually be due to the drug itself. Many medications that are used to treat cardiovascular conditions can cause depressive-like symptoms. The most common side effect that is similar to depression is lethargy, but people may notice additional mood changes as well. Many hormonal agents, including oral contraceptives and steroids, as well as some anti-inflammatory drugs and anti-infective agents, can lead to depressive symptoms.[52]

Some psychotropic medications, such as tranquilizers and antipsychotic drugs, and medications used to treat Parkinson's disease can also lead to depression.[53] Energizing drugs such as cocaine and methamphetamine can often cause depression when a person is withdrawing from a drug or when the drug starts to wear off. Although cocaine is not used therapeutically any more, some of the stimulant drugs such as Ritalin are often used to treat conditions such as ADD and ADHD, and these would have similar risks for depression.

For the majority of patients, any of the aforementioned legal drugs can be used safely and effectively under the supervision of their physician. If a person begins a new medication and notices mood or behavior changes, it must be reported to the physician immediately. It doesn't necessarily mean that the person will be taken off of the drug, but it may affect how the doctor decides to use it, to change it, or to add something else. If the physician is not aware of how the person is reacting to their medications they are less able to be of assistance.

BIPOLAR DISORDER

Bipolar disorder has been recognized for a very long time as a serious mental disturbance. However, over the years the name has changed a few times, and there is still some controversy as to what type of a disorder it really is. We used to refer to BPD as "manic-depressive disease," and many people still do. Some people have conceptualized this as a type of mood disorder, but others have considered it to be a type of psychosis on par with schizophrenia—not the same as schizophrenia, but a psychotic type of disorder. Certainly, BPD can be as serious and debilitating as schizophrenia and sometimes involves distortions of reality similar to a psychosis. However, mentioned previously, even depression itself can have psychotic features and still be considered a mood disorder. It is also true that most people with BPD do not have extreme psychotic-like symptoms, which suggests that it is best thought of as a disorder of mood.

The onset of BPD usually occurs earlier in a person's life than depression, even during childhood, although it can emerge later in adulthood, and women tend to have later onset than men. It tends to be a recurrent condition, and about ⅔ of people with BPD who recover from an acute episode will experience additional episodes of depression, mania, or both. The average number of episodes for a patient during their life is four, although this can vary considerably from patient to patient. It is also true, that, unlike unipolar depression, BPD affects men and women equally, although men tend to show more mania and women more depression.[54]

In order to have BPD the patient has to demonstrate both depressive and manic (or hypomanic) symptoms. If only depression is present, then it is not BPD but rather some form of unipolar depression, and it is very rare that a person presents only manic symptoms.[55] Interestingly, because about half of BPD cases begin with depression, unipolar depression is always a tentative diagnosis.[56] It should also be noted that, like depression, BPD also has some comorbidity with other disorders. One disturbing but important fact is that fully 50% of people with BPD also have a co-occurring substance abuse disorder.

The main difference between BPD and unipolar depression is that it must show both the features of depression and the symptoms of mania, which can range from relatively mild to severe. Unlike the depths of gloom of depression, mania is usually characterized by dramatic and inappropriate increases in mood.[57] People experiencing a manic episode seem to want constant excitement and activity and have what appears to be boundless and unending energy. Interestingly, if you think about it, mania deals with disturbances in the same areas as depression: emotional, behavioral, cognitive, and physical. Symptoms of mania are very dramatic and involve sometimes wild and unpredictable behavior that the person often may not remember. They may do extremely inappropriate and uncharacteristic things that are sometimes immoral (e.g., indiscriminate sexual acting out or public nudity) or even criminal. They may even be violent and hard to control. When a person has a history of at least one major depressive episode and at least one manic episode they are diagnosed as having bipolar I disorder (BPDI).

Over the years, we have found some patients who exhibit symptoms of BPD and whose manic episodes are clearly outside the range of "normal behavior" but are not as severe as seen in bipolar I disorder (BPDI). These less severe symptoms are referred to as *hypomanic*, and if a person has a history of at least one major depressive episode and at least one hypomanic episode they are referred to as having bipolar II disorder (BPDII). To be diagnosed as having either BPDI or BPDII, the person's symptoms cannot be better explained by other disorders such as schizoaffective disorder, schizophrenia, schizophreniform disorder, delusional disorder, or another psychotic disorder.

The manic episode is an important diagnostic feature of BPD and involves a period of abnormally and persistently elevated moods. The person in a manic state usually has episodes of extremely restless energy and can't relax. They often have dramatic mood swings that cause problems at home and at work or in other settings.[58] Although it is not likely that anyone would present all of the following symptoms, some that are seen in mania include:

+ Feelings of grandiosity or inflated self-esteem
+ Diminished need for sleep
+ Increased talkativeness
+ Racing thoughts
+ Easily distracted
+ Increased productivity at work or school
+ Increased involvement in high-risk activities
+ Often use bad judgment[59]

Some additional symptoms are:

+ Abnormal or excessive elation
+ Unusual irritability
+ Increased sex drive
+ Increased energy
+ Inappropriate social behavior[60]

We often think of mania or hypomania as being excited or ecstatic—almost joyous. However, some people with this disorder will exhibit irritability and anger as part of mania or hypomania as well. While true mania is often quite dramatic and even bizarre, hypomania is sometimes not as easy to spot. In fact, some of the symptoms may look fairly normal. There are several things to look for in determining whether or not it is hypomania or just an exaggeration of "normal" behavior. First, is the behavior beyond the range of "normal" behavior expected of most people? Second, is the behavior either different from or significantly out of the norm for what would be considered typical behavior for the person in question? Third, does the behavior create either discomfort or problems for the person displaying it? Fourth, in looking at the total picture and the aggregation of symptoms, does the person show patterns of different symptoms that point to the diagnosis of BPDII? According to Angst,[61] the following are some of the most common manifestations of hypomania:

+ Less sleep
+ More energy and strength
+ More self-confidence

- Increased activity levels, including work
- Enjoying work more than usual
- More socially active
- Spending too much money
- More plans and ideas
- Less shy and inhibited
- More talkative than usual
- Increased sex drive
- Increased consumption of coffee, cigarettes, and alcohol
- Overly optimistic
- Increased laughing
- Thinking fast/sudden ideas

Sometimes, patients who have experienced hypomania will experience sharpened, creative thinking and even greater productivity. For example, the nineteenth-century composer Robert Shuman produced 27 works during one year when he was hypomanic and practically nothing in the years when he was depressed and suicidal.[62]

A person with BPDII will not necessarily experience all of the listed symptoms, but it gives you an idea of what clinicians look for when making a diagnosis. Too often, people think that anyone who is moody and whose moods change frequently is bipolar. To make the diagnosis of either BPDI or BPDII they need to have either mania or hypomania (either presently or historically) and a history of depression. The history of depression alone does not indicate BPD unless the person is currently in a manic or hypomanic state nor has either of those in their past.

A simple way of distinguishing between these conditions is summarized as follows:

Manic Episode

1. Abnormally and persistently elevated, expansive, or irritable mood lasting for at least one week.
2. Persistence of at least three of the following:
   a. Inflated self-esteem or grandiosity
   b. Decreased need for sleep
   c. More talkative or pressured speech (need to keep talking and usually rapidly)
   d. Racing thoughts and flight of ideas
   e. Highly distractible
   f. Increased activity level or psychomotor agitation
   g. Excessively involved in pleasurable activities that have high probability of negative consequences
3. Significant distress or impairment

Bipolar I Disorder

1. The presence of a manic, hypomanic, or major depressive episode
2. If the person is in a hypomanic or depressive episode they must have a history of at least one manic episode
3. Significant distress or impairment

Bipolar II Disorder

1. The presence of a hypomanic or major depressive episode
2. If the person is in a hypomanic episode, then they must have a history of a depressive episode. If they are in a depressive episode, then they must have a history of a hypomanic episode. They cannot have a history of a manic episode.
3. Significant distress or impairment[63]

Some people will have more frequent episodes called *rapid cycling* BPD. This is less common than persons who experience depressive episodes and some manic or hypomanic episodes spread over many years. To be considered for a diagnosis of the rapid cycling variety of BPD a patient must report at least four episodes (either depressive or manic [or hypomanic] or both) in one year. An even rarer condition is called *ultrarapid* BPD, requiring at least four episodes per month. An extremely rare form is called *ultradian* BPD where there are at least four episodes per day.[64]

Further complicating the diagnosis of BPD is when a patient presents as a "mixed state." There is still some controversy about whether this is a separate type or form of mood disorder. Some patients show depressive and manic characteristics simultaneously, but it has not been clear as to what exactly is happening. Some feel that the mixed state is an intermediate condition that exists when a patient is transitioning between mania and depression. Others feel that it is an entirely different affective state rather than either depression or mania alone.[65] Whatever it actually is, it clearly does appear to exist in some patients. This does complicate the diagnostic picture because patients with this condition may appear to be suffering more from schizoaffective disorder or another similar condition. It will take a careful evaluation and a complete and thorough history to make an accurate diagnosis of a mixed state BPD.

Bipolar disorder is a mood disorder in that it represents significant and problematic departures from normal mood states. It involves depression, but it clearly is not the same as unipolar depression. It is a condition that can be extremely disruptive to people's lives while creating a huge disease burden on patients, families, employers, and society. However, for most patients it is a highly treatable condition with appropriate therapy (including medications and psychotherapy).

When previously discussing MDD, I also mentioned a related condition called dysthymic disorder. The symptoms are less acute or severe than in MDD, but have a long-term and continuous history that typically goes back many years. In BPD there is also a similar condition with a long and consistent history called cyclothymic disorder (CTD). According to the *Diagnostic and Statistical Manual of Mental Disorders*, fourth edition, text revision,[66] the following are the diagnostic criteria for CTD.

1. For at least two years (one year in children and adolescents) the patient reports or displays the presence of episodes of hypomanic symptoms as well as depressive symptoms, and the depression does not meet the criteria for a major depressive episode.

2. During the above two-year period (one year in children or adolescents), the patient has not experienced an absence of symptoms in criterion A for more than two months at a time.

3. During the two-year period of the disturbance there has not been a major depressive episode, a manic episode, or a mixed episode.

4. The symptoms of criterion A are not better accounted for by schizoaffective disorder, are not imposed on schizophrenia, schizophreniform disorder, delusional disorder, or psychotic disorder not otherwise specified.

Table 4.1.
Summary of Mood Episodes and Mood Disorders

Episode	Disorder
Major depressive episode	Major depressive disorder, single episode
Major depressive episode + Major depressive episode	Major depressive disorder, recurrent
Major depressive episode + Manic/mixed episode	Bipolar I disorder
Manic/mixed episode	Bipolar I disorder
Major depressive episode + Hypomanic episode	Bipolar II disorder
Chronic subsyndromal* depression	Dysthymic disorder
Chronic fluctuations between subsyndromal depression and hypomania	Cyclothymic disorder

*Subsyndromal refers to symptoms that are not severe enough to qualify for a specific diagnosis.

M. B. First and A. Tasman (Eds.). (2004). *DSM-IVTR™ mental disorders: Diagnosis etiology and treatment*. Chichester, UK: John Wiley & Sons, Ltd.

5. The symptoms are not due to the direct physiological affects of substances (drug abuse or medications) or another medical condition.
6. The symptoms cause clinically significant distress or impairment in social, occupational, academic, or other important areas of functioning.

If you think about it, you can see that while DD is a more chronic and milder condition that is similar to MDD, then CTD is a chronic and milder condition that is somewhat like BPD. In both cases, we think that the milder versions may not actually be the same disorder as the more severe type, but it is not really clear at this time what the actual relationship between them is. Too often, the milder forms of these disorders (DD and CTD) do not reach threshold for treatment. Patients assume that this is the way they are supposed to feel and don't mention it to their health providers, or the health care providers assume that because the symptoms do not reach the criteria for a more serious condition such as MDD or BPD, they must not be clinically significant. Once again, careful examination of the person's history and a complete understanding of how their symptoms create problems for them or for others is critical.

SUMMARY

Depression is manifested in many forms and can be caused by different factors. It can accompany other psychological or medical conditions, and it can make these other conditions more difficult to manage and to treat. However, we have many more proven and effective treatments for *all* of these conditions, as we will discuss later in this book. There is no reason for a person with any type of depression or mood disorder to suffer in silence—there are too many avenues for assistance. Too often, people with serious medical conditions look at their depressive symptoms as being an annoying, unavoidable byproduct of being ill; however, that doesn't mean they shouldn't be treated.

Bipolar disorder, another serious mood disorder, is related to depression and also requires attention and treatment. In order to summarize and clarify the differences and the relationship among the different mood disorders, we will use the following chart.[67]

Chapter 5

Gender and Depression

There are women in middle life, whose days are crowded with practical duties, physical strain, and moral responsibility . . . they fail to see that some use of the mind in solid reading or in study, would refresh them by its contrast with caretaking [sic], and would prepare interest and pleasure for their later years. Such women often sink into depression, as their cares fall away from them, and many even become insane. They are mentally starved to death.
    —Ellen Henrietta Swallow Richards, U.S. chemist and educator;
    quote from around the turn of the twentieth century

Let there be no steps backward. A thought as to the manliness of persevering, of the want of manliness in yielding to depression, came to his rescue.
    —Anthony Trollope, British novelist, 1874

This chapter examines how gender issues are related to depression. Historically, women were expected to experience more emotional problems, and men were thought to have more behavioral, substance-related, and legal difficulties. To evaluate the validity of these beliefs, we examine the research literature and discuss the differences between the sexes with respect to depression.

One in every four to five women will be depressed in their lifetime, and most will have recurrent episodes. It is clear that depression affects a woman's ability to fulfill her responsibilities and to take care of her children, and research demonstrates that the young children of depressed mothers have impaired cognitive and emotional development.[1] However, with appropriate treatment, mothers can be helped, and the difficulties children experience as the result of their mother's depression can be reversed.

Most research demonstrates that about twice as many women (12%) as men (6.6%) are affected by depressive conditions each year,[2] and this is true in the

United States and most other developed countries.[3] In developing countries, where the data is not as available, many do not report any difference between men and women.[4] Because research, treatment, and the availability of services is minimal in less developed countries, it is difficult to determine the significance of these early findings. However, in developed countries, this 2:1 ratio (women to men) is quite consistent for all types of depression. Closer examination shows that in major depressive disorder (MDD) the ratio may be more like 3:1 or 4:1, and with bipolar disorder (BPD) it is more likely to be 1:1.[5] The World Health Organization (WHO) reports that mental illness disability falls most heavily on those, predominantly women, with three or more comorbid conditions. They also found that depressive disorders account for 41.9% of the disability from neuropsychiatric disorders in women and only 29.3% in men. The risk factors that disproportionately affect women include gender-based violence, socioeconomic disadvantage, low income or income inequality, low or subordinate social status, and unremitting responsibility for the care of others.[6]

The gender difference in depression only occurs in the years between puberty and menopause; before and after this part of life there appears to be no difference in the rates of depression between men and women.[7] This, of course, has led many to assume that gender-based depression rates are hormonally linked, and we discuss this later in the chapter. An additional finding is that women are more likely than men to get depressed from a cognitive diathesis-stress pathway.[8] Diathesis-stress pathway refers to a person having a predisposition (*diathesis*) to a particular disorder, and when they experience certain environmental events (stress) they may then develop the disorder. Women are more susceptible to this cognitive diathesis-stress mechanism than are men, which means there are ways of thinking and perceiving that are more common in women, and these have a role in women being more prone to depression. Khan et al. also point out that patient gender significantly modifies the clinical features of depression and that men and women tend to report different types of symptoms.[9] It is clear that not only does gender impact depression but that depression impacts men and women differently. The reasons for this are not totally clear, but over the past couple of decades, new theories and studies have helped us to gain a better understanding of how and why men and women are affected differently by depressive disorders.

THEORIES REGARDING GENDER DIFFERENCES IN DEPRESSION

Artifact Theory

Some people feel that the difference in the rates of depression for men and women is just an artifact; there is no real reason medically or psychologically why more women than men report depression. This suggests, therefore, that clinicians often fail to detect depression in men because men tend to hide their feelings and don't report them.[10] Others report, however, that women are no more willing to identify depressive symptoms or to seek treatment for depression.[11] While it is unlikely that the difference in the depression rates between men and women is solely due to this artifact, as we discuss later, men *are* less likely to ask for help for almost any condition, including depression. Although women may also be reluctant to discuss depression with their providers, the research does suggest that men are probably more frequently "underdetected" when it comes to depression.

Hormone Theory

Many speculate that hormones may be responsible for the differential rates of depression for men and women. This would indicate that hormonal changes can trigger depression in many women.[12] This theory is particularly compelling when it is noted that the gender difference for depression only holds between puberty and menopause, as noted previously. This would also explain other types of depression that women are prone to, such as postpartum depression (PPD), premenstrual dysphoric disorder (PMDD), and premenstrual syndrome (PMS). As tempting as this theory is, many feel that it is too simplistic. Nolen-Hoeksema states that it is unlikely that hormone changes alone are responsible for the higher rates of depression in women.[13] She points out that there are many important life events that occur at and during puberty, pregnancy, and menopause and that these events, too, could have an impact on the rate differences.

Rumination Theory

Nolen-Hoeksema, who has been studying gender differences in depression for many years, has contributed some very compelling ideas about gender and depression. She finds that some depressed people have a tendency to repeatedly think about and dwell on their feelings and to continually consider the causes and consequences of their depression; she calls this "rumination." She also reports that people who ruminate when they are sad are more likely to become depressed and are more likely to stay depressed longer, and she also finds that women are more likely to be ruminators than men and are thus more likely to become depressed.[14]

Societal Pressure Theory

Almost from birth, women in Western cultures are taught to seek an unrealistically low body weight and slender body shape within a society where cultural standards for men's appearance are more lenient. As girls enter adolescence, there is more pressure to look a certain way, and girls and young women start to show more dissatisfaction with their bodies. This, too, is the period of time when gender differences in depression begin to emerge. It is also the time when young women are most likely to develop eating disorders as well as depression.[15] I must point out, however, that the relationship between eating disorders and depression is not clear. Does depression lead to eating disorders? Do eating disorders lead to depression? Do other variables lead to both? The point of this theory is that society places different pressures on women regarding their appearance and behavior, beginning most significantly at puberty and continuing through adulthood. Perhaps it is not hormones but rather cultural pressure to look a certain way that produces the stress that leads women into depression more often than men.

Lack of Control Theory

Women are thought to be more prone to depression because many women feel that they have little control over their life. Research finds that women are more likely to develop learned helplessness than are men,[16] and victimization of any kind often leads to feelings of helplessness or depression. Because women are more likely to be victims of sexual assault, rape, domestic violence, and child sexual abuse, it follows that they could feel a lack of control and helplessness that could lead to depression.[17] Further, there are other aspects of many cultures where women might understandably feel a lack of control over their lives, including such things as educational or occupational discrimination, caretaker responsibilities, and so forth.

Self-Blame Theory

It has been demonstrated that women are more likely to attribute their failures to their own lack of ability and their successes just to luck, which is an attribution style linked to depression.[18] As with other phenomena, these attributional differences emerge in the early teens when the differential rate of depression between boys and girls also begins to emerge.[19] Clearly, if a person attributes their success to factors other than their own skill and ability and their failure strictly to their own shortcomings, they will draw little pleasure from success and will blame themselves for failure. It is easy to understand how this type of attributional style could lead someone into depression. However, other research finds that women today are no different from men relative to self-blame and self-esteem.[20] While this attribution may lead to depression, it is not likely that this is the only factor that differentiates men from women.

Quality of Life and Cultural Theory

In general, more women around the world live in poverty, perform more menial jobs, have less than adequate housing, and experience more discrimination than men, and these are all factors that are related to higher rates of depression.[21] In addition, most cultures and subcultures place the majority of housework and child care responsibilities on women, an obvious source of stress. Women tend to be the primary caregivers in a family, including caring for the acute and chronically ill, which is, of course, yet another source of stress in their lives.[22] The WHO reports that a number of other psychological and physical problems are risk factors for depression in women and include such things as gender-based role problems, stressors, and negative life experiences.[23] They go on to state:

> Depression, anxiety, psychological distress, sexual violence, domestic violence and escalating rates of substance use affect women to a greater extent than men across different countries and different settings. Pressures created by their multiple roles, gender discrimination and associated factors of poverty, hunger, malnutrition, overwork, domestic violence, and sexual abuse; combine to account for women's poor mental health. There is a positive relationship between the frequency and severity of such social factors and the frequency and severity of mental health problems in women. Severe life events that cause a sense of loss inferiority, humiliation or entrapment can predict depression.[24]

As more women with family care responsibilities enter the work force, they often experience a decrease in the quality and quantity of leisure time.[25] In many cultures, young married women caring for small children are especially at risk for depression.[26] Research also demonstrates that, in some cultures (India in this study), women suffer more rejection for developing mental illness than do men, and yet, they are expected to care for a mentally ill husband; however, if the wife becomes mentally ill she is sent back to her family, deserted, or divorced.[27] They also report that Indian women are high risk for depression due to the oppressive relationships built on gender-discriminatory attitudes.[28] Similarly, in China, we find that distress secondary to arranged marriages, unwanted and forced abortions, and enforced nurturing roles leads to more psychological problems in women.[29]

Cultural norms are often an element in determining how gender issues relate to mental health. For example, economic and social policies that produce sudden, disruptive, and severe changes in income, employment, and social capital significantly increase gender inequality as well as the rate of common mental disorders.[30] Even the definition of "abnormality" depends on the relevant culture and its specific gender roles.

Conclusions

Several theories conclude that there are different factors related to the development of depression with a number of them disproportionately affecting women. Like risk factors for most diseases, it is rarely only one cause that produces a problem but rather an interaction between several. The number and severity of risk factors to which a person is exposed work together to determine the actual risk of developing depression—the more risk factors a person has the more likely they are to develop the disorder.

SEXUAL VIOLENCE, REPRODUCTIVE HEALTH, AND DEPRESSION

Sexual Violence and Depression

We know that the harmful impact of sexual violence and abuse in childhood leads to mental health problems in adulthood, and depression is one of the most common reactions.[31] The WHO reports that the lifetime prevalence rate for violence against women ranges from 16–50% depending on the study and its locale and that about 20% of all women suffer rape or attempted rape during their lifetime.[32] Because women are most likely to be victims of sexual violence, they also experience more depression as a result of the trauma of sexual victimization.[33] Although women are most frequently the victims of sexual violence and the resultant mental health problems, some studies in the United States and the Netherlands found that male survivors of sexual abuse suffered worse and more complex problems than women later in their life.[34] Although this problem affects a disproportionate number of women, men are certainly not immune to the difficulties that result from sexual abuse and violence.

It is important to remember that other types of mistreatment of women make them more likely to succumb to problems such as depression. Even incivility leads to problems such as sexual harassment and discrimination in the workplace and in society.[35] The fact that women's roles, gender discrimination, sexual violence, and domestic and intimate partner violence can all lead to depression demonstrates that there are many reasons why women are more likely to experience depression.

Reproductive Health Issues and Depression

Since the beginning of recorded history we know that women suffer emotional problems secondary to reproductive health. Women are twice as likely as men to experience depression during their reproductive years (typically 25–

45), and there is also a high frequency of depression during premenstrual, peri-menopausal, and immediately postpartum periods.[36] Although we introduced these disorders in Chapter 4, we discuss them in more detail here because they are certainly relevant to gender issues.

Premenstrual syndrome (PMS) refers to physical and emotional symptoms that a woman experiences usually during the week prior to the onset of men-struation. These symptoms can be quite problematic, and it is estimated that 3–4% of women suffer PMS severe enough to interfere with work and social functioning.[37] A related condition that is even more problematic is premenstrual dysphoric disorder (PMDD), which is actually a diagnostic category character-ized by depressed mood, marked anxiety, affective lability, and decreased inter-est in normal activities.[38] These severe symptoms are similar to MDD, but the condition is much briefer because it tends to remit following the cessation of the woman's menstrual flow. Some think that PMDD is an abnormal response to the hormonal changes a woman experiences during her cycle,[39] and some women seem to be much more sensitive to hormonal shifts in their bodies and may respond more intensely, both physically and psychologically, when their hormone levels change. Women who are prone to PMDD are also more likely to experience other forms of depressive disorders.[40] Conversely, depressive dis-orders may predispose women to problems such as PMDD, but it may be that women who are more sensitive to hormonal fluctuations are more susceptible to depression. Whether a hormonal change is the cause or the effect is irrel-evant; depression and hormonally related mood disorders are clearly related.

Another issue relative to a woman's emotional well being and her susceptibil-ity to depression is reproductive tract surgery. This type of surgery may impact a woman's mental health due to the identification of the reproductive organs with sexuality and feminine identity. Inadequate professional concerns about the psychological impact from reproductive tract surgeries, such as hysterec-tomies and tubal ligations, may lead to adverse mental health consequences, depression being the most likely.[41] The WHO concluded that infertility and hysterectomies increase a woman's risk for emotional problems; even bladder control problems, which are more common in women than men, are apt to lead to emotional disturbances and depression.[42]

Postpartum Depression

Women all over the world suffer from postpartum depression (PPD) and are frequently ignored and untreated.[43] Some research demonstrates that between 10–28% of mothers experience a major depressive episode during the postpartum period, although larger studies tend to find rates closer to

10%.[44] Hardly surprisingly, most of the research on PPD is from industrialized countries, but we do know that PPD has been detected in developing countries at a higher rate than expected, having a severe impact on a mother's health and that of her baby.[45] The majority of patients suffer PPD for more than six months, and if untreated, about 25% of patients remain depressed one year later.[46]

Postpartum depression receives far less attention in clinical training and professional literature than less commonly occurring problems such as gestational diabetes, preeclampsia, and preterm delivery. Although we pay more attention to PPD today than in the past, it is still often overlooked. In fact, there is still debate about the definition, causes, diagnostic criteria, and even its existence.[47] Postpartum depression is often missed at the primary care level because providers are typically more concerned with the infant's health. Problems may go unnoticed in the mother, and the mother may be too embarrassed or unaware to raise the issue because she is expected to feel happy rather than depressed during this wonderful time.[48] However, PPD is a serious condition for both the mother and the baby, and it should not be ignored. The mother could develop a more serious and perhaps chronic depressive illness, making her a higher risk for suicide. Maternal PPD may affect mother–baby bonding and could possibly affect the child's later development, and children of mothers who had PPD are at a higher risk for psychological problems later in life.[49] Further, in mothers who have experienced PPD the risk of relapse in subsequent deliveries is 1:3 to 1:4.[50]

Nonacs and Cohen report that not only can PPD affect mother–infant interactions but that a mother with PPD is more likely to harbor negative attitudes toward the infant and to report that the infant is more difficult and demanding than do mothers who have not suffered from PPD.[51] Children of mothers with PPD are more likely to present behavioral problems, such as difficulties sleeping and eating, tantrums, hyperactivity, delays in cognitive development, emotional and social dysregulation, and early onset of depression themselves. The mother with PPD could also place significant emotional and financial stress on the family.[52] One long-term study reports that at four years of age, children of mothers who had PPD tended to produce lower scores on cognitive tests.[53]

There are a number of factors that will cause a mother to develop PPD, but women of all ages, all socioeconomic classes, and all races and ethnic backgrounds can be affected. For example, in adolescent mothers, the rate of PPD climbs to 26–32%.[54] Any woman who was pregnant, delivered a baby in the past few months, miscarried, or weaned a child from breast feeding can develop PPD. The best single predictor of PPD is a prior history of depression.[55] Another significant risk factor is a family history of depression and especially if there is a family history of PPD.[56] If the mother has a prior history of depression it increases her risk by 30%, and if she has a prior history of PPD the risk increases to 70%.[57]

Other factors that can contribute to PPD include:

+ Feeling tired after delivery; fragmented sleep; not enough rest; especially if the mother had a C-section
+ Feeling overwhelmed with a new or second baby; doubting ability as a mother
+ Feeling stress from changes in work and home routines; trying to be perfect— "Super Mom"
+ Feeling loss of identity, control, slim figure, attractiveness
+ Having less free time, less control how time is spent; less time with husband and friends; having to stay home more[58]

Things that also contribute to the risk for PPD, even if the mother did not have a prior history of depression, include the existence of anxiety disorders prior to pregnancy.[59] Other comorbidities, including a history of substance abuse or somatization disorders, can also impact the risk for PPD.[60] Some additional factors that increase risk for PPD include:

+ Poor social support
+ Adverse events during postpartum period
+ Marital instability
+ Young maternal age
+ Infants with health problems or perceived "difficult" temperaments

Many factors are involved in the development of PPD, and Leopold and Zoschnick summarize the state of the literature very nicely.[61]

The data suggests that the etiology of PPD is multifactoral. Causative components include both organic and conditional changes arising from both parturition as well as the mother's surrounding situation, which likely combine to influence the patient's psychological function.

MEN AND DEPRESSION

Because depression is a condition that impacts women more than men it is not surprising that most of the research focuses on women. That is not to say men are not affected by depression; they are, and seriously so. During the nineteenth century, when "dangerousness" was used as the main criterion for being placed in a mental hospital, men were more often committed to asylums than women. In the past century there has been a change to an emphasis on "illness" as the basis for identifying a mental condition, and now women are more frequently the focus of mental health treatment.

Today, the more dangerous and violent mentally ill patients are typically placed in jails or prisons rather than hospitals,[62] and, unfortunately, men may be even less likely to be identified as needing mental health treatment than they were in the past. One noticeable trend in developed countries is that low-income women often develop depression, but the men are more likely to turn to alcohol, drugs, and violence.[63]

Often men will not, or perhaps cannot, identify their feelings with any certainty or assurance. They may describe symptoms of depression without even realizing they are depressed. Men are more reluctant to seek help for many reasons including the fear that colleagues and superiors at work might discover their "weakness," and it might have negative repercussions.[64] Men tend to hide their emotions and suppress or resist showing affection—especially to other men.[65] Occasionally, in my practice, men have refused to use their health insurance to pay for treatment, preferring to pay out of pocket rather than chance someone at work finding out they were seeking mental health treatment. Real points out that men who experience depression actually carry two stigmas: first, the stigma of having a mental illness, and second the stigma of showing a "soft or feminine" side by being overly emotional.[66]

The reluctance of men to admit needing or seeking help for mental health problems is unfortunately found for medical problems as well. At every age, men experience poorer health and have a higher death rate. When men are experiencing emotional problems they tend to keep it to themselves, but the gender difference in seeking help can't be the only factor involved in the gender difference in depression. There are a number of reasons why depression isn't detected as frequently in men as in women, and it can create a dangerous situation because men have a higher suicide rate and a higher rate of cardiovascular disease; depression leads to a higher risk for both.[67] While depression increases the risk for coronary heart disease in both men and women, it is men who suffer a higher death rate from this condition.[68] Ford et al. found that men who reported experiencing clinical depression were more prone to coronary heart disease and myocardial infarction (heart attack) even a decade later.[69] A tentative explanation for this increased mortality in men includes findings that men are less equipped to deal with feelings of hopelessness and depression than women, and women are more likely to admit their feelings to others including to health care providers. Women are also more likely to accept support from others when feeling depressed.[70]

While we know that women in childbearing years have a depression rate twice that of men, there are still at least six million men who suffer from depression in the United States today. Men don't admit depression easily, don't ask for help typically, and doctors are less likely to suspect depression when they are seeing a male patient for a different condition. Also, depression in men is often masked by drugs, alcohol, or overworking and is often disguised as irritability, anger, or discouragement.[71] Some men may think that they don't go to as many doctor's appointments as women because men are healthier, but this isn't true. In fact, the real reason has more to do with a discrepancy between a need for care and help-seeking behavior in men.[72] Both poor and rich men are less likely than women to report a recent contact with a health provider.[73] When female college students are depressed they tend to reach out to roommates and friends and tend to seek nurturing relationships. When male students are depressed they tend to isolate socially and occasionally become outright hostile. They are also more likely to resort to self-medication with drugs or alcohol.[74]

A phenomenon called "gender-role conflict" may be part of the reason why men are so reluctant to seek help. This refers to a psychological state that stems from negative consequences of masculine role socialization and a positive relationship between gender-role conflict and men not seeking help.[75] Gender-role conflict means that men are socialized to be strong and self-reliant, but in reality, they have fears, vulnerabilities, and other problems as well. The conflict emerges when men feel they can't get help or support when they need it because it would not be "manly." It is often written that traditional male roles are oppressive to women, but some would argue that the male role is oppressive to men, too.[76]

Work stress and work uncertainty are major sources of stress for many men: not knowing what the future holds, not knowing where you or the organization are going, and not having future career development plans are often serious issues. Other concerns such as not knowing what may be expected of you in the future, not knowing what your boss/colleagues think about your ability, and receiving vague and unclear instructions can create stress as well.[77] Both men and women report that conflicts between family and job responsibilities produce stress, but it seems that men are more negatively affected by this than are women, unless we are referring to a single mother.

In sum, the main problem for men with depression is having their condition recognized and receiving treatment, a much more complicated process than might appear on the surface. It does suggest that screening for depression may be more important to men than to women because women are more likely to self-refer and tend to be more aware of their emotions (except in PPD when they may not be as likely to self-refer). It is also true that while antidepressant medications are equally effective for men and women, the sexual side effects that some men experience, such as erectile dysfunction, decreased libido (sex drive), or delayed or absent orgasm, lead men to stop the medications too soon. Because 40–60% of men in the 40–60 age range experience erectile dysfunction (ED), and one common cause of ED is depression, therefore, avoiding treatment because of concern for ED is probably not a sound reason.[78] However, if the medication used to treat depression causes ED, then treatment compliance becomes a serious issue. Rather than just discontinuing the medication, the patient needs to discuss it with his physician who can change dosages, prescribe a different medication, or add a medication to help this condition. Men need to understand that when treatment produces some unwelcome side effects, such as ED, it does not mean treatment should be stopped but rather that treatment may need to be modified.

Educating men and women about depression, the various medical and psychological treatments, and where to find help and support is a place to start. The tragedy is how few people do receive help for a condition that is highly treatable with safe and effective therapies.

GENDER AND SUICIDE

With respect to gender issues and suicide, there are some differences that bear examination, but, as we know, depression is a significant risk factor for both men and women. As we learned in Chapter 1 of this book, women report attempting suicide two to three times as often as do men.[79] In fact, self-inflicted injury, including suicide, ranks 9th out of the 10 leading causes of disease burden for females age 5 and older worldwide.[80] On the other hand, men are four times more likely to die by suicide than women.[81] In combining numerous studies, the WHO finds that, with the exception of China and parts of India, men commit suicide more often than women, and the world rate is 3.5:1.[82] However, it is also reported from international studies that women attempt suicide more frequently than do men.

Some would assert that women are more likely to use suicide as a "cry for help" or as an attention-seeking device, while men attempt suicide with the intent of killing themselves. Although this may occasionally be true, it is unlikely that this simple explanation can account for patterns throughout so many different cultures. Failed suicide attempts by males are probably not reported as often as those by females because men are less likely to reach out to friends, family, or professionals when then need help, a pattern that is also common in many cultures.

Whether a person is trying to kill themselves or is seeking attention, we should never ignore a suicide attempt. Most people who attempt suicide probably do not want to die—they just want to escape the pain they are living with. They need someone to help them generate options that offer some hope of relief. Friends and family can assist with support and direction, but something this serious and potentially tragic needs to be in the hands of a trained and experienced professional.

SUMMARY

Women are twice as likely as men to become depressed for a variety of reasons. While gender differences as well as hormones do factor into the equation, it is largely a woman's experience with "role overload" that puts them in the position where more is expected of them than they can realistically fulfill. For example, work and home conflicts, caregiver burden, single parenting obligations, and so forth are the things that create a burden of stress that increases a woman's susceptibility to depression.[83] Social and cultural factors, unequal power and status, and sexual and physical abuse enter into this picture as well.[84] It has been demonstrated that estrogen has an effect on the stress hormone cortisol, which may actually accentuate the effects of stress on the body.[85] Further, the likelihood that a woman will be a victim of abuse or violence also affects the probability of developing depression.[86] As mentioned previously, not only are there a number of factors that can negatively impact women, but women also tend to ruminate over their difficulties more than men, which also affects their vulnerability to depression.[87]

Earlier we described the diathesis-stress model, which suggests that some people have a predisposition to a certain type of disease. Given the right environmental circumstances, this predisposition, coupled with the specific stressors, will produce the disease in question—in this case, depression. Nolen-Hoeksema suggests that boys and girls (or men and women) have the same risk factors for depression but that girls experience more of them during childhood, making them more vulnerable in adolescence.[88] As we learn more about depression, we find that, while there are many differences between men and women relative to depression, there are similarities as well. Some have even concluded that men and women become depressed for the same kinds of reasons, and they also get well for the same reasons.[89] This conclusion seems to fly in the face of the data that shows a preponderance of depression in women. However, Kessler et al. give some suggestions that appear to tie the data together.[90] They find that women with a history of depression do not differ substantially from men with a history of depression in either the probability of being chronically depressed or in the probability of having an acute recurrence in the past year. Therefore, because women had a higher rate of depression in the past year, this must be due to the fact that women had a higher probability of first onset. This makes considerable sense if one looks at the risk factors. Nolen-Hoeksema found that when risk factors for depression are present they lead to depression in both men and women but that the risk factors do occur more frequently in women.[91]

According to Spangler et al., women are more likely to hold negative perceptions and thoughts that could lead to depression—the cognitive diathesis-stress pathway.[92] However, they also noted that there is no evidence that women have different cognitive diatheses (predispositions) than do men—why, then, the differences in occurrence rates? In addition to women reporting more negative events prior to the onset of depression, they had more negative events during the past year than did men. Perhaps it is not just that women think more negatively, but they also have, or perceive that they have, more negative events in their lives than do men. Nolen-Hoeksema also suggests that cognitive factors seem to be more important for women than men in leading to depression.[93]

Another set of studies concludes that women are more likely to be genetically inclined to depression. Bierut et al. find that the lifetime prevalence for MDD is 22% for women and 16% for men, and for severe MDD the rate is 9% for women and 3% for men.[94] They found evidence for a contribution from both genetic and environmental factors unique to the person in the development of depression in women, and there was a heritability estimate of 36–44%. However, for men, depression was only modestly familial, and environmental factors appear to play a larger role for men than for women.

Some writers assert that one of the reasons for gender differences in the rates of depression is the gender bias in the treatment of mental disorders. The WHO reports that doctors are more likely to diagnose women with depression even when they score the same on tests or present with identical symptoms as men.[95] They also find that while women have higher levels of distress and are more likely to complain of and be diagnosed with emotional problems than men with the same symptoms, once men acknowledge that they have a problem they are just as likely to get help. Clearly, the difference is partly due to the tendency of men not to see or to admit to problems as readily as women. It has been suggested by some that men develop alternative disorders to depression. While they do have higher rates of alcohol and drug abuse, it doesn't appear that these problems are a substitute for depression. There is good evidence that substance abuse is more common in young men who are single or separated, while gender differences in depression are most obvious during the years when people are most likely to be married.[96]

Others point out that from articles in women's magazines to the health section of the daily paper there is a shift toward the "medicalization" of deviation from women's traditional roles. Meanwhile, men's depressive illness is increasingly described in terms of connoting problems with work, aggression, or athletics. Women and their problems are more often described from a traditional female role perspective and, thus, are attributed to the difficulties of being a wife or mother. Men are seen as getting depressed because they are not performing on the job or on the athletic field.[97] Another result of the "medicalization" of women's depression has been the greater likelihood of treating her condition with medication rather than dealing with the social conditions that are contributing to the problem. Further, it is felt that this trend does not help restore women to health but rather perpetuates the situations that caused the problem to begin with, even if there is some temporary relief to the symptoms she experiences.[98]

There does appear to be a gender bias in the diagnosis of mental health problems; women who display deviant behavior are labeled as being "mad," while men displaying deviant behavior are "bad."[99] Today, a normal healthy adult is usually judged by male norms, which leads to some interesting complications. A woman who either conforms too closely or rejects the female norms is judged as psychiatrically "ill."[100] As far back as 1961, psychiatrist Thomas Szasz pointed out that the overuse of medical diagnoses and treatments for "problems in living" tended to cloud the frequent issues related to unhappy living conditions.[101]

In sum, according to the American Psychological Association Task Force on Depression, the following issues make women a higher risk for depression:

- Socioeconomic class, biological and environmental variables
- Her personality structures, cognitive styles, and problem-solving strategies
- Post-traumatic stress stemming from sexual or physical abuse
- Being married and having children
- Economic state (poverty is a "pathway to depression")[102]

Recognizing that these problems exist is a start, but providing the treatment necessary and making it accessible is the answer to the issues. Men and women both suffer from depression, and treating them appropriately is vitally important. Whatever is responsible for the differences between men and women with respect to depression is not as important as making sure that people suffering from depression are recognized and diagnosed and that proper treatment is provided in a timely fashion.

Chapter 6

Life Cycle Issues and Depression

You are as young as your faith, as old as your doubt; as young as your self-confidence, as old as your fear; as young as your hope, as old as your despair.
—General Douglas MacArthur

Age-based retirement arbitrarily severs productive persons from their liveli-hood, squanders their talents, scars their health, strains an already overbur-dened Social Security system, and drives many elderly people into poverty and despair.
—Claude Pepper, statement in the U.S. House of Representatives

The more we learn about depression, the more interesting it becomes, and it is hardly surprising to find that age and developmental level are factors that influence depression and its treatment. Depression in children and adolescents doesn't always present itself like it does in adults or the elderly, and while it is true that all age groups can be victimized by depression, how it looks, its course, its outcomes, and its treatments may vary from age group to age group.

In this chapter, we look at the different ways that age is related to and impacted by depression and also how age affects depression. Because most of the ideas presented in earlier chapters relate primarily to the adult experience of depression, we concentrate on children, adolescents, and the elderly in this chapter. People tend to neglect and ignore mental health issues in the elderly, and depression is often not recognized or treated in children and adolescents; these issues are important to understand and explore further.

DEPRESSION IN CHILDREN AND ADOLESCENTS

"Compared with adult depression, depression in children (6–12) and ado-lescents (13–18) may have a more insidious onset, may be characterized more by irritability than sadness, and occurs more often in association with other conditions such as anxiety, conduct disorder, hyperkinesis and learning problems."[1] Depression in these younger age groups often has uncertain cause but may include things such as genetics, childhood events, and current psychosocial adversity.[2] Understanding the nature and quality of depression in children and adolescents is important to provide appropriate treatment and to return their life to normal. Substantial research suggests that mood disorders often begin early in life,[3] and therefore, dealing more effectively with depression early on may make mental health issues later in life less problematic and easier to treat. It has been found that depression in childhood will not only lead to adult depression but that, sometimes, childhood depression continues into adulthood.[4] This suggests that when children with depression go untreated or are inadequately treated there is a tendency for depression to continue into adulthood, and one report found that depression occurring in youth actually predicted a more severe depression in adult life.[5]

In terms of prevalence, about 2–6% of children suffer from depression, with the proportion of depressed youngsters increasing with age and showing a sharp rise at the onset of puberty. In preadolescents, the proportion of boys and girls who are depressed is about equal;[6] although some studies have shown that preadolescent boys are more likely to be depressed than girls.[7] Most, however, would agree that after the onset of puberty depression becomes more common in girls.[8] In general, the incidence rate of depression in adolescents is anywhere from 0.4–8.3% depending upon which study you are examining.[9] The difference between boys and girls starts to emerge between the ages of 13–15, but major differences appear between the ages of 15–18, and this difference was found in samples taken from university settings, as well as those from non-university settings.[10] This, of course doesn't mean there were 13–15-year-olds at the university but rather that when the students were studied, their health records and interviews recalled earlier depressive episodes.

In a national survey of 12–17-year-olds it was found that 14% of adolescents (about 3.5 million youngsters) have experienced at least one episode of major depression in their lifetime, and 9% of adolescents (about 2.2 million youngsters) had a major depressive episode in the past year. It was also reported that 40.3% of those who had a major depressive episode in the past year received treatment. Importantly, during the month prior to the onset of a major depressive episode, youngsters were more likely than nondepressed adolescents to use illicit drugs, cigarettes, and alcohol. In fact, 21.2% of those who became depressed reported using illicit drugs compared to 9.6% of nondepressed teens. The same pattern held with smoking cigarettes (22.8% vs. 10.7%) and drinking alcohol (28.4% vs. 16.5%). With respect to gender, it was found that 13.1% of adolescent girls reported having been depressed compared to 5% of the boys. Relative to age, 5.4% of the 12–13-year-olds reported having been depressed, while 9.2% of the 14–15-year-olds and 12.3% of the 16–17-year-olds had suffered from depression.[11]

One problem with detecting depression in youngsters is that it often doesn't look like the depression seen in adults, and it is frequently missed by parents, teachers, and health professionals. In fact, it has been demonstrated that parents report less depressive symptoms in their children than the children report themselves. In general, parents appear to be relatively insensitive to their children's depressive symptoms.[12] This is complicated further by the finding that children and teens not only present different symptoms than do adults, but they also present different symptom patterns from one another. For example, prepubescent children are usually found to have a greater depressive appearance, more somatic complaints, psychomotor agitation, separation anxiety, phobias, and hallucinations. Adolescents have greater anhedonia, feelings of hopelessness, hypersomnia, weight changes, increased use of alcohol and drugs, and a higher lethality of suicide attempts, although not greater severity of suicidal ideation or intent.[13]

The World Health Organization (WHO) has reported that throughout the world girls tend to report more depression, suicidal ideation, and suicidal attempts than boys, although boys will try to express their depression more often through anger and high-risk behaviors and are more likely to commit suicide.[14] Because of these different symptom patterns, the accurate diagnosis of mood disorders in youngsters is often difficult, and this is also true of bipolar disorder (BPD), which has been largely neglected in children and adolescents until very recently.[15]

There is evidence that children are experiencing depression more often now than in the past, but of course, it is never easy to tell if we are simply recognizing it more than we did in the past or if more children are getting depressed. It is reported that children born since WWII have higher rates of depression, become depressed at earlier ages, and are more likely to commit suicide than adolescents and youth of earlier generations. In fact, in the past, it was thought that children were not cognitively developed enough to become depressed. Today, we find that youngsters in the highest quartile of depression are twice as likely to be in the bottom quartile in reading and math achievement and in the highest quartile of teacher's ratings of concentration problems. They were also rated in the lowest quartile of peer-rated likeability. This study also reports no gender difference between prepubescent boys and girls with respect to depression, but they find that children in a lower socioeconomic group were more likely to be depressed than middle- or upper-class children.[16] Reinherz et al.

also reports no difference between young boys and girls in terms of the rate of depression, but girls were more likely to experience a more severe depression than boys.[17]

Factors Related to Depression in Children

There are many factors that have been linked to depression in children, including the feeling of being devalued. In cultures or social groups (including families) where children feel that their role is devalued, they are more likely to suffer depression. Similarly, depressed adults are more likely to report physical, emotional, and sexual abuse in their families when they were children and teens than adults who are not depressed. Other factors that are linked to childhood depression include family conflict, lack of parental support, neglect, and poor parenting skills and practices.[18] Given these findings, it is hardly surprising that children and adolescents who possess a poor self image are also more prone to depression. Children who are rated by teachers as being hostile toward other kids are more prone to depression, and hostile children who perceive themselves as unpopular are also more likely to be depressed. In fact, there is much evidence that not being popular often leads to depression in children.[19] Others report that there is a strong relationship between peer harassment and cognitive vulnerability to depression in children. This is especially a problem during mid-childhood to adolescence when peers are so important.[20] It is hardly surprising that when youngsters feel that they are not accepted by peers and are not valued by them either, that they are more likely to feel badly about themselves and are more susceptible to the kinds of thoughts and feelings that will lead to depression. Health is also a factor, especially in boys, because those who have many health problems are more likely to become depressed. For all children, however, early illness, injury, and other physical problems are related to later depression.[21]

One finding that is somewhat encouraging is that neither family social status nor marital status of parents were predictive of depression in children.[22] The reason why this is encouraging is that two factors that may be predictive of adult depression seem less apt to create problems for children and teens. Particularly because there are increasingly more single-parent families today, it does appear that family and economic status alone are neither predictive of depression and that it must be other things that are causing it to emerge.

There are several other studies that identify factors related to childhood depression, including cognitive variables such as low self-efficacy, feelings of hopelessness, and cognitive errors.[23] Youngsters who are prone to behavior problems, are anxious and dependent, who have school problems (including retention), and who use additional school services are prone to depression.[24] In young men, insomnia is also indicative of a greater risk for subsequent depression, which could persist for up to 30 years.[25] We have talked about the factors that might predispose a child to depression, but it has also been found that both the transition to adulthood and the transition to adolescence have high onset rates for depression.[26]

As one might expect, there are family factors that are related to child and adolescent depression. For example, older children and adolescents whose mothers are depressed are five to six times more likely to develop depression than their peers.[27] In related studies, it is found that depression in a parent more than doubles the risk for anxiety disorders in children, as well as depression and addictive disorders. Further, children of depressed parents develop a five-times greater rate of cardiovascular illness than a control group. More optimistically, they report that treating parental depression can prevent or relieve depression in the child, and when the parents improved, so did the children.[28]

Among the more severe family circumstances, the loss of a parent, and especially the mother, often leads to later episodes of major depression in children.[29] More commonly, however, increased family conflict and the child's poor perception of their role in the family is related to an increased risk of major depression.[30] Generally, the whole family milieu, as represented by the child's perception of family acceptance and the availability of parenting, is a key factor in the later development of depression.[31] One study found that in African American young women, the youngster's perception of parent–teen conflict often results in a negative impact on the psychological and physical well-being of the young women.[32] While others report that higher levels of perceived family conflict are related to higher levels of adolescent depression, researchers also find that higher levels of parental attachment are associated with lower levels of adolescent depression.[33] Other studies show that children with depression report significantly less cohesive and more disengaged families, and they report feelings of emotional separateness and a lack of closeness in their families.[34]

One problem that frequently leads to depression in children and adolescents is eating disorders. As discussed in a previous chapter, this problem primarily affects girls and young women, but it has been frequently reported that eating disorders coexist with depression.[35] Young women are often exposed to unrealistic examples of what an "attractive" body should look like, and because so few of them look anything like this "ideal," it creates dissatisfaction with their body, which leads to eating disorders and depression.[36] In fact, the WHO reports that in many places around the world, lower self-esteem in girls and anxiety over body image leads to more eating disorders and depression.[37]

Depression in children and adolescents seems to be well established as an unfortunate reality of today's mental health climate. Depression in childhood may not look exactly the same as it does in adulthood, but they are related in the sense that childhood depression does make a person more at risk for adult depression. This is especially true if the childhood depression was severe.

While there is no doubt that depression in children and teens is more frequently seen today than in the past, the reasons for this are not as clear. For example, there are more children on earth today than in previous decades, so we can expect the absolute number of cases to increase. However, we also know that the relative frequency is also increasing, and this means we are seeing a higher percentage of depressed children than in the past. The question we asked before, "Is childhood depression more common today than in the past, or are we just detecting it better?" can be answered, and the answer appears to be, "Yes." That is, there are relatively more cases, *and* we are detecting it better. If you review the various risk factors, many of them are more commonly found today than in the past; therefore, we should expect more cases. Even though access to appropriate mental health services is beyond the reach of many people, primary care physicians and pediatricians are far more aware and vigilant about mental health issues than they were in the past and are identifying more cases than they used to.

Certainly, this is a mixed blessing. It is not good news that there are more children who are depressed, but it is good news when we detect it earlier and this leads to more timely and appropriate treatment. All of us must continue to insist that the mental health needs of all citizens, but especially children, be recognized and met.

Treatment Issues in Children and Adolescents

In later chapters, we discuss a range of available treatments for mood disorders, but we should mention here some of the special treatment considerations for children and adolescents. The most obvious issue is whether treatment is safe and effective for children. While this issue is important for all patients, it becomes a more sensitive issue when dealing with children. We know that children can react to prescription medications differently than adults. Different levels of maturity and metabolic rates, developing bodies and nervous systems, children being less sophisticated about medical/psychological issues, and being legally unable to speak for themselves are all issues that make dealing with depressed youngsters even more problematic than dealing with adults.

Similar concerns are associated with other forms of treatment. For example, medical procedures (e.g., psychosurgery) are rarely used on children, as would be expected. Children do not respond well to many forms of psychotherapy because they often lack the verbal facility and insight to benefit from them.

It is very common to use more behavioral forms of treatment with children. This does not mean that you can't try verbal types of therapy with children or adolescents, but the treatment needs to be appropriate for the age and developmental level of the child or youth. We also frequently use family therapy and parental counseling when addressing children's and adolescent's issues.

In dealing with depression in children and teens, it is reasonable to be more optimistic today because we do seem to be detecting mood disorders more reliably and are able to treat them more effectively. There have been some concerns about the safety and possible overuse of antidepressant medications with youngsters, and we address this issue in more depth in a later chapter. Suffice it to say that treatments today are better and safer than in the past, but we must be careful and vigilant about their use and appropriateness.

DEPRESSION IN OLDER ADULTS

Another group of citizens whose mental health needs have been neglected is the elderly. There are so many misconceptions about mental health issues in the elderly that it is nearly impossible to know where to begin. Some feel that the elderly are retired and basically have it pretty easy; there is not much for them to be depressed about! Many, and probably most, elderly are worried about finances, health issues, family matters, the nation, the world, and so forth, and these concerns tend to increase over the years. If our earlier assumption is correct, that the more risk factors a person has the more likely they are to develop depression, then it seems that the elderly should be more depressed than the rest of society. Their health may be failing; they may be cut off from their families and friends; their own friends and family are probably dying off, moving away, or living in nursing homes or adult care facilities; and their own mortality is probably becoming more apparent. They may be living on fixed incomes and having difficulties meeting their financial needs. Being retired also means they often do not have productive outlets for their energy, and it may be difficult to feel that they do anything meaningful or important in their life or in the community. However, it has been demonstrated that illness or other adversity is not a sufficient explanation for depression by itself, and this is true in the elderly as well.[38]

While there are many reasons why older people get depressed, perhaps the greatest tragedy is that they remain one of the most undertreated groups of people in most cultures. It is sad to think there are people suffering from a highly treatable condition who are not being treated because of short-sighted misconceptions among society, politicians, and even medical and mental health professionals.

Symptoms of Depression in the Elderly

The symptoms of depression in older adults can be numerous and often mimic physical diseases, which also makes depression more difficult to identify. Although no single patient would manifest all of the possible symptoms of depression, the following list represents symptoms that can be part of a constellation of depression in the elderly:

- Agitation
- Anxiety
- Persistent, vague physical complaints
- Memory/concentration problems
- Social withdrawal
- Changes in appetite; weight loss or gain
- Sleep problems (insomnia, hypersomnia, fragmented sleep, and others)
- Irritability and demeaning of others
- Decreased personal care
- Confusion, delusions, hallucinations
- Feelings of discouragement and hopelessness
- Sadness, lack of playfulness, inability to laugh
- Anhedonia
- Prolonged grief
- Loss of self-worth
- Reduced energy and fatigue
- Abnormal thoughts, excessive or inappropriate guilt
- Suicidality

It is certainly understandable why someone experiencing some of these symptoms can be depressed. It might be surprising to see the more serious symptoms, such as delusions and hallucinations, on the list of symptoms of depression, but as mentioned earlier, some severe forms of major depressive disorder (MDD) have psychotic symptoms, and this can be true in the elderly as well as in younger patients.

Incidence of Depression in the Elderly

The National Institute of Mental Health (NIMH) Epidemiologic Catchment Area Survey estimated that at least 1 million of the 31 million Americans over the age of 65 have MDD, and an additional 5 million have significant depressive symptoms.[39] Drawing data from primary care settings, they find that 6.5–9% of older adults have MDD,[40] and evidence of major depressive episodes and subsyndromal depression (not quite enough symptoms to reach diagnostic threshold) in nursing homes is about 50%.[41] Teachman reports that both depression and anxiety disorders show a gradual increase with age until the mid-30s, when the rate declines a bit, until older adulthood, when the rate for both increases again.[42] This was not due to personality factors but probably indicates exposure to and experiencing varying degrees of risk factors in the different age groups. This suggests that when people reach their older years, the risk factors increase again. Therefore, elderly persons are more susceptible to depression, and by being depressed, their risk for suicide is significantly increased.[43]

It may be "understandable" why older people might develop depression, but we must remember that being depressed is not a normal condition of aging.[44] The NIMH suggests that not only is depression not normal in the elderly, but it is frequently ignored or dismissed by family, friends, and health professionals as well.[45] This often leads to a situation where depression in older adults is often either untreated or undertreated, occasionally resulting in avoidable but tragic outcomes such as suicide.

In all fairness, symptoms of depression are similar to symptoms of other diseases or conditions and are also like some normal patterns of aging (e.g., slowing down, less sleep, not as much energy, etc.), and depressive symptoms are sometimes confused with the side effects of medications a person may be taking. However, the NIMH points out that when depression in the elderly is appropriately diagnosed and treated, the results are usually very good.[46] It has been demonstrated that after recovering from major depression, recurrence is likely in 50–90% of older adults unless they are maintained on medication, and if they are continued on medication for two years after remission, the rate of relapse significantly decreases.[47] It is also my belief that, as is found in younger patients, maintenance psychotherapy can have the same protective effect in reducing relapse rates as does continued medication. To be certain of this, more study in this area is clearly warranted.

Specific Problems with Depression in Older Adults

One of the problems in the treatment of the elderly for all conditions is that very often bias and stereotyping enter into and distort the picture. People often have expectations and assumptions about the elderly that are not founded in fact and are often wrong. Unfortunately, these misconceptions frequently guide decisions and treatment considerations in older patients. One study found that there was not much age bias in the diagnosis of depression, but there was certainly a prognostic bias in the sense that clinicians were much more pessimistic about the prognosis of older patients, and this was reported even though the research data clearly suggests a positive prospect for treatment outcomes in the elderly.[48] For example, as we know, women are more prone to depression when transitioning into menopause,[49] and thus, when older women are depressed it is thought that they must just be having "hormonal" problems. As we learned in the last chapter, this is an inadequate and oversimplistic view of women and depression, and when discussing the elderly, it is not even a reasonable assumption because most women go into menopause well before they would usually be considered to be elderly. Clearly, employing simple explanations that result in a woman not being appropriately treated for her depression at any age is not good practice.

One factor that often interferes with accurate diagnosis of depression in older people is that they express their depressive symptoms in primarily somatic terms.[50] Therefore, the treating professional is likely to conclude that these symptoms are secondary to physical conditions that should be the focus of treatment. Of course, because many older patients have a myriad of physical conditions to provide symptoms, it is understandably easy to miss depression. However, Blazer et al. find that both somatic and psychological symptoms are common in this group when they experience depression, and this would imply that health professionals are quicker to focus on the physical symptoms and are ignoring the psychological and emotional symptoms that are presented.[51]

Impact of Depression on Older Adults

The Helpguide suggests that depression affects the quality of life in the elderly in many ways in addition to the impact of the symptoms.[52] Depression can increase the impairment that a person suffers from other medical conditions, can impede improvement from other conditions, and can increase the likelihood of death from physical illness. In the elderly, depression also tends to last longer than in younger patients. It is found, however, that psychotherapy can decrease the secondary problems and keep depression from further complicating other medical conditions; certainly, depression does impair an elderly patient's ability to participate in the treatment of other conditions.

With these findings it is hardly surprising that the health care costs for older adults who suffer depression are approximately 50% higher than similar patients who are not depressed. It is also true that depressed patients rate the health care they receive as worse than similar patients who are not depressed, they visit emergency rooms more often, and in general have more appointments with their physicians. Research demonstrates that by treating depression in older adults it not only helps improve their physical condition but leads to improvement in comorbid anxiety conditions and substance abuse problems as well.[53]

When older people are depressed they also show a broad range of cognitive symptoms. For example, they demonstrate a broad base of deficits relative to controls of similar age and also experience more rapid declines on tests of complex psychomotor functions, copying, and perceptual integration; this even occurs to a much greater degree than in younger depressed patients.[54] This is particularly important because some of the symptoms of depression are very similar to the symptoms of dementia, also a major concern in the elderly. The WHO reports that the leading mental health problems of the elderly are depression, organic brain syndrome, and dementia, and most of these patients are women.[55] This is most likely true because women live longer, and therefore, there are more existing cases in the older age groups who are female. This is true for both depression and Alzheimer's disease.[56,57]

Gender Differences in Depression in the Elderly

There is also some evidence that elderly men and women experience other differences relative to depression. According to the NIMH, when men retire, they may have problems with depression if they see themselves as the wage earner for the family and are highly identified with their job.[58] Retirement often leads to a sense of loss of an important role, to decreased self-esteem, and to additional stress resulting from other numerous losses. Further, men often look at their employee peers as their primary social reference group, and when they retire they feel cut off from an important source of companionship and support. Men seem to experience more of the physical symptoms of depression in general, and this is also true in the elderly. This is significant because the elderly typically experience more physical problems, but when the symptoms of depression are largely physical, it is usually very difficult to determine what is physical disease and what is depression.[59]

It should not be surprising that older men and women both experience depression but that the issues related to the depression and the expression of the disorder may be different. Depression is the same disorder in men and women, as mentioned earlier, but the symptoms of depression are expressed differently by males and females, in the elderly as in other age groups.

Suicidality in the Elderly

One of the important issues regarding depression in the older adult population is that depression places them at higher risk for suicide;[60] this comes as a surprise to many. Even if depression is recognized in elderly people, often the risk of suicide is not considered. In one study, it was found that 14.7% of elderly had symptoms of tiredness of life, 5.9% wanted to die, and 1% had suicidal ideation or gestures.[61] Many feel that if a person has lived a full life and they rationally decide that the pain of continuing to sustain their life is no longer worth it, then they should be permitted to end their life in a quiet and comfortable manner. However, as reasonable as this sounds, it must also be pointed out that suicidal ideation and the wish to be dead are usually symptoms of a psychological disorder—especially depression. This suggests that if these are symptoms of a treatable disorder, then providing appropriate treatment is a more reasonable approach to these feelings than helping them to commit suicide.[62] Obviously, this is a complex social, legal, and psychological issue that is far beyond the scope of this book. While I personally feel that we should always try to respect the needs and wishes of patients, we should not be too quick to confuse the right to die with a treatable depression. If a person who wishes to end their life receives appropriate treatment for their depression and they start to feel better, there is a very good chance that suicide will not seem such an attractive option. Regardless of our personal feelings about "right to die" issues, our first concern must be to accurately diagnose and treat psychological conditions such as depression in an effective and timely manner.

Social Factors and Depression in the Elderly

Gallo and Rubins report that older patients may be reluctant to discuss feelings of sadness, grief, or anhedonia with doctors because they may be embarrassed or don't want to waste the doctor's time.[63] A combination of poor health and their concerns about being able to afford health care were found to influence depressive symptoms in older adults living in the community.[64] These were normal, elderly citizens who had not been identified as needing treatment for depression nor had they been living in an institution or in another care facility. However, simply being older and in declining health are not sufficient reasons to simply accept depression as a normal and understandable state;[65] depression in the elderly is a real problem and needs to be treated as such.

That is not to suggest that problems of living that are common in the elderly cannot produce difficulties, because they certainly can. If we look at community-residing elderly who are in poor health and who have relatively low financial and social support, we will certainly see an increase of psychological distress, which often leads to depression.[66] One of the biggest concerns faced by the elderly is the fear of being a burden on others. Declining health and lower financial resources certainly contribute to their fears, and these issues can produce troubling stress and emotional distress. However, it has also been demonstrated that these difficulties can be offset to some degree by improving the quality of social support available to the person.[67]

Self-Help Activities to Help with Depression in the Elderly

It is important to *listen* to patients to hear what they need and what kinds of things are important to them, and Helpguide suggests a number of things that can help older adults with depression.[68] Of course, not every suggestion will fit every person, but the list provides many ideas that could be helpful to many older adults—depressed or not:

+ Mild exercise—with doctor's approval, of course
+ Music (to listen to or even participate in)
+ Pets or pet visits
+ Gardening or other hobbies
+ Reminiscing
+ Visiting others
+ Good nutrition (including appropriate vitamins—with doctor's approval)
+ Volunteering to help others
+ Joining and participating in a religious/spiritual community

As simple as these suggestions are, it is sad they are not more frequently used. Most of these take little effort or planning, but busy family and friends simply forget or neglect to help with even the simplest of these. The elderly usually appreciate even the smallest acts of kindness and often respond gratefully and enthusiastically.

Activities for Family and Friends to Help With

As mentioned previously, one thing that frequently worries elderly patients is the fear that they are a burden to those around them. This often leads to their isolating and refusing help. However, it is important for family and friends to stay involved and encourage them without nagging. Activities that others can do for an elderly depressed patient include:

+ Offer emotional support
+ See that the depression gets diagnosed and treated
+ Make sure that medications are taken on time as prescribed
+ Encourage treatment compliance with all aspects of treatment
+ Remind the patient to stay away from alcohol, particularly if they are on medication
+ Invite the patient to do activities with you, and be persistent
+ Reassure them and comfort them
+ Watch for suicidality, and don't dismiss it if you see something that concerns you[69]

It is often difficult to deal with depressed people because frequently they feel so poorly that they don't act as if they even want help. They can be so discouraged and pessimistic they may feel that nothing will help anyway. This is why persistent encouragement is so important, but if you become a pest they can just refuse to listen to you. It is essential to remember that it is not the job of family and friends to "treat" the depression—leave that to the professionals. What family and friends can do that professionals cannot is to be just that—family or a friend in a supportive role that only those people close to the patient can fulfill.

Preventing Depression in the Elderly

For any condition, the best treatment is always prevention. The most helpful approach is to encourage older persons to stay active and to keep life as normal as possible while dealing with the things that confront them. To prevent depression, a few of the things that can help the elderly are:

- Facilitate social interaction; join clubs, go to religious services, etc.
- Stay in contact with family and friends; invite people over to visit
- Participate in absorbing activities—do things that interest you and with people you enjoy
- Volunteer to help others
- Learn new skills (one of my patients is learning Spanish at age 80)
- Share jokes and humorous stories—laughter may not be the best medicine, but it is definitely one of the better ones
- Maintain a healthy diet
- Do physical exercise at least three times per week—do what you can and always with medical approval

Summary

Dealing with depression in older adults is rarely easy, especially when this condition is often ignored or minimized. It is important to remember that depression in the elderly is neither inevitable nor untreatable, and the quality of a person's life and health can be dramatically improved by treating this disorder. Unfortunately, in our society, getting old is not traditionally valued unlike in cultures where the aged ones are venerated and supported. We often do everything we can to avoid aging, and when people get old and difficult to manage some tend to "ship them off" or ignore them. However, for many older persons, adult communities and retirement villages offer stimulation and wonderful places for people to live among peers who have similar needs and interests.

The age, wisdom, humor, and life experiences of those who came before us are a wealth of information that we might never learn without them, and it is a treasure to be savored and not hidden, neglected, or ignored. The best way to deal with depression in the elderly is to treat them as capable adults who should be a part of society and our culture in general and who deserve the care and treatment that is appropriate for their age and condition.

CONCLUSIONS

In this chapter, we examined how depression can occur in different forms within various age groups. Depression is common to all age groups, and no one group is immune. We have also found there are some differences as to how depression is manifested in different age groups and also what are some of the relevant causal factors. The most important thing to remember is that when patients fall outside of the typical adult grouping, the likelihood of their depression being recognized, diagnosed, and appropriately treated is not encouraging. Children and adolescents are more prone to depression than we used to think, but often their depression is not detected because the symptoms may be similar to another condition or developmental stage, or the symptoms are minimized and ignored. For example, how often do we hear that a child or adolescent who is showing depressive symptoms, "is just going through a phase, and they will grow out of it," or, "All teenagers are like that"?

Interestingly, the same is often said of the elderly. Their depression is sometimes written off as "to be expected at their age" or is minimized by saying things such as, "You know how cranky old people are." However, as stated previously, depression is *not* normal in any age group. It is a condition that can and should be treated; to do less is unacceptable in a civilized and responsible community.

Chapter 7

Special Groups and Depression: Race, Ethnicity, and Sexual Orientation

Someone is always at my elbow reminding me that I am the grand-daughter of slaves. It fails to register depression with me. Slavery is sixty years in the past. The operation was successful and the patient is doing well, thank you. The terrible struggle that made me an American out of a potential slave said, "On the line!" The reconstruction said, "Go!" I am off to a flying start and I must not halt in the stretch to look behind and weep.
    —Zora Neale Hurston (1891–1960), African American novelist,
        short story writer, folklorist, playwright and anthropologist

Oppression does not make for hearts as big as all outdoors. Oppression makes us big and small. Expressive and silenced. Deep and dead.
                —Cherrie Moraga (1952–), Hispanic American
                        lesbian feminist author

Depression does not discriminate; it can affect anyone of any group and sometimes without any apparent reason. Chapter 7 examines depression as it affects different racial and ethnic groups as well as the gay and lesbian community. Information on how depression affects special groups of people in our society has been sparse until very recently, but by looking at gender and age differences with respect to depression, we know this disorder can appear differently within distinct groups and can be caused by slightly different factors. Because people of minority status often face numerous and different types of risk factors, their rate of depression varies as well; however, they also share risk factors commonly found in other social and ethnic groups. For example, women of childbearing years are at higher risk for depression regardless of their race, ethnicity, or culture. We can see that certain personality traits may be related to depression across groups as well. For example, it is reported that in White, Asian, and

African American college students perfectionism was a significant predictor of depression regardless of the race or ethnicity of the student.[1]

As our country and the rest of the world become more diverse, mental health concerns become increasingly important as a public health issue. Demographically, the adult minority population in the United States is expected to move from 23% in 2004 to 40% in 2015, and minority children are expected to move from 33% in 2004 to 48% in 2015. In 2004, 67% of the U.S. population were white, non-Hispanic; 14% were Hispanic; 12% were African American; 5% were Asian/Pacific Islander; 1% were Native American/Alaskan Native; and 7% were "other." In 2003, people of Hispanic origin passed African Americans as the largest of the minority groups. The most diverse population groups in the United States are on the East and West coasts and along the border with Mexico.[2] We are not only seeing an increase in minority populations in general but within the minority elderly age group as well. In fact, Asians and Latinos are the two fastest growing groups of elderly immigrants.[3]

CULTURAL DIFFERENCES IN DEPRESSION AND RELATED PROBLEMS

As the population becomes more culturally diverse, increased problems such as prejudice and discrimination are more likely to occur. One of our concerns is how minority status might affect the diagnosis and treatment of mood disorders. One report found that 43% of African-Americans and 28% of Latinos feel that health care professionals treat them badly because of their race or economic background as opposed to 5% of whites.[4] A related finding is that ethnic minorities in the United States are less likely to utilize mental health services—especially Hispanics and Asians.[5]

People from different cultures often look at and respond to mental illness differently. Their response may indicate an unwillingness or inability to seek appropriate help but will also reflect the extent to which families and friends will be supportive of one who is having psychological problems. In some Asian cultures mental illness reflects badly on the family and may even interfere with one's marriage chances. Statistically, African Americans tend to be overdiagnosed with schizophrenia and underdiagnosed with bipolar disorder (BPD). They also tend to have a slower metabolism with respect to some antipsychotic and antidepressant medications, which makes them more likely to experience side effects and less likely to tolerate adequate therapeutic doses of their medications. Living in a remote location can also limit treatment opportunities, and about one-third of Native Americans or Native Alaskans do not have a doctor or a clinic where they can seek even the most basic or preventive health care.[6]

Suicide, always a concern in depressed persons, is also affected by racial and cultural differences. For example, the annual suicide rate is higher for males in general, but Mexican and Puerto Rican males had lower suicide rates than whites,[7] possibly because they are predominantly Catholic cultures. Some studies find no difference in depression between whites and minorities, and other studies find higher rates among minorities;[8] thus, it is clearly not an unambiguous situation. This fact is probably most reflective of the fact that there is not the depth and breadth of research and theory that would lead to a coherent body of knowledge. Fortunately, this is changing, and we are finding more and better scholarship in this area in recent years.

Depression and Social Class in Minorities

Differences in depression rates and symptoms between racial groups can be explained, at least in part, by socioeconomic status (SES).[9] In fact, Kennard et al. assert that most differences in depressive symptoms are due to SES rather than ethnicity.[10] They go on to point out that many of the cognitive models hold up well across ethnic groups, for example, feelings of low self-efficacy, hopelessness, and cognitive errors that predict depression across all ethnic groups. They also find that cognitive-behavioral interventions work equally well across various groups. However, Beaudet points out that the relationship between SES and depression is ambiguous and not as clear as some suggest.[11]

We can assume, however, that independent of social class, one's ethnic background will have some effect on the way the symptoms of depression are manifested and that ethnicity may play some part in the etiology of depression. Any person with more than one risk factor has a greater likelihood of developing depression, which puts people of minority status frequently in "double jeopardy." For example, if a person is elderly and African American they have two factors that can place them at risk for various conditions, including depression.[12] If a person is a member of a minority ethnic group, and they also happen to be female *and* elderly, they then have several risk factors working against them simultaneously. This does not, of course, guarantee that they will develop depression, but it does make them higher risk.

African Americans and Depression

For African Americans, racism, poverty, and poor health have been found to significantly infringe on the quality of life,[13] and as we know, the lower one's quality of life the more likely they are to be a victim of depression. Because African Americans are disproportionately found to be victims of racism, poverty, and poor health, they are more likely to suffer depression. It is reported by

McMan's Depression and Bipolar Webpage that 40% of all African American children are raised in poverty and that African American families earn about 60% of the median income in the United States, possessing only about 10% of the family wealth in this country.[14] They are also more likely to pay for mental health services out of pocket, to terminate treatment prematurely, and to be hospitalized for mental problems, and they are frequently treated with older, less preferred medications. Understandably, many African Americans do not trust the mental health system.

It is difficult to ascertain the exact role of race in the etiology of depression, but when factors other than race are accounted for, one study reports that African Americans are less likely to suffer from major depressive disorder (MDD) and dysthymic disorder (DD) than are whites;[15] however, other studies report different results. In a study of adolescents, Wight et al. found that even when SES was controlled for, depression was found at higher rates among African American youths.[16] They assumed the differences were due to experiences of discrimination and exposure to victimization, which fits into the supposition that being higher risk is dependent upon the number of risk factors a person has. One other study found that if there was perceived or reported family conflict it was predictive of depression in adolescent African American young women; apparently due to the indirect effect on parental attachment.[17] What this means is that in this particular group they are predisposed to depression if they have experienced a disturbance in the parental attachment bond.

Pottick et al. found that clinicians were 60% more likely to diagnose a mental health problem in boys if they were black or Hispanic than if they were white, regardless of the race of the clinician.[18] Another study reported that clinicians tended to find less pathology in blacks than whites with similar symptoms, and though this may seem to be contradictory with Pottick et al.'s report, the explanations are very compelling.[19] Blacks were less likely to receive a mental health diagnosis and were far more likely to be judged as delinquent and referred to the juvenile justice system. Therefore, if clinicians *only* judge symptoms, they tend to see more pathology in black or Hispanic youths than in whites. However, if they are making diagnoses for the purpose of treatment, they will more likely send black youths to the legal system and whites to the mental health system. Some have argued that blacks are less likely to benefit from treatment, but there is evidence to the contrary. Miranda et al. found that there is a growing body of experimental literature that supports the idea that minority groups will respond equally well to cognitive-behavioral therapy as whites.[20] Therefore, there is no therapeutic reason to refer blacks and other minorities to the legal system because they might not respond to treatment.

African American males, like white males, are less likely than females to seek medical and mental health care regardless of income level. Even when treatment is pro bono, men are less likely to seek treatment than are women.[21] There is no evidence that there is a genetic basis to racial differences in depression, but there is good evidence that some of the social and other high-risk factors that are related to depression may exist to a higher degree in the black community.

Hispanics and Depression

In the United States, the Hispanic population is over 36 million people, which is an increase of over 700% in the last 40 years. In terms of mental health issues, one-third of these 36 million people have no health insurance, half do not have a personal physician, and about 30% of immigrant Hispanics are depressed.[22] We often think of Hispanics as one group, but it is actually a very heterogeneous group of people. Being of Hispanic origin can mean they are of full or partial Hispanic heritage, they are Spanish speaking, or they have immigrated from Latin American. The major subgroups of Hispanics in the United States are: Mexican (60%), Puerto Rican (10%), and Cuban (3%).[23]

As mentioned earlier, we know less about depression and how it affects minority groups than we do about the majority white population, but this is an area where the literature is expanding and improving. Hispanic immigrants (both legal and illegal) are one minority group that receives considerable media attention and are the subject of heated debate. One study found that among immigrant Mexican Americans, mental health, in general, was poor, with 40% indicating levels of anxiety and depression that might impair normal functioning. However, the basis for depression did seem to have gender relativity in this group as it does in the white majority population. In Mexican American men, social marginalization was more often associated with higher levels of depression, while stress that was related to the separation from family was more often related to depression in women.[24] One would expect there to be differences in the salient issues regarding depression in different groups of people. In most Latino cultures the family is very important, so feelings of hopelessness are more likely to be related to interpersonal difficulties.[25] As shown in Hiott et al.'s work, this tendency may affect women more than men, but it is still a factor that applies to both.[26] In Latino men, higher levels of machismo and restrictions on emotions are associated with higher levels of stress and depression, a pattern that is very similar to what was found in common with non-Hispanic white men.[27]

In any minority group, issues of discrimination often lead to feelings of personal distress and lower self-esteem,[28] and these factors similarly tend to lead to depression and other mental health disorders. Unfortunately, the majority group in any population typically does not recognize "discrimination" as a potential risk factor for mental health issues such as depression. This obviously compounds the problem and makes the effects more difficult to manage both personally and socially. One interesting finding is that Mexican immigrants who have lived in the United States for less than 13 years have far lower rates of depression than Mexican Americans who were born here.[29] The most obvious interpretation of these data is that the cumulative effect of discrimination over many years is significant, but there is not yet enough evidence to prove the actual cause of this difference.

Hispanics experience mood disorders at about the same rate as whites,[30] but this fact by itself may be misleading, because we know there is inadequate treatment of depression in Hispanics,[31] and we know Hispanics face significant disparities in health care compared to whites.[32] This suggests that, even though some studies find that Hispanics and whites have about the same rate of mood disorders, we are missing many more Hispanic cases because they are less likely to attract the attention of the mental health care system due to language differences, health literacy barriers, somatic presentation of depressive symptoms, and the use of cultural idioms of distress. Interestingly, when appropriately diagnosed, Hispanics are usually amenable to treatment for depression, often preferring psychotherapy to medication. This group seems to respond well to both types of treatment, individually or combined, which is an important reason for making sure that they are identified and treated—there is a good chance of their responding favorably to treatment.[33]

As mentioned previously, much of the research on depression in minority groups is very recent and presents many of the problems that all new areas of research face, such as a lack of a coherently organized and cohesive body of theory to direct and motivate research. Researchers should be lauded for breaking ground in this important but difficult area of study because much of the literature on mental health issues in Hispanics has been plagued by problems such as weak methodology and stereotypic interpretations.[34] However, there are still ample opportunities for researchers and theorists to make substantial contributions in this area.

Asians and Pacific Islanders and Depression

In recent years, we have seen an increase in immigration from various parts of Asia and the Pacific Islands. It is reported that 40% of Southeast Asian refugees are depressed, 35% have anxiety disorders, 14% have post-traumatic stress disorder (PTSD), and that many of the Southeast Asian refugees experienced very traumatic events in their former homelands.[35] Another troubling statistic is that the suicide rate for elderly Chinese is 10 times than for elderly whites.[36] Among college students, Asian Americans score higher on measures of depression and social anxiety than do whites. In fact, depression is the most common mental health problem reported by Asians, a rate often higher than that of whites. In general, Asian Americans report higher rates of serious mental health problems than other racial and ethnic groups.[37]

As with other minority groups, Asians are not a homogeneous group and also underuse mental health services in the United States.[38] According to the U.S. Department of Health & Human Services, only 17% of Asian Americans with psychological problems sought assistance, and less than 6% did so from a mental health professional.[39] Stigma and shame, as well as the challenge of finding services, make it difficult for Asian Americans to acknowledge problems and to follow through with obtaining appropriate services.[40] Blair found that Southeast Asian and Korean Americans reported a higher rate of depression than people of Chinese, Japanese, and Filipino heritage.[41]

Treating depression in those of Asian ancestry is difficult for many of the same reasons we found with the Hispanic population. Accessing adequate care, agreeing to see a mental health professional, and dealing with language or cultural differences are all important hurdles to clear. Also, people of Asian background are more likely to present with somatic symptoms of depression than other ethnic groups,[42] which means they are less likely to recognize the psychological basis of their problem. Professionals who treat depression psychotherapeutically frequently use cognitive types of strategies in order to address differing cultural concerns. Adjusting the strategy to the cultural distinctions of the relevant group, as well as being sensitive to the unique individual differences of the person in treatment, is good practice for treating Asians or people from any other group as well. It also accentuates the importance of training clinicians with more awareness and knowledge of dealing with cultural differences in the context of treating psychological disorders.

DEPRESSION IN THE LESBIAN, GAY, AND BISEXUAL COMMUNITY

Lesbian, gay, and bisexual (LGB) persons are often grouped together as a minority and, as such, are often the object of discrimination and prejudice. They are, of course, a heterogeneous group that includes men and women from all racial, cultural, social, and ethnic backgrounds. Stereotyping and treating LGB persons unfairly can contribute to the multiple risk factors for depression that they are exposed to. There is a heterosexual bias in the training of mental health professionals of which most people are not even aware. This means that the training most mental health professionals receive is only (or predominantly) focused on the heterosexual population. The majority of mental health practitioners do not have appropriate training to deal with the LGB community or other minorities for that matter.[43] This particular group of people might best be thought of as the hidden minority because other than their sexual orientation they are simply part of their own racial, ethnic, cultural, or subcultural group.[44] Of course, if they are also a member of another minority, this compounds the issue of discrimination and the fears they must face, increasing the risk for mental health problems such as depression.

There is evidence, similar to what is found with other minority groups, that links perceived discrimination, based on sexual orientation, with depression, attachment anxiety, and avoidance behaviors.[45] Attachment anxiety is characterized by an excessive need for approval from others and a fear of interpersonal rejection or of abandonment.[46] It is often related to the onset of depression. Other studies have demonstrated that being a gay male is not only stressful, but it is associated with higher levels of psychological distress, which, as we have demonstrated earlier, is related to a higher incidence of depression.[47] Certainly, being part of an out-group can be stressful, but the additional weight of fear and discrimination can have a wide range of psychological consequences as well.[48]

Gay and bisexual men show evidence of a higher prevalence of depression, panic attacks, and psychological distress than heterosexual men. However, lesbian and bisexual women are more prone to develop generalized anxiety disorder than heterosexual women. Interestingly, one difference between the LGB community and other minority groups is that they tend to use mental health services at a higher rate than does the majority of the heterosexual community.[49] This, then, is one difference between the LGB community and the heterosexual community that is a positive and encouraging trend.

One subgroup of the LGB community that is less visible and often outside of the range of accessible help is the LGB youth. They often have to deal with invisibility or total rejection as well as conflict with family and friends. Gay youth are the only group of adolescents who often face total rejection from their families with little prospect of ongoing support.[50] Obviously, these youths belong to two very high-risk groups—being young and homosexual; people who have these two characteristics are two to three times more likely to attempt suicide than other young people. In fact, it is estimated that they may comprise up to 30% of completed suicides annually. When we are able to determine the motives behind these suicides, they often seem to involve the discrepancies with which the gay youth must live continually.[51] They must face discrimination, humiliation, rejection, and abandonment, or they can live a life of lies, deception, emptiness, and emotional isolation. A majority of homosexual suicide attempts occur before age 20, and nearly one-third occur before the age of 17.[52]

With respect to the adult segment of the LGB community, about 25% of lesbians and 20% of gay men have attempted suicide. In fact, gay males are six times more likely to attempt suicide than are heterosexual males, and lesbian women are twice as likely to attempt suicide as heterosexual women.[53] Another study found that when people were questioned as to whether or not they had ever attempted or *contemplated* suicide, 40% of gay males and 39% of lesbian women affirmed that they had.[54]

One fact that seems surprising, given the stress and discrimination that LGB people face daily, is that the rate of psychological problems in this community is not higher. In fact, some studies do not find many differences in depression rates between LGB people and heterosexuals. Thompson et al. report that gay men are less defensive and less self-confident than heterosexual men, while lesbian women are more self-confident than heterosexual women.[55] They also found no difference in personal adjustment between the homosexual and heterosexual groups. Although this is at odds with other studies, it does suggest that being gay or lesbian does not necessarily mean they experience higher levels of psychopathology.

A study that looked at Latino lesbian women and gay men reported that although certainly at risk for depression, they showed resilience through coping, high self-esteem, and relatively low levels of depression. It also reported that people who perceived more social support experienced less depression.[56] This is a finding that is consistent with other studies of gay men as well as studies on heterosexual men. Aspects of collective self-esteem were also related to lower levels of psychopathology,[57] an important finding that demonstrates that collective, positive self-esteem can directly affect depression rates within the Latino LGB community in a positive direction—that is, it helps.

An ethical issue associated with treating LGB clients is that a therapist must be aware of any negative biases they may harbor about this client group and deal with it through diversity training, personal counseling/supervision, continuing education courses, more supervision with this type of client, and so forth. A therapist may feel they should try to convert the LGB client to a "normal" lifestyle and may argue that the LGB lifestyle is so stressful and demeaning that changing the sexual orientation of the client is really in the client's best interest. However, unless the client brings this topic up and requests such a change, the therapist should never presume to dictate the agenda for therapy just because it fits with the therapist's values. So-called conversion therapy has never been very successful and is considered unethical by mental health professionals. In fact, the only way that it wouldn't be considered unethical is if the client introduces the topic themselves and asks to set this as a goal in therapy. It is vitally important that a therapist find ways to affirm the client before sexual orientation is disclosed or becomes an issue in treatment. A therapist must do this with all clients, but it is of the utmost importance if the client is from a group that is typically marginalized by society and the health care system.

SUMMARY AND CONCLUSIONS

As you can see, the more we learn about depression, the more complicated it becomes, and especially when cultural differences are introduced into the equation. While certain risk factors may be more applicable to one group or another, we do know that the more risk factors that are present the more likely a person is to suffer from depression. It has also been demonstrated that acceptable treatments seem to work for most groups regardless of age, race, ethnicity, gender, or sexual orientation. We have found, however, that treatment by a professional who is unfamiliar with a particular group's culture may be problematic and most certainly wouldn't be as effective. Although people of a minority group are usually not as likely to seek and receive treatment, a group of clients that seems to go against this general trend is the LGB group.

Regardless of a patient's origin and culture, each client deserves the respect of the treating professional. If a professional is uncomfortable with the values of a particular client, and it is creating a problem in treatment, the professional must refer the client to a different provider who is experienced and comfortable with the issues being addressed. Most clinical settings deal with a more diverse client population today than ever before, and therefore, this is a more common issue in treatment today than it has ever been before. Mental health professionals need to think about diversity within their practice, institutional, and educational settings and in their research. To the extent that we are educated and sensitive to culture, race, gender, age, and lifestyle differences, we will be better able to address these issues in treatment. There are many books, articles, training programs, and workshops available to increase one's knowledge and skills—the best professional takes advantage of these opportunities.

Chapter 8

Treatment of Depression: Psychological Therapies

In a strange way, I had fallen in love with my depression. Dr. Sterling was right about that. I loved it because I thought it was all I had. I thought that depression was the part of my character that made me worthwhile. I thought so little of myself, felt that I had such scant offerings to give to the world, that the one thing that justified my existence at all was my agony.
  —Elizabeth Wurtzel; American author and actress

There is no perfect solution to depression, nor should there be. And odd as this may sound . . . we should be glad of that. It keeps us human.
  —Lesley Hazelton, The Right to Feel Bad

This chapter deals with some of the various types of psychological treatments for depression and how they can be helpful in dealing with this difficult, costly, and harmful disorder. The basis of the psychological approach is that a problem has resulted from a flawed psychological process that leads to a disorder of mood—in this case, depression. Of course, there may be an underlying biological problem as the ultimate cause, but it becomes a psychological problem because of how this biological dysfunction affects psychological processes. Some people subscribe to the reductionistic fallacy of feeling that because all psychological processes can be reduced to biological factors then biology is the only way to understand these types of problems. Of course, this isn't true at all.

A ridiculous example of this fallacy is to take it a level or two further. If human behavior can be reduced to biology, and human behavior is the fundamental basis of social behavior, and social behavior is the basis for societal problems like war, then war must be based on flawed biology! It is true, however, that psychological problems that have a social or interpersonal cause can lead to biological changes in the central nervous system and to other parts of the body as well. The only answer to the question, "Is depression a biological or psychological problem?" is, "Yes." In addition to using medications in treatment of the biological aspects of depression, it is clear that psychological treatments are at least as important in helping people to deal with and recover from the complex elements of depression.

Psychologists consider three types of data when developing treatment approaches: thoughts, feelings, and behaviors (although there are social and interpersonal factors, biological, and even evolutionary issues to consider as well). Each psychotherapeutic approach is formulated and structured in a manner that addresses therapeutic change within one, two, or all three of these factors—thoughts, feelings, and behaviors. The basic idea in therapeutic change is to help people make changes that will positively affect their life. However, treatment may focus on primarily one area as a way to initiate change. Later, I discuss different models and show how these models work to effect therapeutic change.

EARLY HISTORY OF PSYCHOTHERAPY

Psychotherapy is a relatively recent tool in the armamentarium of mental health therapies. Historically, we have seen many different, sometimes bizarre, and often horrific types of therapies used to treat the mentally ill. Because many of the early thinkers assumed that faulty biology was at the base of mental illness, most of the early treatments were biological. Some evidence was discovered in prehistoric humans that suggests a type of brain surgery where a hole was cut in the skull as a form of treatment; this is called *trephining*. It is assumed this surgery "fixed" a problem in the brain, or perhaps released a troublesome "spirit." Because some of the skulls had calcified edges on the holes it is obvious that the patient survived the treatment long enough for the cut bone edges to calcify.

Over the millennia, people have conceptualized and treated mental illness in many different ways. The early Greeks were inclined to treat the mentally ill with kindness and support, but as history entered into the Middle Ages; the treatments became much harsher and less supportive. While we don't know as much about history in other parts of the world, we do know that in Europe during the Middle Ages official thought about mental illness was generally governed by the position of the Church. Typically, it was assumed that if someone was behaving in a "crazy" manner they were possessed by demons, in league with the devil, or were inflicted by a mental disease as punishment for some type of sin. Thus, the treatment was generally vicious and often fatal. If one was possessed, the host body had to be rendered so unpleasant that the invading demon would leave to find a more hospitable home. If the person was in league with the Devil or was being tormented because of sin, they were "obviously deserving" of severe punishment. In the name of treatment, people were tortured, maimed, and even killed.

At least in Europe it wasn't until the Renaissance and the Age of Enlightenment that attitudes and treatment of the mentally ill started to change. Philipe Pinel and others started to "unchain the insane" and to treat them kindly and supportively. Some called the new approach to treatment "Moral Therapy," but it was really just kindly, supportive care, and any true therapeutic gains were probably based more on good fortune or the placebo effect than any true therapeutic benefit. Eventually, mental illness was removed from the religious realm and returned to the medical sphere, which led to primarily biological treatments, including some medications (not very effective ones by today's standards), and other treatments such as convulsive therapy (performed with electricity or drugs), physical restraint, nutrition, hydrotherapy (placing patients in warm baths where they were strapped in place for hours), psychosurgery (lobotomies where incisions were made in the brain to separate part of the frontal lobes from other aspects of the brain), and other very strange therapies by today's standards.

During this era, there were interesting biological theories, such as phrenology, where the human psyche was studied by examining the shape, bumps, and depressions in the skull. The rationale was that an elevation meant that there was a corresponding "strength" in the brain at that point, and if there were an indentation at the "depression location," this would indicate a "weakness" that would result in the person having depression. By having an "accurate" map of the brain, a phrenologist could then "diagnose" mental problems a person might be experiencing. Another theory called *physiognomy* was widely accepted and is based on the belief that a person's personality could be determined by looking at their facial characteristics. Even today when you hear someone say something such as, "You can't trust him, his eyes are too close together," this is a vestige of the old physiognomic way of understanding people. Somatotyping was also a popular theory in the past that believed a person's personality and personality problems could be diagnosed by studying the body type of the individual.

These types of theories were in vogue until Freud came along and began to postulate purely psychological mechanisms for understanding human personality and pathology. However, even Freud, whose training was as a physician and physiologist, postulated that there were biological factors underlying all psychological processes. He did state that the psychic energy system was derived from the biological energy system but became independent of it and was parallel to it throughout a person's life. From this time forward, we have seen the growth of psychological theories about human psyche and the pathological processes that emerge from it.

Freud was exposed to exploring the functional (nonmedical) aspects of mental pathology when he studied with the French psychopathologists (Charcot, Janet, and Liebeault) who were trying to understand the psychological aspects of what was then called "hysteria" but today is known as a conversion disorder. This interesting disorder is manifested as a physical symptom but without any underlying physical pathology. In addition, the French psychopathologists were the first to discover that hypnosis actually produced temporary relief from the symptoms of hysteria. His work led Freud back to Vienna where he worked under the supervision of Josef Breuer in order to become a consulting neurologist. In fact, it was Breuer who discovered the "talking cure" for hysteria when he found that, even without using hypnosis, hysteric patients experienced relief from their symptoms by simply talking about them and about themselves and events in their lives. Freud learned from Breuer and credited him with his early discoveries. From this beginning, Freud undertook the enormous task of developing a purely psychological theory of human personality and psychopathology, which developed into a new way of understanding and treating mental illness—psychoanalysis.

PSYCHOLOGICAL TREATMENTS FOR DEPRESSION

There are literally hundreds of different approaches to psychotherapy for depression, but most of them fall into one of the following groups: psychodynamic, humanistic/existential, cognitive and cognitive/behavioral, the purely behavioral, and family and/or group methods. In this section, we examine how each of these approaches deals with the treatment of depression, and we examine the similarities and differences among them as well. Each of them offers unique elements to help us understand depression, how it can be treated, its complex nature, and the need to possess a broad-based and thorough understanding of all available treatment methods.

Psychodynamic

The psychodynamic approaches generally assume that depression results from something in our past that is often related to loss. It is sometimes challenging for a person to deal with their loss because the real, imagined, or symbolic loss is often buried in the subconscious, and they may not even be aware of the source of their depression. In general, the more traditional types of psychodynamic therapies (e.g., psychoanalysis) will try to uncover the subconscious root of the problem, bring it to conscious awareness, and then work to resolve the original conflict, thus, relieving the patient of their symptoms.

Some of the newer psychodynamic approaches work more directly with information from a person's present daily life and relationships, but the logic is much the same—an underlying problem must be identified. The person must find ways to deal with this and similar issues so that the same problems don't keep re-emerging. Unlike the spectacular cures often found in the popular media, the "cure" is never as simple as an insight that leads to an "Ah-ha" experience, suddenly changing a person to a fully integrated and healthy individual. This makes for a good movie, but it is never that simple.

Psychodynamic theorists typically assume that depression is due to an unconscious grief reaction due to a real or imagined loss. The psychodynamic therapist will try to focus a person's conscious awareness and help them to work through and resolve these issues.[1] The older psychodynamic approaches focused very heavily on the feelings and emotional aspects of the person's experience, but, as mentioned previously, some of the newer approaches include cognitive and social concerns as well.

The research literature has not been very supportive of psychodynamic therapy as a treatment for depression. In this day of empirically validated treatments and managed care companies counting the number of visits a patient receives, the longer-term therapies are not widely used. Also, the more insight-oriented therapies that rely on subjective factors to determine treatment success are more difficult to empirically validate. However, the longer-term psychoanalytic types of therapy have only *occasionally* been found to be helpful in the treatment of unipolar depression.[2] It could be that some depressed patients are not up to the verbal interchange and analytic thinking that is necessary in this type of treatment,[3] and some patients may drop out of treatment too early because of their frustration with a lack of quicker results.[4] However, in all fairness, this form of treatment works very well with some patients who prefer a psychodynamic type of therapy, but it is the shorter-term therapies that have been more readily supported in the empirical literature.[5] In response to these findings, some professionals in the psychodynamic camp have begun developing and working with more time-limited and directive forms of treatment, hoping to improve the efficacy of this form of therapy.

For the time being, the conclusion is that psychodynamic therapy is very important historically, but it has not fared as well in the research literature as some of the newer, more directive forms of treatment. Although many professionals would accept the basic ideas behind the psychodynamic approach to therapy, the majority seem to feel that the newer forms of therapy are a more efficient and effective way to accomplish psychotherapeutic change. It remains to be proven that the newer and more time-effective psychodynamic forms of treatment are as efficient as some of the more empirically validated forms of therapy. The jury is still out.

Humanistic/Existential Therapies

During the mid-to late 1960s, American society was in the midst of dramatic and sweeping social changes. The United States was reeling from the economic success and growth of post–World War II, and the Baby Boomer generation was coming into its own. Social issues such as racial and gender equality were front-page concerns, and every town and city in America was challenged to adapt to the new ways of thinking and treating one another. At the same time, the birth control pill became widely available, and, in the pre-AIDS era, sexual liberation, coupled with women's liberation, opened up an entirely new standard of sexual freedom and expression. This was also the era of the emergence and greater acceptance of recreational drug use; it was the generation of "Sex, Drugs, and Rock & Roll."

Then came the Vietnam War, one of the most controversial and least supported of America's military adventures. All of these factors coming together at the same time were much like the book by Junger and the subsequent movie titled *A Perfect Storm*, where all of the factors coincide in such a way as to produce something so dramatic and intense that it might never happen in the same way ever again.[6] The 1960s were much like a social and cultural version of the "perfect storm," and the social changes that accompanied it were sweeping and deeply ingrained in the American psyche.

Inevitably, there were accompanying political changes and events that were quite impressive and some tragically so. This was the era of assassinations—a much beloved President (John F. Kennedy); the President's brother who was then a candidate for President himself (Senator Robert F. Kennedy); a non-violent, black social activist (Dr. Martin Luther King); another very influential black social activist (Malcolm X); and one of the leaders of the American Nazi Party (George Lincoln Rockwell) were all victims of assassination during this decade. In addition, former Alabama Governor and Presidential candidate George Wallace was shot in an attempted assassination that left him paralyzed for life. However, as explosive as the political scene was, this was a time when politicians began to actively consider and even court the vote of younger Americans. Black power, women's power, youth power, and so forth were on the lips of people seeking to redress wrongs and change the world forever.

Psychology was certainly not immune to these social pressures, and it began to adapt to these influences as well. Some in psychology jumped on the political and social bandwagon, and most college campuses were hotbeds of political and social unrest. A few psychologists became deeply involved with the recreational drug movement and encouraged the use of drugs as a way of expanding and enriching one's consciousness. Dr. Timothy Leary, a well-known Harvard psychology professor, was one of the leading exponents of the use of the hallucinogen LSD as a legitimate method for studying and expanding consciousness. However, most psychologists were not as visible or as extreme in their views as Dr. Leary, although some did join into the spirit of the times. As many younger people began to challenge the status quo and the "power elite" and were calling into question some of the basic assumptions that had been accepted as American "truths," psychology began to look at its traditional methods and assumptions and to question some of the values that American psychology seemed to accept as fundamental.

Where strict determinism was basic to the psychodynamic and behavioristic approaches to psychology, many American psychologists were challenging the premise and legitimacy of the deterministic approaches of main stream psychology. Interestingly, they began to borrow ideas from more philosophical approaches to examining behavior. Drawing from fields in philosophy such as existentialism, humanism, and phenomenology, this "new psychology" began to grow and find many supporters among students, the public, and professional psychologists as well.

In the period between World War I and World War II, there were some psychiatrists in Europe who tried to find a philosophical basis for psychology that didn't depend so deeply on the subconscious as Freud's psychoanalysis did—they found a home in existentialism, which focused on consciousness, choice, the rationality of the individual, and the worth and uniqueness of each person. Others gravitated toward rational humanism, which affirmed the importance of rational moralism and the value and worth of the individual. From phenomenology came the notion that the only reality that could be known was that through our own unique and subjective perception. That is, reality is as reality is perceived. Although very different from traditional American psychology, a new and unique approach to psychology and to therapy emerged.

Some very influential and important American psychologists became involved with this new movement. Carl Rogers developed a totally new approach to personality and psychotherapy based on the "self" as an experiencing, rational, feeling entity. Abraham Maslow contributed a completely new way of conceptualizing human motivation as well as the idea that people could be and were often motivated by the highest of human values and that to understand humankind we needed to stop focusing only on pathology and examine the very best that humans could be—those he called "self-actualizers." Interestingly, both Rogers and Maslow were important as innovators, teachers, researchers, and leaders. In fact, both were elected presidents of the American Psychological Association during this era.

Another who was influential during this time was Fritz Perls, who was considered the Father of Gestalt psychology. This was an approach very much in opposition to traditional American psychology that focused on a person's ability to integrate their experiences into a coherent sense of themselves, much as Rogers had. Another important contributor of this era was Rollo May, who took existentialism and applied it to an understanding of psychology, presenting his ideas in a manner that was accessible to an educated lay public and that led to a broader acceptance of his ideas among psychologists and others. As a group, these approaches tended to be more positive, less interested in systematic research, less concerned with determinism, and more concerned with health, growth, and the importance and uniqueness of the individual.

In terms of psychotherapies, there were many variations, but they all tended to resist the deterministic, therapist-guided approaches of the psychoanalysts and the behaviorists. Individual rationality, personal growth, and integration were the important bases for therapy. While psychoanalysts tended to view human nature as being guided and determined by sexual and aggressive impulses, which were largely subconscious, they see human nature as basically negative. The behaviorists, on the other hand, looked at human nature as a *tabula rasa* (blank tablet) upon which experience would write its messages. Thus, for them, human nature is neutral. For most of those in the humanistic and existential camps, human nature is largely positive and healthy. These therapists then try to find ways to unlock and release the healthy things inside a person and to help them flourish. Therapy tends to be very nondirective and client-centered. Many of these thinkers even resisted the idea that the people they were serving were "patients." They rejected the medical model of mental illness and considered the people that they treated as "clients." In fact, Carl Rogers called his approach to treatment "Client-Centered Therapy." One important American psychiatrist who we mentioned earlier, Thomas Szasz, was very influential in challenging psychologists and psychiatrists to reject the medical model that labeled psychological difficulties as diseases and to more realistically think of them as "problems in living" for which people needed guidance and help and not medical treatment.[7]

As influential and important as the humanistic and existential approaches have been, there is not much empirical evidence that they have been very helpful in treating mood disorders. As is true with any of the approaches to psychotherapy, there is probably a very specific type of patient who is likely to benefit from these approaches, but that does not include the majority of patients. However, many of the practitioners of these approaches disagree with the idea that the only therapies of value are those that can be validated by empirical research. It is their position that truth can be sought and found in ways other than the scientific method, and they reject the idea that they need to prove their approach experimentally, when they know experientially that what they do is of value to their clients. Suffice it to say that these approaches are not as widely utilized today as they were in recent decades, but there are still practitioners who use these types of therapy with reportedly good results. More accurately, it can be assumed that there are many therapists who integrate some of the approaches to therapy from this background with the more conventional therapies in order to take advantage of both perspectives.

Cognitive and Cognitive-Behavioral Approaches

For many decades, psychoanalysis and some of the newer psychodynamic approaches were the primary methods for psychotherapeutic interventions. There were behaviorally oriented practitioners who were looking at ways to apply behavioristic models to psychotherapeutic processes, but most of these clinicians were in the academic realm, and many of the interventions were found in the applied research literature. Consequently, most of the people who were "in the trenches" conducting the practice of psychotherapy were from the psychodynamic background.

A few people had deviated from this heritage but had not embraced the behavioral model and were trying to find alternative ways to conceptualize and treat psychopathology. As you recall, the three primary sources of data for therapists are thoughts, feelings, and behaviors, and the one area that they had not been utilized much in the past was the cognitive realm—dealing with people's thoughts and ideas. Of course, the psychodynamic therapists dealt with thoughts, but feelings seemed to be at the bottom of what was being targeted for therapeutic interventions. Some theorists and practitioners began dealing with cognitive models, and while they aroused some notice, they did not have a major impact in the field for many years. Some of the real innovators drew from earlier "rebels" in the psychoanalytic realm and introduced a new way of conceptualizing mental illness and psychotherapeutic change. Earlier therapists such as Alfred Adler, Karen Horney, Harry Stack Sullivan, and Eric Ericson deviated substantially from the Freudian dogma and dealt with conscious thought and belief systems as a focus of therapy. From this background, one psychoanalytically trained therapist, Albert Ellis, developed an approach he called Rational/Emotive Psychotherapy, which looked at how faulty beliefs could lead to disordered thinking and behavior and then at how therapeutic change could result from altering these pathological belief systems.[8]

Another of the early leaders in this field was Aaron Beck, a traditionally trained psychiatrist who focused on the dysfunctional thought patterns associated with depression and on how the treatment of depression needed to focus on these thoughts. This was particularly interesting because depression is considered to be a disorder of mood, and yet, Beck felt that the best way to understand and treat depression was to focus on the thought patterns associated with it.

Finally, George Kelly's approach gained considerable attention in the academic ranks, although it wasn't as influential in practice. His approach was so different and innovative that many people could not understand how to apply it, but it had a significant impact on how some of the later theorists and clinicians would conceptualize and treat psychological problems. As one of the first to incorporate "systems thinking" into his approach to understanding personality and to dealing with and modifying cognitive systems and subsystems, he also tied his interventions into the social realm, which was a harbinger of things to come.

As the cognitive approach gained ground, it became clearer that this approach would be more applicable and more powerful if coordinated with behavioral interventions, and this is when the cognitive-behavioral approach started to take hold. The next generation of psychologists, produced in an environment that challenged the traditional psychoanalytic approaches and also wanted something more broadly applicable than the strictly behavioral types of interventions had been, started to integrate the different ideas that were now available, beginning a whole new movement. Albert Bandura's work on Social Learning Theory set the stage for much of what was to follow. Having a behaviorally based approach that also focused on cognitions was controversial but very compelling. Others started to pick up on these ideas, and they started to gain ground. Beck's work started to broaden and to incorporate some of the behavioral approaches, such as those developed by Peter Lewinsohn and his coworkers. In fact, one very innovative psychologist, Martin Seligman, took his work on learned helplessness and applied it to an understanding of depression. He quickly realized, however, that this simple concept was not enough to deal with something as complex as depression, and he began to study under and collaborate with Aaron Beck. What emerged from all of this work and collaboration was a cognitive *and* behavioral approach to understanding depression.

Beck and many of these clinicians have done considerable research and have contributed much to our understanding and ability to treat depression. How he (and others) blended the two approaches is clear in his treatment structure, which involves several phases of therapy for depression:

Phase 1: Increasing activities and elevating mood
Phase 2: Challenging automatic (viz., dysfunctional) thoughts
Phase 3: Identifying negative thinking and biases
Phase 4: Challenging primary attitudes[9]

Today, Cognitive-Behavioral Therapy (CBT) is the most widely accepted of the psychological forms of treatment for depression, and there is substantial literature supporting its efficacy and efficiency as a treatment method. Some have demonstrated that CBT results in a faster recovery from depression than other treatments and that cognitive factors are more important in understanding depression than demographic or psychosocial factors.[10] Historically, it has been felt that medication was the first line of treatment and that meds would produce better and quicker treatment results than psychotherapy; however, even these beliefs have been challenged in the research literature. Segal et al. pointed out that people who have had major depressive disorder (MDD) in the past can fall into a major depressive episode with even minor negative moods and mild sadness.[11] They can slip into negative ways of thinking about things, which then lead to another episode of major depression. However, they also found that patients who had been treated with CBT were less likely to relapse than patients who were treated with just medication.

Another comprehensive study reported in the Archives of General Psychiatry by DeRubeis et al. compellingly demonstrated that CBT works as well as medication in patients with moderate to severe depression.[12] They found that half-way through the 16-week study 50% of patients on medication had shown improvement while only 43% of those in CBT showed improvement. By the end of the study, however, both groups showed 58% improvement rates. However, the most important finding of this study was that the CBT had very lasting results. The patients who were treated with CBT were no more likely to relapse than patients who were *still* being treated with medication. However, those patients treated with medication alone had significantly higher relapse rates than the therapy-alone group when the medication was discontinued.

If one looks carefully at the literature, it is clear that either CBT alone or CBT with antidepressant medications is considered to be the first-line treatment for depression. However, we must not fall into the trap of thinking that this is the *only* way to successfully treat depression, because that is simply not true. Some patients may prefer or be more likely to respond to other forms of treatment, and, of course, there are very skilled practitioners who use other techniques effectively and successfully. However, these observations do not detract from the huge body of literature that supports CBT as the most effective treatment for depression in a majority of patients.

Neobehavioral Approaches to Treating Depression

As soon as cognitive therapies and behavioral treatments were joined together it seemed they were inextricably and forever linked in the minds of most psychologists. However, there remained a small group who felt that the purely behavioral approaches had been abandoned too abruptly and deserved more consideration and study. Hopko et al. pointed out that, in the last quarter of the twentieth century, the cognitive approaches gained such strength that behavioral therapies were considered inadequate by themselves.[13] In fact, some were not so sure that the cognitive approaches were even necessary and questioned how and even if they worked as advertised. Rehm asserted that cognitive therapies "do not seem to be effective for the reasons we think them to be effective."[14] He went on to claim that, in CBT, most of the improvement occurs early in treatment when the behavioral interventions are the primary focus of treatment. That is to say that the main therapeutic changes have occurred before the cognitive elements have even been introduced.

The behavioral theorists and therapists have a long and distinguished history in the realm of depression, although they were considered to be on the fringe of mainline thinking and treatment. As early as 1953, B.F. Skinner suggested that depression must be associated with an interruption of established sequences of healthy behavior that have been positively reinforced by the social environment.[15] Another behaviorally oriented psychologist, Ferster, feels that behavioral models of depression suggest that decreases in response-contingent reinforcement for nondepressive behavior are the principle causal factor in evoking depressive behaviors.[16] Ferster went on to point out that, when someone continues to be depressed over time, there must be some combination of reinforcement for depressive behavior coupled with a lack of reinforcement or even punishment for healthy alternative behaviors.[17] This "functional analysis" of operant behavior gave the behaviorally oriented psychologists and clinicians a way of conceptualizing depression and for developing a method for treating it.

Peter Lewinsohn and his coworkers were among those who continued to work toward developing a behavioral model of depression that was theoretically sound and empirically and clinically validated. He summarized the approach by pointing out that behavior therapy for depression was largely aimed at increasing access to pleasant events and positive reinforcers as well as decreasing the intensity and frequency of aversive events and consequences.[18] He goes on to suggest that there are three fundamental therapeutic behavioral approaches that are a part of behavioral treatment for depression:

1. Reintroduce clients to pleasurable events and activities
2. Appropriately reinforce the correct behaviors—extinguish others
3. Help improve social skills

Research has found that these techniques tend not to work very well if you only use one of them, but if you use several, they then tend to be effective.[19]

Drawing heavily from the earlier work of Lewinsohn, other researchers and clinicians have continued to try to merge the strictly behavioral approaches with the mainstream of psychological treatment for depression. Hopko and his colleagues point out that, even in many of the early studies, simple behavioral activation of depressed patients proved to be successful in improving their conditions.[20] This somewhat newer approach called Behavioral Activation (BA) guides the implementation of procedures that are intended to increase patient activity levels and access to reinforcement. The idea is that the change in activity levels will lead to improvement in thinking, mood, and quality of life. As we learn more about these behaviorally based treatment methods, we find that the basic behavioral activation strategies, such as pleasant-event scheduling, can be as effective in treating depressed outpatients as the cognitive therapy and personal skills training approaches.[21] The three fundamental principles of BA are:

1. Extinction of depressive behaviors
2. Fading (gradual removal of therapeutic structure so that the functional behaviors become a permanent part of the behavior repertoire)
3. Shaping (the gradual approximation of the desired final behavior patterns)

These basic principles will guide and direct the therapeutic interventions, but some still question the extent to which behavior change alone will accomplish the broader therapeutic goals. However, studies such as those done by Jacobson et al. have demonstrated that cognitive changes may be just as likely to occur using environment-based interventions as cognitive interventions.[22] Many feel that most of the important therapeutic change in CBT occurs during the early and primarily behavioral parts of CBT therapy, therefore, the behavioral aspects must be very important.[23]

Recently, another newer approach called Brief Behavioral Activation Treatment for Depression (BATD) has been introduced and discussed.[24] This approach usually lasts for 8–15 sessions, and early in the treatment the intention is to try to weaken access to positive reinforcement for dysfunctional behavior (e.g., sympathy) and to avoid or minimize negative reinforcement (e.g., avoiding responsibilities). The therapist will work with the client to establish rapport and to educate and explain the treatment approach.[25] Both BA and BATD are very similar in form and function, but the BATD is more structured around a brief time frame. Both the BA and BATD approaches include:

+ relaxation skills
+ increasing pleasant events
+ social and other problem solving

+ skills training
+ contingency management
+ incorporation of verbal-cognitive methods such as
    + cognitive restructuring
    + self-instruction training

In addition, both BA and BATD use additional strategies such as:

+ rating mastery and pleasure of activities
+ assigning activities to increase mastery and pleasure
+ mental rehearsal of assigned activities
+ therapist modeling
+ periodic distraction from problems or unpleasant events
+ mindfulness training or relaxation
+ self-reinforcement
+ additional skills training
    + sleep hygiene
    + assertiveness
    + communication
    + problem solving

As can be seen from these lists, the newer behavioral therapies tend to be very technique-oriented and are based on a philosophical approach that is grounded in behavioristic theories and empirical research. The practitioners and aficionados of these approaches have done some very impressive work in developing new techniques and validating them. It is hard to imagine that any specific approach will work equally with every type of problem, but it is clear that this approach has survived many new fads and keeps re-emerging with new ideas and supportive research.

OTHER PSYCHOLOGICAL APPROACHES TO TREATMENT

Interpersonal Psychotherapy

Interpersonal Psychotherapy (IPT), first introduced by clinical researchers Gerald Klerman and Myrna Weissman, has been very influential and has demonstrated success rates close to CBT. According to this approach, there are four events that may lead to depression:

+ interpersonal loss
+ interpersonal role dispute
+ interpersonal role transition
+ interpersonal defeats[26]

Clearly, this approach is grounded in the belief that depression is linked to interpersonal difficulties, the implication being that treatment must address interpersonal issues if the depression is to be treated effectively. While not as widely used or accepted as CBT, IPT is proving to be a credible and empirically supported approach that is gaining adherents in the clinical realm and clinical research and is often included in clinical training programs.

Couple's Therapy

It is not uncommon for troubled relationships to either lead to or complicate depression. Research demonstrates that recovery from depression is often slower for people who do not receive support from their spouse.[27] An advantage of Couple's Therapy is that it can be used in addition to any of the individual therapy approaches ranging from behavioral to psychodynamic. Some research has demonstrated that couple's therapy can be as effective as IPT, individual therapy, or medication in the treatment of depression.[28] Couple's Therapy is helpful in treating depression, but it is difficult to evaluate because it not only relies on two people as therapy clients, but either or both clients may also be involved with individual treatment, which is another factor that makes it hard to evaluate Couple's Therapy on its own.

Attachment-Based Family Therapy

Attachment-Based Family Therapy (ABFT) emerged from research that demonstrated that adolescent African American females often experienced depression when there was conflict in the family and the attachment with parents was disrupted. This approach works with the entire family (or at least the parents and targeted adolescent patient) focusing on the troubled family dynamics in order to help the adolescent deal with depression. Research by Diamond et al. found that in a sample that was predominantly depressed female adolescent African Americans, ABFT was very effective in reducing anxiety, depression, and family conflict.[29] One would expect this type of therapy to work well with any adolescent who has attachment issues in a dysfunctional family, although, there is not yet enough credible research to make this assertion. One study that compares more general family therapy with CBT and supportive therapy found that in the treatment of MDD, cognitive-behavioral therapy was significantly more effective than either family or supportive therapy.[30] This does not mean that family-based therapies should not be used but that we must determine which types of patient groups and problems are best served by family types of therapy.

Group Therapy

It is somewhat misleading to put Group Therapy as a singular form of treatment for depression because it may involve any type of approach from psychodynamic to behavioral to cognitive to humanistic/existential, and so forth. Thus, coming from any background, a therapist can conduct treatment with groups of patients. Some groups will focus on one type of problem, for example, depression, while others will include people with many different types of disorders. Group Therapy was much more widely used in the 1960s and 1970s and is still used to some extent today. It is logistically more difficult to administer, but it is also very difficult to evaluate because it involves many different people and because it may accompany other forms of treatment at the same time. Much of the research has been less than supportive of group therapy as a primary treatment approach for depression, but some have found it to be a helpful adjunct to medication and individual therapy. Group Therapy has been particularly helpful in dealing with specific topic areas, such as grief, and has been very beneficial with certain medical issues such as breast cancer and cardiovascular disease.

SUMMARY AND CONCLUSIONS

One basic assumption about all of the psychological forms of treatment for depression is that, as a predominantly psychological/emotional disorder, the most appropriate form of treatment should be psychological. In the past, there was considerable debate over the relationship between treatment and etiology. Even today, we see ads for antidepressant medications on TV often making a point of stating that depression is a "medical illness" that is treated with medication. Of course, this has nothing to do with the reality of depression, but it has much to do with the drug companies trying to sell their products. As we saw in earlier chapters, there are some types of depression that are caused, precipitated, or complicated by biological factors, but there are many types of depression that are primarily caused by psychosocial factors. Some people used to argue that if depression can be treated with medication then it must be a biological illness; conversely, others argued that if depression can be treated psychologically then it must be a purely psychological phenomenon. People were making the fallacious assumption that an effective treatment modality was all the evidence needed to support the etiology implied by that theory. In other words, if the treatment works, then the underlying theory must be correct, and the causes implied by the theory must be valid as well. Clearly, this is faulty reasoning. We know that depression is caused by many factors and is never a simple condition. Further, we know that there are many very good forms of treatment for depression, and clinically, what we are most concerned with is treating the condition effectively *regardless* of the cause.

Most practitioners today are comfortable with the fact that there are different types of treatments available, and the job of the practitioner is to match an effective treatment with the patient and their needs. If one treatment doesn't seem to work very well, then try another, but make sure the patient stays with a treatment long enough to experience some results or to determine that it is not going to work. One of the most common causes of failed treatment, either medical or psychological, is when it is discontinued prematurely. By failed treatment we mean there is not a significant improvement in the symptoms of the disorder.

Looking at the research literature one is tempted to assume that every therapist should use CBT, a very successful and effective treatment for depression. However, in the hands of experienced and competent therapists very good results have been demonstrated with all of the types of therapy that we have discussed. For a patient to find a practitioner with whom they are comfortable, and who is well-trained, appropriately credentialed, experienced, and competent, and then to also feel that the treatment approach is reasonable and comfortable provides a very good foundation upon which to build an effective course of treatment. Good treatment results depend upon an effective treatment team, the primary team members being the patient and the treating professional. This is true regardless of the type of therapy that is practiced.

Chapter 9

Treatment for Depression: Medical Treatments and Others

I am in that temper that if I were under water I would scarcely kick to come to the top.
—John Keats (1795–1821), British poet

Medicine heals doubts as well as diseases.
—Karl Marx (1818–1883), German political theorist and social philosopher

For all of recorded history (and even before, I am quite sure) people have suffered from depression, and for as long as people have born the burden of this disorder there have been attempts to find answers and remedies to cure it. From trephining (primitive brain surgery) through bleeding and other well-intentioned but worthless and often dangerous treatments, people have searched for answers and largely without any positive results. Historically, mental illness has been viewed as a moral failing, a characterological weakness, evil, malingering (faking), and other typically negative states. Depending on the time period in question and the prevailing culture, treatment was relegated to the legal system, the church, the family, and finally, even medicine. Fields such as psychology and psychiatry were not even relevant until the late nineteenth century, and in the absence of reasonable and effective treatments, the mentally ill, including those with depression, were treated (or not) based upon the prevailing views and theories in society at large.

When treatment gravitated into the medical sphere, it is hardly surprising that the tendency was to seek medical answers and to pursue medical treatments. In terms of depression, more things than any of us can even imagine were tried as treatments. The search for effective medicines has always been at the forefront, but there have also been efforts to find surgeries and other physical forms of treatment that might be helpful in the treatment of depression. This chapter examines some of the present forms of medical treatment, and we examine the research that has helped us to understand and evaluate the effects of these treatments. We do not go into in-depth discussions over the historical forms of treatment but focus on what is being done today, how the treatments are being used, and how they work. We begin with the most common form of treatment for depression today—medication. Not only is medication the most frequent form of medical treatment, but it is the most frequent form of treatment for depression *of any modality.*

PSYCHOPHARMOCOLOGY FOR DEPRESSION

In recent decades, drug companies have been permitted to advertise medications, targeting their ads to the general public. This has certainly been true of the antidepressant drugs, and most of us have seen the ads that "promise" to treat this "medical disease" by providing a drug that will make a person happy and self-fulfilled once again. While it is certainly true there are many very effective drugs for the treatment of depression, this approach to selling drugs offers very unfortunate and misleading expectations about the nature of depression and its treatments. The hype that is perpetuated in advertising does a disservice to patients by not providing a clear and accurate picture of depression and of treatment and probably leads to gross overuse and misuse of otherwise effective and helpful medications.

Prior to the 1950s, there were not very many medical treatment options for depression. There was psychosurgery, which had proven to be dangerous and ineffective; electroconvulsive therapy (ECT), which was (at that time at least) somewhat effective but dangerous and frightening for patients; and finally, medications, which at that time were not very effective. Basically, there were two types of drugs that were used: the central nervous system (CNS) depressants, such as tranquilizers, barbiturates, and other sedatives, which could calm someone who was agitated or anxious but certainly didn't help depression and may have made it worse; and the CNS stimulants, such as amphetamines. Because many people who are depressed feel lethargic and fatigued, it seemed like the energizing drugs might be a benefit. While they did tend to make people more aroused, they did little to help the depressed mood or thoughts. Thus, what resulted were depressed people who were anxious, agitated, and impulsive. However, with so few options available, people continued to experiment with various doses, combinations of treatments, and new approaches. Unfortunately, few of these were very helpful.

The Early Antidepressants

In the 1950s, some accidental findings ushered in two new classes of drugs that provided not only effective treatment for depression but the hope that we were finally starting to understand the neurophysiology of depression. With no apparent preconception of what might happen, physicians noticed that iponiazid, a drug that was being tested on patients with tuberculosis, seemed to make patients feel happier.[1] With further testing they also found that this same effect could be observed in depressed patients.[2] Research demonstrated that this class of drugs called monoamine oxidase inhibitors (MAOI) improved the mood and decreased the symptoms of depressed patients. They subsequently discovered that monoamine oxidase in the CNS could build up and inactivate the neurotransmitters norepinephrine, dopamine, and serotonin (recall that neurotransmitters are those chemicals in the brain that carry messages between nerve cells). It appears that the MAOI prevents the breakdown of neurotransmitters, returning them to a normal level in the brain, which then leads to a decrease in depressive symptoms. It has been demonstrated that at least 50% of depressed patients will show improvement with the use of MAOIs.

Unfortunately, it was also discovered that the MAOIs have some very serious side effects and particularly when people eat or drink certain foods with a chemical called tyramine. If a person on an MAOI eats a food such as certain fish, bananas, certain wines, and other foods, a serious rise in blood pressure can occur that can even cause death. In fact, the MAOIs can interact with so many foods, drinks, and other medications that physicians in the United States rarely use these drugs anymore. Look at most over-the-counter medications in your medicine cabinet, and very frequently you will see that you should not take that medication if you are on an MAOI. Physicians in Europe are much more likely to use this drug than those in the United States, but it is still used with caution. We have also found that these drugs are effective, and that, for patients who have not responded well to conventional antidepressant medications, they can still be a valuable treatment alternative—as long as they are used carefully. In fact, a new approach using a skin patch for an MAOI called Emsam (selegiline) has been shown to be safe without dietary restrictions at low doses because it doesn't break down the tyramine in the digestive system. This drug bypasses the digestive system and goes straight into the bloodstream.[3] However, at the higher doses they do follow dietary restrictions. Some of the other MAOIs that are used are Marplan (isocaroxazid), Nardil (phelelzine), and Parnate (tranylcypromine). By blocking the action of MAO and increasing the levels of the neurotransmitters norepinephrine, dopamine, and serotonin, there is a therapeutic effect that decreases depressive symptoms and improves functioning.

In the 1950s, another class of medications was accidentally discovered to be helpful for depression. Researchers were studying the effects of a drug called imipramine on schizophrenia. They found that it had little effect on schizophrenia, but it seemed to help unipolar depression.[4] This drug and related compounds became known as tricyclics because they all share a three-ring molecular structure. These drugs have proven to be very effective in treating depression with about 60–65% of depressed patients being helped by them.[5] It was also found that when patients discontinue a tricyclic drug too soon they often relapse. Thus, many physicians keep their patients on these drugs indefinitely. Another complication is that the drugs rarely reach therapeutic effectiveness in less than a few weeks, and sometimes it takes more than a month. While these drugs are certainly safer to use than the MAOIs, they are not without side effects, and some of the side effects make the drugs difficult to use with some patients (e.g., heart rhythm irregularities, dizziness, agitation, dry mouth, constipation, etc.).

The tricyclics seem to work by blocking the reuptake of the neurotransmitters norepinephrine, serotonin, and to a lesser extent, dopamine. When a nerve cell releases a chemical to stimulate the adjacent neuron (nerve cell), the chemical enters the synaptic cleft (the space between the neurons) and is picked up by the adjacent neuron at a receptor site on that neuron. In order to keep from overstimulating the receiving neuron, the sending neuron has a reuptake pump that reabsorbs the neurotransmitter back into the sending neuron. However, if this reuptake pump is too effective then it takes too much of the neurotransmitter out of the synaptic cleft, and there is inadequate neural transmission. Thus, there are not enough of the neurotransmitters to have the desired effect on the adjacent neurons. When those neurotransmitters are norepinephrine, dopamine, and serotonin, then decreased availability of these substances can result in depression. By blocking the reuptake of these neurotransmitters, tricyclic medications reduce depressive symptoms. Examples of tricyclic antidepressants are:

+ Aventyl, Pamelor (nortiptyline)
+ Elavil (amitriptyline)
+ Norpramin (desipramine)
+ Sinequan (doxepine)
+ Surmontil (trimipramine)
+ Toframil (imipramine)
+ Vivactil (protriptyline)

The tricyclics do have some unpleasant side effects and can be lethal in overdose. In recent years, with the introduction of new antidepressant medications with fewer side effects, the tricyclics have not been used as often. However, tricyclics are being used in lower doses for chronic pain disorders, fibromyalgia, and insomnia, particularly if a patient has insomnia that is related to pain. Finally, some people with migraines find that taking tricyclic medication helps decrease the frequency of headaches. Thus, while these drugs are not used as often for depression, they are still used as a second-line treatment when a patient is either treatment resistant to the newer medications or cannot tolerate the newer medications because of side effects. Further, the tricyclics are used frequently for other medical purposes besides depression and have proven to be helpful in these areas as well.

A related class of drugs called tetracyclics (they have a four-ring molecular structure) work by blocking the reuptake of serotonin and norepinephrine. They have similar advantages and disadvantages of the tricyclics and often with side effects that create problems (e.g., significant weight gain). However, for some patients these drugs work very well, without significant side effects. Two of the drugs in this class are maprotiline and Remeron (mirtazapine).

Second-Generation Antidepressants

In addition to the tetracyclics, there has been an influx of newer antidepressants that have been very much a part of the treatment landscape in recent years and have had a major impact on the treatment of depression and anxiety disorders. The first of these drugs to create a stir (and resultant controversy) was Prozac (fluoxetine), which came on the market in the United States around 1987. What made this drug different was the fact that it worked as a reuptake inhibitor *only* for serotonin. Thus, Prozac and other drugs like it are called selective serotonin reuptake inhibitors (SSRIs). While Prozac was the first drug in this category to be widely recognized, it was not the first SSRI to be developed. In fact, three other drugs were actually marketed before Prozac: indalpine, zimelidine, and fluvoxamine. The first two were removed from the market because of side effects, and fluvoxamine is still on the market. However, Eli Lilly, the manufacturer of Prozac, did some very aggressive marketing and made Prozac the first of the SSRIs to have a major impact on the treatment of depression. There is one other drug that is serotonin-specific but is chemically a tricyclic, and that is Anafranil. This drug is used in Europe as an antidepressant but not as often in the United States because there are many other medications that don't have the side-effect profile of the tricyclics. However, Anafranil is sometimes used as a treatment for obsessive-compulsive disorder.

Prozac and the other SSRIs were quickly and aggressively marketed, became very popular, and were probably overused. They are not as dangerous as other antidepressants when overdosed, do not have the same troubling side effects as the tricyclics, and do not have the dietary restrictions of the MAOIs. That is not to say they are perfect. They also take anywhere from 2–6 weeks for full effect, and they produce their own side-effect problems. Most commonly, people taking these medications sometimes complain of nausea, digestive problems, sexual dysfunction, and other, usually mild, difficulties. Many side effects go away in a few days, and the ones that don't can often be eliminated by simply changing to a different medication. Because they are effective, relatively safe, easy to use, and available, these drugs are used widely and enthusiastically. Interestingly, most of the prescriptions that are written for the antidepressant drugs are written by primary care physicians (PCPs), family physicians, and OB/GYNs rather than mental health professionals. This is not necessarily a problem but is an indication of how widely these drugs are used. Certainly, the introduction of the SSRIs dramatically changed the treatment of depression and related conditions.

The SSRIs that are used today in the United States include:

+ Celexa (citalopram)
+ Lexapro (escitalopram)
+ Luvox (fluvoxamine)
+ Paxil (paroxetine)—also available in controlled-release
+ Prozac (fluoxetine)—also available in a weekly dosage option
+ Zoloft (sertraline)

These medications are attractive by being selective to the reuptake of serotonin; they don't affect other systems and, therefore, were not as "dirty"—this means that by being less general in effect they are less likely to cause side effects and other problems. Serotonin is very important in understanding the neurophysiology of depression, but it became clear that serotonin is not the only neurotransmitter involved with depression. Other systems, particularly dopamine and norepinephrine, were also involved in depression, and thus, new drugs dealing with these systems also began to emerge.

One class of drugs that inhibits the reuptake of both serotonin and norepinephrine are called the serotonin and norepinephrine reuptake inhibitors (SNRIs). This class of drugs deals with a broader array of neurophysiological systems and seems to work differently in treating problems in addition to depression; this group includes such drugs as Cymbalta (duloxetine), Desyrel (trazadone), and Effexor (venlafaxine—also available in extended release). In addition to being used as antidepressants, they have each found a specialized niche for the treatment of other conditions. For example, it was inadvertently found that Cymbalta seemed to relieve the pain of peripheral neuropathy, which is nerve pain that occurs in the peripheral parts of the body (e.g., arms and legs) and is common in conditions such as diabetes where circulation in the extremities is compromised. It may not eliminate the pain, but it often reduces it. Desyrel (trazadone) has also been helpful in treating a completely different type of problem. As an antidepressant, trazadone was difficult to use because it was so sedating that patients had difficulty functioning normally. But in lower doses this drug is widely used to stabilize sleep patterns in those suffering from insomnia, and unlike traditional sleep medications, trazadone is not addictive. Finally, Effexor, a proven antidepressant, is very effective in treating anxiety conditions. Consequently, for those patients who suffer both anxiety and depression, it is a very useful medication. Many of the SSRIs are used to treat anxiety disorders as well, but this is a niche that Effexor has filled, too.

The final class of the newer antidepressants is the dopamine reuptake inhibitors (DRIs). These medications block the reabsorption of dopamine in the CNS, keeping more of it available in the nervous system. For people who are treatment resistant to the SSRIs, these are often good second line drugs. In fact, because they work so differently than the SSRIs they are sometimes used in combination with an SSRI, often with very good results. The main drug in this category is Wellbutrin (bupropion), which also comes in a sustained release (Wellbutrin SR) and in an extended release (Wellbutrin XR) form. This drug is used frequently due to the low frequency of sexual side effects and weight gain, which often leads patients to discontinue antidepressant medication treatment. Wellbutrin is the same medication (bupropion) that is in the drug Zyban, which is used to help people stop smoking. Wellbutrin was also recently approved by the FDA for use in the prevention of major depressive disorder (MDD) and for the treatment of seasonal affective disorder (SAD).[6] Even the drugs that are not approved for the prevention and treatment of these conditions (especially the SSRIs) are frequently used "off label" for treating these conditions. This means that even though they have not been "officially" recognized to treat a specific condition, the common practice has been to try these drugs and let the clinical results determine whether or not the drug is working.

In addition to antidepressant medications, occasionally prescribers will use one of the benzodiazepine drugs (tranquilizers) with a depressed patient who is also anxious. Drugs such as Ativan (lorazepam) or Klonipin (clonazepam) are typically used to combat anxiety, although other benzodiazepam tranquilizers could be used as well (e.g., Valium or Xanax). These work by increasing the activity of gamma-amino-butyric acid (GABA), which is a neurotransmitter that inhibits the excessive firing of certain types of neurons.[7] Very frequently the antidepressant medications will help with anxiety, but they usually are slow to take effect. Because the benzodiazepines work very quickly, they are often used at the beginning of antidepressant treatment until the slower-acting drug begins to take effect. The benzodiazepine drugs, while effective, also have troubling side effects such as the development of drug tolerance and addiction. As such, they are not used for longer-term treatment unless nothing else has proven effective for managing the anxiety symptoms.

DRUG TREATMENT FOR BIPOLAR DISORDER

While one of the characteristics of bipolar disorder (BPD) is depression, it is not as easily treated as unipolar depression because BPD involves either mania or hypomania, which are conditions not treated with antidepressant medications. In fact, the use of some antidepressants (e.g., SSRIs) in a depressed patient with BPD may actually trigger a manic episode.[8] It has also been found that corticosteroids such as prednisone, levadopa and other medications used to treat Parkinsonism, and Ritalin (methylphenidate) and other drugs used to treat attention deficit disorder (ADD) and attention–deficit/hyperactivity disorder (ADHD) can also trigger a manic episode in bipolar patients.[9] Thus, in BPD the typical strategy is to stabilize the manic or hypomanic condition first and then to treat the depression. There are several different approaches to treating the symptoms of mania and hypomania.

The mood stabilizers reduce the excitement and agitation of the manic or hypomanic patient and stabilize them emotionally. Although it is not certain how these drugs work, they are used very effectively with many patients. Basically, there are three categories of medications used as mood stabilizers: carbamazapine (Carbitrol, Epitol, and Tegretol), lithium (Eskalith and Lithobid), and the drugs derived from valproic acid (Depakene, valproic acid; Depakote, divalproex; and Depakote Sprinkles, divalproex). For a person suffering from BPD, these drugs are often the first line of treatment.

Some anticonvulsant medications that are used to treat epilepsy and related conditions also have a mood stabilizing effect. While these drugs suppress excessive and abnormal firing of neurons, how they work specifically with BPD has not yet been established. The drugs in this category are Lamictal (lamotrigine), Neurontin (gabapentin), and Topomax (topiramate).

In addition, some of the typical and atypical neuroleptic medications are used to stabilize the bipolar patient who is in a manic state. These drugs are frequently used as antipsychotic medications and seem to work in BPD because they block the dopamine receptors. Because symptoms of BPD can be produced with overactivity of dopamine, these drugs can prevent the overstimulation of nerve cells that are sensitive to dopamine. Thus, they tend to produce antipsychotic and tranquilizing effects in agitated patients. Some of the drugs in this category that are used for the treatment of BPD include some of the atypical neuroleptics:

+ Abilify (aripiprazole)
+ Clozaril and FazoClo ODT (clozapine)
+ Geodon (ziprasidone)
+ Risperdal (risperidone)
+ Seroquel (quetiapine)
+ Zyprexa (olanzapine)

These drugs are used more often than the typical neuroleptics because they have a better side-effect profile, particularly with respect to the more serious side effects. However, they are not without their own concerns, particularly clozapine, which can have very serious side effects. However, even clozapine can be used safely under the careful supervision of a physician (usually a psychiatrist) who will use blood tests to make sure that the medication is not creating other problems. Specifically, clozapine can cause agranulocytosis, which is a dangerous reduction in white blood cells. Taken under careful supervision, this can be a very helpful and effective drug.

The typical neuroleptics, Haldol (haloperidol) and Permitil or Prolixin (fluphenazine), are used to treat BPD patients by blocking the dopamine receptors; however, they are associated with more frequent problems and serious side effects. One additional drug recently on the market, Symbyax, combines the stabilizing effect of the atypical neuroleptic olanzapine and the antidepressant effect of fluoxetine; it is like taking Zyprexa and Prozac at the same time. The typical drug treatment of the bipolar patient involves the stabilization of the patient's mood and behavior by using the antimanic types of drugs and working on the depressive symptoms with an antidepressant.

ANTIDEPRESSANT MEDICATIONS AND SUICIDALITY

One of the concerns that has been an issue since the beginning of the use of antidepressant medications is whether or not the medication itself increases suicidal risk. This is a tricky issue to study because depressed patients are already higher risk for suicide than someone who is not depressed. However, because antidepressant medications take weeks or sometimes even months to work, it is not clear that patients are at higher risk *because* they are on the medication. Is it because they are still depressed, and the medicine isn't working yet? While the evidence surrounding this issue is conflicted and has not led to consistent and accepted conclusions, it is clear that suicide rates have decreased since the SSRIs have come on the scene.[10] One study showed that, after 1988 when Prozac first came on the market, as Prozac sales increased, the suicide rate decreased. These data also showed that women were more likely to benefit from Prozac but probably because they were more likely to seek treatment.[11] Because of continuing concerns, however, the FDA has put warnings on antidepressant medications regarding the possibility that a person might be more prone to suicide after having started the medication and should be monitored closely. This is especially true for children, teens, and young adults. If we look at the entire body of research on this issue, it is apparent that the real risk for suicide is more the depression than the medication, but there is a possibility that as people begin to feel better and become more energized, if they are still depressed, they might attempt suicide. However, this is true whether people are on medication or not, and this is not a new finding—we have known this for years.[12] Of course, patient welfare and safety is always the primary concern in any treatment, so closely monitoring a depressed patient is considered appropriate care under any circumstances. The greater risk is to not treat someone when effective treatment is available.

We should also be considerate of the best forms of treatment if we want to minimize the risk of suicide—especially among high-risk groups. For example, if we use cognitive-behavioral therapy (CBT) with fluoxetine (Prozac) we find that suicide rates are decreased with fluoxetine but that CBT does better than fluoxetine alone, and CBT + fluoxetine is the best of all. The research findings show that there is no scientific evidence causally linking SSRIs to increased suicide rates. The caution, however, is understandable, and it certainly is better to be careful than to have tragic outcomes. However, we must be mindful of the fact that there are people young and old who could benefit from treatment but who are not receiving it because of a misplaced fear of increased risk of suicide. One thing to consider is, because medication is frequently the first line of treatment, we forget that increased suicidality typically involves conflicts that medications aren't going to fix but that psychotherapy might help. This is especially true of adolescents who can learn to become a therapeutic tool for themselves.[13] Good psychotherapy can be used to teach people the skills that will help them deal with life outside of therapy in such a way as to reduce their own suicidal risk—this is difficult to do with medication alone.

SUMMARY OF FINDINGS ON MEDICATIONS

While the medications that have emerged since the 1950s have proven their effectiveness in clinical practice and in the research literature, there are various reasons for using one medication over another. For example, no two patients are the same, what works for one person may not work for another, and it is difficult to predict which medication will work for a specific patient. Often, medications aren't effective because they are not used properly. One factor that is occasionally helpful is if we find that a close relative has been treated with a particular medication, and it was helpful; this may well be a good drug to use as a first trial. On the other hand, if the medication didn't work well, or there were negative side effects with the relative in question, then it would not likely be the first medication that should be tried. Conventional wisdom dictates that the *main* reason medication is not initially effective is the drug is either not being used at a high enough dosage or is not continued long enough. All of these medications take weeks to work, and sometimes the adjustment of the dosage may take several months to reach the correct level. Of course, when someone is depressed and seeking relief, they will sometimes pressure their prescribing professional into changing their medication if they don't experience quick results. Sometimes this is the correct thing to do, particularly if there are problems with side effects, but frequently people change medication before they have given the drug a chance to work.

In recent years, the SSRIs have usually been the first course of medication treatment. They tend to produce milder side effects than other types of antidepressants and are a lower risk for fatal overdoses and heart rhythm disturbances, which can be dangerous for people with cardiac disease. Research has demonstrated that the SSRIs are at least as effective as the tricyclics and because they are safer and less problematic, they are usually used first.[14]

While medication is not the only form of treatment for depression, there are some advantages to the use of safe and effective medications:

+ They have proven to be effective in the treatment of mild, moderate, and severe forms of MDD.
+ Patients frequently respond more quickly to medication than to psychotherapy.
+ It is easy to administer.
+ These medications are not addictive and when used appropriately are generally quite safe.
+ They can be used in combination with psychotherapy.[15]

This does not mean that medication is the only or even necessarily the best form of treatment. As we learned earlier, medication alone, as the treatment for depression, frequently results in relapse when the drug is stopped. None of the medications are without side effects, and this always has to be balanced with therapeutic advantages. Medications are often used quickly by PCPs because they are easy to use and relatively safe, but this means that there are probably people being treated with medication who hadn't been offered psychotherapy or a combination of treatments. Primary care physicians know the patients and often deliver the first line of treatment to most patients. However, medication alone for many patients will not be adequate treatment, and the involvement of a mental health professional could make a significant difference in the success for treating depression.

Some of the "take-home messages" for those using medications for the treatment of depression include:

+ No one antidepressant medication will work effectively for all patients—you may need to try several.
+ Being persistent and being willing to try different drugs will typically improve results.
+ At a standard dose of most antidepressant medications, 30% of patients with severe depression will achieve remission on the first drug that is tried.
+ It often takes 12 weeks (not just 4–8 as previously thought) to fully benefit from a given medication.
+ If the first drug doesn't work, the second one does 25% of the time.
+ Switching from one SSRI to another is as effective as switching to another class of antidepressant drugs.
+ If the first drug doesn't work, adding a second one will help about one-third of patients.
+ If the first drug doesn't work, adding another drug is slightly more likely to be successful than changing drugs.
+ If the first and second drugs combined don't work, adding a third drug will work about 20% of the time.[16]

A patient's compliance with their treatment regime is key to the successful treatment of depression. Sometimes patients who are being followed at the primary care level do not understand the importance of continuing their meds or the need to discuss side effects, and they are not being seen in the office often enough. Nearly half of depressed patients in primary care stop taking medication in the first three months, and 60–70% stop in six months. They either have side effects that they don't like, they believe they are better, or they feel that the drug isn't doing anything.[17] One survey showed that 50% of PCPs say they always inquire about depression when the patient sees them for another problem, and the rest said they sometimes asked. However, over one-third of patients in the same study claimed they had never been asked about depression. The PCPs say that they give clear directions as to how to take antidepressant medications, including the instruction to continue taking the medication after they start feeling better. Many patients deny that they had ever been told about the medications. Either some PCPs aren't effectively doing their job, or some patients are not hearing or remembering the instructions.[18] It is very clear that depression management at the primary care level is vitally important and needs to be done correctly.[19] One extensive study, the STAR*D study, found that depressed patients responded equally well to treatment by a PCP or a psychiatrist when they adopted a management program that included self-monitoring of symptoms and drug side effects.[20] This does suggest that it is possible to manage depression at the primary care level but that having an appropriate and specific program for patients to follow is essential to optimize compliance.

OTHER MEDICAL TREATMENTS

Electroconvulsive Therapy

Electroconvulsive therapy (ECT) has the longest history in mental illness other than medication and has the most research associated with it. The use of strong electric currents with minimal anesthesia, producing violent convulsions and side effects such as serious memory loss, has given ECT a bad reputation, and it was rarely used for many years. The introduction of much better equipment, more patient-friendly techniques, education, better anesthesia, and the control of a patient's convulsive responses have led to more frequent use of ECT today. It is now considered to be an effective and fast-acting treatment intervention for unipolar depression.[21] Up to 90% of depressed patients improve with ECT when it is the first line of treatment. When used as a last resort, effectiveness drops off to about 45–50%, but it is still a very impressive result.[22] This treatment has not produced damage visible on brain scans in humans or animals. However, there is frequently permanent memory loss for events during and immediately prior to treatment. Although ECT is proven to be an effective treatment, it is not commonly used, and in the United States, only about 100,000 treatment episodes per year are recorded.[23]

In summary, controlled studies demonstrate that ECT is as effective as medication and often more so. Although actual ECT treatment in a clinical setting tends not to be as effective as in clinical trials, it is probably due to the fact that in real clinical settings the treatment is not carried on as long as it needs to be. Other considerations in support of ECT include the fact that it has fewer side effects than drugs and is less risky for people with cardiac disease. In fact, ECT may be the preferred treatment for pregnant women, older people, and those who are physically ill. It is rarely used with teens, and general guidelines for adolescents dictate that it should only be used after two drugs have failed, the patient is suffering from severe depression, and the patient and the guardian both agree to ECT treatment.[24] Because there is often some memory loss, and the medications we have today are much more effective and safer than in the past, ECT is still rarely the first line of treatment for depressed patients.

Deep Brain Stimulation

This very sophisticated new treatment involves the surgical implantation of a device that will deliver an electrical current to a specific part of the brain to normalize its activity. Presently, it is only being used experimentally, but it has started to show encouraging results. The FDA approved it for use in treating tremors in Parkinson's disease as well as other movement disorders. It is also being investigated for use with unrelenting pain disorders, certain forms of epilepsy, as well as for strokes and paralysis. At this time it is only being used as an investigatory treatment for psychiatric disorders, including depression.[25] However, it appears to offer some promise and may prove helpful in the treatment of depression where nothing else has worked.

Rapid Transcranial Magnetic Stimulation

Rapid transcranial magnetic stimulation (rTMS) involves placing an electromagnetic coil on the scalp while a pulsed, high-intensity magnetic current is passed through the coil to change the way the brain functions.[26] Because it produces no seizures and does not require anesthesia, it seems to be a more palatable form of treatment than ECT. The results of its treatment for depression are far too preliminary to form an opinion. However, because it appears to be safe and less invasive than some of the other medical treatments, there is hope that it might be an effective and safe treatment for depression.

Magnetic Seizure Therapy

Magnetic seizure therapy is a new approach that combines ECT and rTMS as a form of treatment that induces seizures, but it has fewer side effects than ECT alone. This is a very promising new technique, but it is so new that it is still in development, and much remains to be done to determine its efficacy and safety. As advances in microtechnology blossom, new treatment methods emerge almost continually. We will need to watch the research and clinical literature to see how this approach develops.

Vagus Nerve Stimulation

The vagus nerve is one of the cranial nerves that apparently has something to do with depression. Vagus nerve stimulation (VNS) involves a surgical implantation of a device that stimulates the vagus nerve in a programmed sequence and at regular intervals. Supposedly, it affects the levels of serotonin and norepinephrine, but little is actually known about how it works. The earliest literature suggests that it may effectively treat depression that has not previously responded to more conventional forms of treatment, and it was approved for use by the FDA in July 2005.[27]

Light Therapy

It has been demonstrated that some people develop depression during the late fall and winter, with it remitting in the spring. This is apparently due to the increased production of melatonin, a hormone that is released by the pineal gland when it is dark but not when it is light.[28] This hormone plays a part in sleep and in the hibernation of animals. However, some people seem so sensitive to melatonin that when the days get shorter and darker the extra production of melatonin seems to make them slow down, grow more tired and less motivated, and can lead to depression.[29] This condition is known as seasonal affective disorder (SAD) and is more prevalent the further north or south of the equator that a person lives.[30] If the amount of light that a person is exposed to affects the amount of melatonin produced, and excess melatonin is related to depressive symptoms, then adding a light source to a person who is prone to SAD should help reduce the level of depression.

The use of artificial light for several hours every day in the winter is call light therapy, or phototherapy. Some researchers report that this form of treatment for SAD often will reduce or even eliminate the symptoms of depression. If one looks online or in catalogs that sell this type of equipment, it is easy to find a light box for several hundred dollars that will (according to the manufacturers) work miracles. Most professionals would hesitate recommending such an expense before other methods have been tried first. In fact, if one looks at all of the research, the conclusions are not quite as emphatically supportive as some would lead us to believe. In fact, there are mixed findings and unclear results that make it difficult to interpret the data and to draw conclusions from it.[31] Some clinicians have found it just as helpful to encourage their patients to pursue activities outside during the daylight hours, such as walking. I have instructed my own patients to turn on all of the lights inside their house in order to keep the ambient light consistently high throughout the house and to get out for physical and social activities as often as possible. Simple little things such as following good nutrition, avoiding alcohol or recreational drugs, getting appropriate sleep, and even hand washing can help. Hand washing? Think about it; washing one's hands is a very good way to keep from getting sick. If you become ill during the winter months, it is very easy to slip back into habits of staying in bed, avoiding activity, and socially isolating.

Exercise

It has been known for centuries that vigorous activity can help elevate someone from the depths of despair. However, we are only now beginning to understand how exercise serves as a therapeutic activity in the treatment of depression as well as other conditions. One study demonstrated that both exercise and social contact resulted in a decrease in scores on the Beck Depression Inventory. However, only the exercise condition resulted in the decrease of the physical symptoms of depression.[32] We now understand how important exercise is for both physical and mental health, and most mental health practitioners include vigorous regular exercise as a component of the total treatment program that they recommend to their patients with depression (as well as many other conditions). These recommendations include a number of different considerations:

+ Begin exercising now, and continue it on a regular schedule.
+ Choose activities that are moderately intense.
+ Select activities that are continuous and rhythmic (e.g., walking, jogging, biking, swimming, etc.).
+ Be wary of competitive sports—they won't help much with depression.
+ Add a mind-body element (relaxation, yoga, meditation, etc.).
+ Start slowly and build up—don't overdo it.[33]
+ Of course, when recommending a new exercise program, always make sure that the patient's physician is in agreement.

It seems clear that exercise does improve depressive symptoms for many patients, but it is not always clear as to why this is the case. Exercise affects us physically, neurophysiologically, cognitively, and emotionally. For example, vigorous exercise releases beta endorphins, which make people feel better and more positive, and exercise boosts the levels of the "feel good" chemicals in the brain such as serotonin. Exercise can also serve as a release or a distraction from the things that are bothering a person and can get them to focus on something other than their own problems—at least for a short while. One reason exercise is particularly important to depressed patients is that it gives them a feeling of accomplishment—something to feel good about. Often exercise can involve other people, and the socialization is also very helpful for those who are depressed.

ALTERNATIVE TREATMENTS

One study found that only 40% of people with MDD receive adequate conventional treatment, and 54% of those with depression use alternative treatments. Of those who use alternative treatments, 26% use manual therapies such as chiropractic, massage, and accupressure. About 20% of people surveyed use herbs and teas, and 16% use vitamins and nutritional supplements. Other forms of alternative therapies are yoga, meditation, tai chi, traditional Chinese medicine, Ayurveda, and Native American healing rituals.[34]

In one study, the reasons people gave for choosing alternative treatment methods for their depression included:

+ Side effects from conventional medications (45%)
+ Conventional medications were ineffective (43%)
+ Could not afford conventional treatment (17%)
+ Preferred natural approach (65%)
+ Alternative practices were consistent with patient beliefs (59%)
+ Patients became familiar with these methods during their childhood (45%)
+ Read or heard something about the techniques (39%)
+ About one-third of patients in this study said that their physicians had recommended alternative treatments, usually the manual types of treatments—they almost never recommended herbs or vitamins.[35]

Certainly, there are many people who use and swear by alternative treatments for depression. Most of the proponents of these treatments are quick to point out that they are not recommending them as replacements for normal forms of treatment but do urge patients and mental health professionals to keep an open mind, particularly for those patients who do not respond quickly or completely to conventional treatments.

St. John's Wort

Hypericum Perforatum, or St. John's Wort (SJW), has been used in Europe for some time for the treatment of depression and has been used more frequently in the United States in the past couple of decades. Most of the evidence in the past has been anecdotal or based on minimal and inadequate research. In recent years, however, there have been some very good studies evaluating the effects of SJW. It appears that SJW can be helpful in the treatment of mild to moderate depression and has greater efficacy than placebo. It is also equal to low doses of tricyclics (but not at higher therapeutic doses), and there is very limited data that examines head-to-head trials against the newer antidepressants.[36] Other researchers have found that the MAOI activity with SJW is minimal and that the mechanisms of action are unclear. Further, it has been determined that cotreatment with SSRIs is not wise because it can lead to serotonin syndrome, which occurs when serotonin levels are too high.[37] The conclusions on SJW are:

+ It is better than placebo, sometimes.
+ It is equivalent to low doses of tricyclics.
+ In two large studies that compare SJW to SSRIs, the SSRIs were clearly superior.
+ Basically, the side-effect profile is safe, although there can be some adverse effects and some interactions with other medications.[38]

Interestingly, many people who use SJW will do so because they think it is safer than the medications they might receive from their physician because it is natural. However, "natural" alone does not make it safe, and because the FDA does not have authority over natural supplements, the manufacturers are not held to the same standards of production and proof as are regular medications. In fact, because we know much more about the normal medications that are used to treat depression, it seems more reasonable to start with conventional treatment before trying something that is alternative, unproven, and has less research supporting its safety and effectiveness. This substance may well have a place in the treatment arsenal for depression, but at this point, the evidence is not very compelling.

Omega-3 Fish Oil

In recent years, there has been increasing interest in the use of omega-3 oils as supplements for better health. The two main types are eicosapentanoic acid (EPA) and ducosahexanoic acid (DHA). There is evidence that these substances benefit people by decreasing risk for heart disease, high cholesterol, some types of cancer, as well as other conditions. There has also been some attention given to omega-3 fatty acids, particularly to EPA, as a potential preventive agent and/or as a treatment for depression. In fact, some would consider EPA to be an effective add-on treatment for unipolar depression and recurrent unipolar depression, and most of the research evidence to date has focused on EPA.[39]

One line of research has looked at the *per capita* consumption of fish and the incidence rates for depression. Hibbeln reported in *Lancet* (the British medical journal) that the correlation between fish consumption and major depression is $r = -.84$, $p < .005$.[40] This is a highly significant finding that strongly suggests the more fish one eats the less likely one is to suffer from major depression. He also reported that mothers who ate more fish were less likely to suffer from postpartum depression (PPD). For example, in Japan, where people eat more than 140 lbs. of fish per year, the rate of PPD for new mothers is 2.0%. In the United States, where people consume a little more than 40 lbs. of fish per year, the rate of PPD is 11.5%; in South Africa, where people only eat a little more than 15 lbs. of fish per year, they have a 24.5% rate of PPD. Of course, this finding must be followed by the warning that for prospective mothers, pregnant women, and new mothers there is a risk for heavy metal contamination (e.g., mercury) in fish.

Summarizing the research on omega-3 fatty acids and depression, Stoll reports the following.[41]

+ There is lower blood omega-3 fatty acids in patients with MDD.
+ Epidemiological evidence points to a lack of omega-3 fatty acids as a world-wide risk factor for depression.
+ Neurochemical effects of omega-3 depletion are consistent with models of depression.
+ Research reports an antidepressant effect of omega-3 fatty acids.
+ Double-blind studies report antidepressant effects from fish oil in BPD.
+ Reduced rates of seasonal mood shifts in Iceland and Japan; both are in the northern latitudes and have very high rates of fish consumption.

These data make it sound like everyone should take omega-3 fatty acids for a variety of reasons. However, rather than making an immediate dietary change, it makes more sense to discuss these substances as part of a total health and nutrition program with one's physician or nutritionist. For example, many people who are familiar with the positive effects of omega-3 oils will only eat fish once a week because of the potential for contamination. However, if you take *processed* fish oil tablets, which are contaminant free, you will also receive the benefits of omega-3 fatty acids without the fishy aftertaste.

Some people add flax seed to their diets, which also has an omega-3 fatty acid called alpha-linolenic acid (ALA), but it does not contain either EPA or DHA and has not been shown to have the antidepressant effects of EPA, although it does have other positive health benefits.

Circadian Rhythm Treatments

There is evidence that many people with depression experience disturbances with their sleep/wake cycle and other bodily rhythms. Modifying these patterns with the hormone melatonin is a way of restoring normal sleep patterns in depressed patients with insomnia.[42] There is some evidence that using melatonin in the afternoon, along with bright light in the morning, may help patients with SAD.[43] Many people don't realize that melatonin is a hormone and may not be entirely safe even though it is produced in the body and sold without a prescription.

Patients for whom nothing seems to work as treatment for their depression have experimented with modifying their own sleep patterns intentionally. For example, Wirz-Justice and Van den Hoofdakker report that patients who haven't responded to conventional treatments deprive themselves of partial or full episodes of sleep and feel an improvement in their general mood and functioning.[44] This type of "treatment" may be helpful but needs to be supervised by a health professional who is experienced in dealing with depression and sleep problems.

Additional Alternative Substances

Three other substances that may be potential treatment aids for depression are folate, vitamin B12, and S-adenosylmethionine (called SAM-e, pronounced "sammy"). There is evidence that low levels of folate (and perhaps B12) may be related to depression and may cause a poorer short-and long-term response to prescribed antidepressant medications. Folate (and perhaps B12) supplementation may play a modest role in the treatment of depression in patients if they have normal levels of these substances. They may also shorten the latency of response to antidepressant medications, improve treatment response, and prevent relapse. There is also preliminary data that suggests that SAM-e may have an antidepressant effect and may be useful as a supplemental treatment. However, the evidence is not overwhelming, and there may be a risk of stimulating a manic episode in a patient with BPD and possibly some problematic interactions with other medications.[45] Clearly, supplements like these should *only* be taken with the knowledge and approval of the treating physician. The final word on folate is that by itself it may not have an antidepressant effect, but used as a supplement it might give a boost to conventional antidepressant drugs and, therefore, have a role in the treatment picture.[46]

SUMMARY

One of the interesting problems we have is the wealth of effective and safe medical treatments that are available today. Every year we see new and better medications that provide a different approach to managing depressive symptoms. Some of the older treatments such as ECT are becoming better and safer, and some of the new experimental approaches hold significant promise for the future. Having depression identified as a medical condition has led to some wonderful treatment advances and to a better understanding of the neurophysiology of depression. The drugs and medical treatment methods that are available today are so much better than those in the past—even a decade ago—that more people are being diagnosed and treated than ever before.

However, with all of the impressive advances there are some cautionary notes as well. For example, the newer antidepressant medications are so much safer and less problematic from a side-effect standpoint that they are being used much more frequently and for a wider range of problems, and this may mean that they may be used more frequently than they need to be. They are also being prescribed primarily by non–mental health professionals such as PCPs and OB/GYNs. When used in a primary care setting, patients are often not placed on a high enough dose to be effective, may discontinue medication too soon, typically aren't prescribed multiple antidepressant medications, and may not be seen as often as they should. While not every patient suffering from depression needs to see a psychiatrist, it is not clear if the more difficult cases are being referred out when appropriate. In some communities, particularly those in remote or rural areas, they may not have access to a psychiatrist at all.

Another problem resulting from the increased use of antidepressant medications is the promotion of the misconception that medication alone is an appropriate treatment for depression. As was discussed in Chapter 8, research consistently shows that psychotherapy is an important *primary* form of treatment for depression. Patients who are treated with drugs alone tend to relapse when medication is discontinued, while patients treated with psychotherapy are far less likely to relapse. Drugs are one very effective way to treat depression, but we cannot lose sight of other less invasive and safer forms of treatment.

Chapter 10

Pulling It All Together: What Do We Know?

Every age yearns for a more beautiful world. The deeper the desperation and the depression about the confusing present, the more intense the yearning.
—Johan Huizinga (1872–1945), Dutch historian

I cling to depression, thinking it a form of truth.
—Mason Cooley (b. 1927) U.S. aphorist

This book has looked at depression and other mood disorders from a variety of perspectives, and it is obvious that depression is a common disorder affecting many people. In order to fully understand depression, we have examined the biological, psychological, and social issues and have looked at who develops depression and why certain groups are affected as they are. We read about the life experience of several patients who have suffered from depression, and hopefully, we have learned about how depression can affect people's lives and those around them. Although it is a complex disorder, there are many effective treatments available today, and in this chapter, we draw some conclusions integrating and summarizing what we have learned. We also look at some of the social and financial issues that are related to the diagnosis and treatment of depression.

EFFECTIVE TREATMENTS FOR DEPRESSION

According to the National Institute of Mental Health (NIMH), more than 80% of people with depression will improve with appropriate treatment.[1] That is an impressive statistic and is probably surprising to most people—even to most professionals. The operative phrase here is, of course, "appropriate treatment." As was mentioned in Chapter 1, only about 20 out of every 100 depressed people receive appropriate treatment, and of these 20, 16 (80%) should expect to get better. This disturbing conclusion suggests that only 16% of people with depression will show an improvement of their condition by having received appropriate treatment.

What is particularly frustrating is that when appropriately treated, people with depression usually improve—getting into treatment is the problem. One ambitious program compared four groups of patients: those who received cognitive therapy, interpersonal therapy, imipramine (a tricyclic antidepressant), and a placebo (no real treatment). In the three treatment groups, 50–60% of patients reported a complete elimination of symptoms, while only 29% improved with placebo.[2] I frequently point out to my patients that if a person has a strep infection and they don't do anything it might go away on its own, but if you take an antibiotic it will usually go away more quickly and with fewer risks and complications; this analogy fits the treatment of depression as well. Because we have effective treatments for depression, we now need to provide the correct treatment to those who need it, a task easier said than done. The treatment for a mood disorder basically has three goals:

1. Relieve symptoms
2. Restore the person's ability to function socially and in the workplace
3. Reduce the likelihood of recurrence[3]

Likewise, there are three stages of treatment for any mood disorder:

1. Acute treatment—relieving symptoms and restoring the person to a normal level of functioning
2. Continuation treatment—stabilizing the patient and preventing relapse
3. Maintenance treatment—preventing a new episode from emerging (preventing recurrence, which is not the same thing as preventing relapse)

While these lists seem similar, they are not the same. The goals of treatment should link up with the stages of treatment. It is important to combine both lists when treating people suffering from mood disorders and to work toward several goals simultaneously: relieving the immediate distress, helping return the person to a state of wellness, avoiding the condition worsening, and preventing future episodes if possible. Good and appropriate treatment should always cover the full range of the disorder regardless of the treatment modality that is used.

As we know, medication is the most common form of treatment for depression, and results suggest that an antidepressant medication has a 70% chance of working on a depressed patient. Psychotherapy works as well as medication but may take longer to produce results; however, the effects of psychotherapy will last longer than the effects of medication. Typically, the most severe cases of depression are best treated initially with medication, but some studies have shown that the combination of medication and psychotherapy is more effective than either treatment modality alone.[4]

Although psychotherapy has been shown to be more effective and longer lasting than medications, physicians still keep prescribing medication as the primary form of treatment for depression. The use of antidepressants increased from 2.5 million prescriptions in 1980 to 4.7 million in 1987,[5] and their use has continued to rise. Of the 2.4 billion prescriptions written in the United States in 2005, 118 million were for antidepressants; between 1995 and 2002, there was a 48% increase in the use of antidepressant medications. In fact, more prescriptions were written for antidepressant medications than for drugs treating high blood pressure, high cholesterol, asthma, or headaches.[6] Evidence strongly supports that the use of antidepressant medication has significantly increased with the introduction of the second-generation antidepressants.[7] Of course, we must keep in mind that antidepressants are prescribed for other conditions as well, including anxiety disorders, pain disorders, peripheral neuropathy, migraine, fibromyalgia, and others, so the increased prescribing is not just for depression, although the majority of prescriptions are written for depression.

Why does the trend of prescribing more of the antidepressants continue when compelling evidence demonstrates the importance of nonpharmacologic treatment methods? First, powerful advertising campaigns from drug companies plant the idea that their medication is the *only* type of treatment that really works. Second, it is cheaper for insurance and managed care companies to have doctors prescribe medication than to pay for several sessions of psychotherapy, and their policies and practices reflect that bias on their part. However, most evidence supports the idea that psychotherapy is cheaper in the long term for the insurance companies by reducing relapse rates, but their policies don't suggest they are aware of this fact.

We must also remember that there are disadvantages to taking medication as a treatment for depression, the most obvious being side effects. There is no medication that is totally without side effects, including antidepressants. Although the newer drugs typically have fewer side effects, they can still be problematic, and it is the main reason most people discontinue taking them. Also, for medication to be effective, it requires strict adherence to a medication regimen plus repeated visits to the physician to monitor progress. Finally, there is no antidepressant medication that works quickly; all of them take weeks or even months to reach therapeutic efficacy.[8] Another problem is that while psychotherapy is better than medication at preventing recurrence, people receiving medication as the sole treatment are protected from a recurrence if they *never* come off of the medication and as long as the medication continues to be effective.[9] While most antidepressant medications appear to be safe over time, it still seems prudent to take medication only when you need to; if there are effective treatments that don't require medication, then they ought to be considered.

Although patients receiving cognitive therapy or interpersonal therapy will relapse at a rate lower than when on medication alone, about 30% of patients who respond to treatment of any kind will relapse within a few years after their depression lifts.[10] Swartz concludes that depression recurs in about half of the cases within two years of stopping treatment—that is, any type of treatment.[11] However, the longer a person is in treatment, the less likely they are to relapse. Thus, to effectively treat depression, treatment must begin as early as possible and continue beyond the point at which there is symptomatic relief; this is true for both medication and psychotherapy.

Improved research on effective treatments indicates that, in general, cognitive, interpersonal, and biological therapies are all effective treatments for mild to severe unipolar depression.[12] Even more impressive is the range of other psychological and biological therapies that appear to be very helpful even when not used as a first-line treatment. We must move past the notion that the only way to treat depression is with drugs. One study reports that the use of psychotherapy in addition to medication is likely to be both clinically effective *and* cost effective while improving the quality of life for patients with depression and their significant others.[13] Most research indicates that psychotherapy should be a primary, first-line treatment for depression rather than being employed as an adjunct.

In recent years, we have seen more research looking at combinations of treatments, a more realistic approach to evaluating the treatment of depression. Due to the complexity of depression and the fact that most people with depression have comorbid physical or psychological problems, a unitary treatment of any type may fall short of dealing with the whole problem. With respect to medications and suicidal risk, Emslie et al. found that the combination of fluoxetine (Prozac) and cognitive-behavioral therapy (CBT) may be *safer* than fluoxetine alone.[14] Therefore, not only is a combination of treatments becoming more common, but it is viewed by many as not only effective but safer, too.

MAKING TREATMENTS MORE EFFECTIVE

There are some factors regarding the use of medication, psychotherapy, and other forms of treatment that can be modified and "fine tuned" to make them more responsive to individual patient needs. One approach that has been influential in the past few years is called personality-guided behavior therapy.[15] One of the criticisms of behaviorally oriented therapies is that they are too "techniquey" and don't adequately take patient differences into account. When deciding on a treatment approach, whether medical, psychological, or both, care should be taken to be sure that the patient's perspective, values, preferences, and personality are considered; this provides the best chance of being effective.

Another thing that needs to be done to make treatments more effective is to make sure that adequate and appropriate psychological and medical therapies are available to all of the people who need them. Focusing more on underserved communities is necessary to improve the effectiveness of treatment in general, as only about 20% of people who report depression have received any type of counseling or psychotherapy in the past year. This rate is even lower in the minority communities. We know that African Americans, Hispanics, and the poor are especially lacking in adequate treatment and tend to either discontinue or be dropped from treatment at too early a stage.[16] Because the disease burden of depression on families and on society is significant, especially for those who are on public assistance or disability, providing effective treatment to those who suffer from depression will help to relieve some of this burden.

One area of concern is the number of people who are caregivers and suffer from untreated depression. Better in-home care of the elderly and those with chronic illnesses has extended life spans and replaced the need for institutional care for many. The increased burden on those who must fulfill the caregiving responsibilities can lead to symptoms of depression, and unfortunately, this is a group of people who often neglect or ignore their own personal, psychological, and medical needs. Caregivers are frequently the recipients of sincere sympathy and concern, but they need more than that. Primary care physicians (PCPs) can overlook symptoms of depression in caregivers because the situation provides an easily accepted explanation for their feelings. The caregivers themselves are the worst at ignoring their own needs and must be frequently reminded that they will be less able to care for their loved one or friend if they become ill themselves. Suggestions to help caregivers take care of their own needs include:

- Join a support group; there are many relevant support groups in most communities, and they are frequently a valuable resource.
- Acknowledge your feelings, and rather than feeling guilty about having them, try to understand and accept them.
- Ask for help; this is one of the most difficult tasks for many people but it can be very helpful—after all, none of us can ever do it all alone.
- Look into caregiver training programs; these have become more common and often are associated with other programs for patients.
- Take advantage of adult day care and respite programs; to caregivers who think that this is unacceptable, I point out that not only does this help the

patient to keep from feeling guilty, but the patient may look forward to and enjoy the change in activity and surroundings.

+ Seek counseling or medication if that is appropriate—the sooner the better.
+ Make time for rest and recreation; if people don't take care of themselves, their bodies will eventually make the decision for them—illness, stress, or exhaustion will finally take over, and the caregiver will then become the *recipient* of care.

Another group of people who can benefit from treatment for depression are those with chronic impairments from illness, accidents, or other forms of disability. Depression is a common comorbid condition for serious or chronic illnesses or other disabling conditions, and unfortunately, it tends to be ignored or explained away without treatment. However, regardless of the source, depression can and should be handled in a timely fashion in order to have a better chance of treating it effectively and with fewer complications (e.g., recurrence). As Kahan et al. found, people with long-term impairments show considerable benefits from treatment for depression, and whether depression is a primary or secondary condition, it is often a complicating factor for other medical conditions.[17]

One other point that is important enough to bear repeating has to do with the treatment of depression in the primary care setting. As we discussed in the previous chapter, the primary care office is the most common site for the treatment of depression, and this carries with it both advantages and disadvantages. We know that the three primary reasons for antidepressant medications failing are that they are not used at high enough doses, they are discontinued too soon, or they are continued for many years unchecked or unchanged. A PCP may not be familiar enough with the drugs to feel comfortable with being aggressive with dosages, and they may not be willing to try to "push through" the side-effect problems to see if they will decrease or disappear. Further, the PCP may not know enough about a specific drug to counsel their patient to give the medication the necessary time to become effective—it may take a little longer. These types of situations can often lead the PCPs to discontinue or change medications too quickly. It is also true that if patients don't say anything about their medication and the PCP is focused on a different presenting problem, the side effects or the lack of progress from the drug might not get discussed. The drug may then be continued far beyond the point where it is effective or perhaps even necessary. I have seen patients on a single antidepressant at a low dose for over a decade without any obvious benefit, but the patient continues taking it because they are afraid to discontinue it. If the PCP doesn't ask, the patient will often keep silent. The patient may no longer need the medication, or they might benefit from an additional treatment modality, but if the patient and the doctor are not discussing these options, nothing will change. Finally, we know that depression is often best addressed by two or more different treatments simultaneously, but that is sometimes a problem in the primary care setting, especially if the PCP is inexperienced with combinations of medications or psychotherapy.

The PCP, however, has a significant advantage in knowing the patient and their health history, and they are in an excellent position to know what the patient may need but may not have all the treatment options to offer. Education in the new psychotropic medications is sometimes limited to the information presented by the drug reps who bring lunch to the office in exchange for an opportunity to demonstrate the drug (or drugs) their company is offering, but the PCP may be the only available professional who is able to prescribe psychotropic medication for a depressed patient. As discussed earlier, it is sometimes difficult to make an appointment with a psychiatrist who has a full calendar or if the patient lives in a remote area. Finally, PCPs can feel pressured to choose the least expensive treatment for some of their patients, which may mean prescribing generic medications instead of referring their patients for treatment to a mental health provider who may be more knowledgeable. Even from the patient's standpoint, it is less expensive to pay one monthly copayment for a prescription instead of several weekly copayments for therapy. This pressure for cost containment may come from insurance or managed care companies or even from the patient, who perhaps cannot afford multiple copayments, but these pressures may sometimes dictate treatment decisions.

One other issue to face in the primary care setting is that in this day of more "efficient" medical services, primary care is often provided by "physician extenders"—that is physician's assistants (PAs) or nurse practitioners (NPs). These professionals are well trained and competent to provide many medical services, but they typically have far less training in the mental health area than do the PCPs. Some NPs or PAs have had additional training in psychopharmocology (psychiatric medications), but they almost always work with psychiatrists or in clinics and not usually in primary care settings.

SOME OTHER WAYS TO IMPROVE THE TREATMENTS FOR DEPRESSION AND OTHER MOOD DISORDERS

Earlier we discussed bipolar disorder (BPD) and how its treatment needed to differ from the standard treatment for depression. Although psychotherapy is usually a primary form of treatment for depression, it is not typically the first line of treatment for BPD. It is also true that because the primary treatment for BPD is usually medication, other forms of treatment, such as "talk therapy," are sometimes underutilized. However, Miklowitz et al. point out that in patients with bipolar depression the use of intensive psychotherapy as an adjunct to psychopharmacology significantly improves treatment results.[18] In the past, people with BPD were not usually offered psychotherapy because:

+ early models of BPD emphasized the genetic and biological factors, making only medical approaches "appropriate";
+ there was a misconception that virtually *all* patients made a full recovery between episodes of their BPD; and
+ therapists often held the misconception that bipolar patients were not good candidates for psychotherapy.[19]

We now know that during manic episodes patients are too disorganized and too impulsive to benefit from psychotherapy and that patients experiencing hypomania often feel so good they don't want to change. Therefore, when offering psychotherapy to bipolar patients, we are typically referring only to depressed bipolar patients between manic or hypomanic episodes. However, there is considerable evidence of additional uses for psychotherapy in BPD patients, and there are a number of approaches that have been effective. One thing that can be very helpful is psychoeducational treatment when the patient is between episodes to help them learn how to recognize and manage their condition before it becomes too severe.

Until the last three decades, BPD was considered very resistant to treatment, and psychotherapists had little luck treating it.[20] Antidepressant drugs were of limited benefit,[21] and in fact, some antidepressant drugs would occasionally trigger a manic episode.[22] Even electroconvulsive therapy (ECT), which has been helpful in treating depression, was only occasionally helpful for manic or bipolar depressive episodes.[23] Fortunately, both in terms of medication and psychotherapy, there have been some major advances in the past 20 years.

Generally, the research literature has supported manualized psychotherapeutic treatments and usually indicates specific models for use with BPD, such as interpersonal social rhythm therapy, cognitive therapy, and family-focused therapy. It has also been valuable to use cognitive-behavioral therapy (CBT) in relapse prevention, and this has shown to reduce the frequency of manic episodes but not depression. Further, patients who received group psychoeducational treatment showed fewer bipolar episodes than patients who didn't.[24] Some of the characteristics of effective brief psychotherapy for BPD include:

+ Offer specific formulations that apply to the patient's problems.
+ The model and rationale for therapy is discussed with the patient.
+ There is a clear rationale for therapeutic methods, and the techniques are applied in a logical order.

+ There is an emphasis on skill development and the transfer of training.
+ Positive changes are attributed to the patient's efforts and not to the skill of the therapist.
+ Patients continue the use of treatment techniques beyond the termination of therapy.[25]

Although not frequently considered to be a first-line treatment for BPD, there are several good reasons why psychotherapy should be used. First, as with most mood disorders, there are often comorbid conditions that may not respond to the medication for BPD but may be treatable with appropriate psychotherapy. Second, if patients can learn to recognize and cope with symptoms during the early onset of an episode, then aggressive treatment may lessen the impact of the episode both on the patient and the family. Finally and most importantly, psychotherapy can help patients and their families learn how to cope with a chronic and recurring condition. Most people with BPD will experience approximately three episodes every decade, so it is important that they learn how to recognize and deal with them when they occur.[26]

Because BPD is complicated to treat, the treatment goals need to be broad enough to encompass all of the relative elements of the disorder. The first and main goal is to try to reduce the frequency and severity as well as the impact of the bipolar episode. Second, the goal is to improve the social and mental functioning between bipolar episodes.[27] What is emerging as a comprehensive treatment model for BPD is the use of Lithium or other mood stabilizers or antiseizure medications, possibly coupled with antidepressant medications if the manic symptoms are already under control. For agitated patients, some of the atypical neuroleptic drugs may be helpful. Finally, psychotherapy should be part of the total treatment of the bipolar patient. While medication will be the main treatment for BPD, even with adolescents, psychotherapy is very important for them as well. It is not clear whether BPD in children is related to adult BPD, but everything that can be done to treat it early should be done.[28]

TREATING POSTPARTUM DEPRESSION

Although frequently ignored and misunderstood, this unfortunately common form of depression is very treatable under most conditions. Several types of postpartum mood disorders include what is commonly called the "Baby Blues," which is very common and is not an "official" diagnosis. This may last from a few hours to a few days but typically goes away within two weeks. Reassurance and emphasizing the importance of adequate sleep and rest is usually appropriate treatment. A mild medication may be used for insomnia, but if the mother is nursing this should be considered carefully. The main concern is to monitor the mother to make sure that the depression doesn't worsen.

A rare and more serious form of a postpartum mood disorder is postpartum psychosis (PPP), which is found most often in those who have experienced serious psychological conditions such as schizophrenia or BPD prior to pregnancy. Fortunately, if women who suffer from these conditions are on appropriate medication and are monitored closely, they can experience pregnancy and delivery with few problems. However, when a mother experiences PPP, she must take medication and may need to be hospitalized. Electroconvulsive therapy has also proven to be an effective treatment for PPP and for more severe forms of postpartum mood disorder.

Postpartum depression (PPD) can be treated effectively if it is detected, but unfortunately, many mothers do not report how badly they feel, or perhaps their physicians are so focused on the health of the baby or the physical recovery of the mother that they might not notice a psychological problem in the mother. Some mothers may feel guilty because they do not feel as happy as was expected; they feel self-conscious, embarrassed, or afraid; or they may not know how to identify or explain what they are feeling. According to the World Health Organization (WHO), around the world, communication between health care workers and female patients is very authoritarian, which makes it difficult for some women to discuss emotional and psychological distress with their health care professional.[29] While this situation is improving in North America and Europe compared to other parts of the world, it remains an issue of concern everywhere.

If PPD is not treated appropriately the depression is more likely to continue longer and may become a more complex and difficult problem. Also, inadequate treatment of PPD increases immediate and future risks to the mother and to the child as well. Further, as with many other conditions, early detection and treatment of PPD leads to a more favorable prognosis.[30] Although the etiology of PPD is somewhat unique, there is no reason to believe that it needs to be treated differently from any other form of depression. Typically the treatment phases are:

1. Acute: 6–12 weeks; oriented to symptom relief
2. Continuation: 4–9 months; stabilize the patient and return to normal functioning
3. Maintenance: 9+ months; prevent recurrence—may not be needed in most cases[31]

The main treatments for PPD include medication, psychotherapy, or both.[32] For mothers who are breast feeding or want to avoid medication and are experiencing mild to moderate PPD, good results have been reported from using cognitive-behavioral psychotherapy, interpersonal psychotherapy, group psychoeducational therapy, and support groups.[33] Similarly, O'Hara et al. found that interpersonal psychotherapy was an effective treatment for PPD by reducing depressive symptoms and improving social functioning.[34] In terms of medication, exactly the same approach is used with mothers suffering from PPD as other forms of depression. Typically, the second-generation drugs are tried first and then others depending upon the side-effect profile and the specific symptoms.

It has also been established that psychosocial treatment for prospective mothers can produce a protective effect prior to delivery, thus reducing the frequency of PPD. Zlotnick et al. found that four interpersonal therapy-oriented group sessions reduced the occurrence of PPD in a group of financially disadvantaged women, suggesting that by using more treatment opportunities before the baby is born, the health of the mother and baby can be improved.[35]

When feeling overwhelmed or angry, a mother shouldn't release it on the baby or her family, but there are some active choices she can make that can very likely help:[36]

- Use relaxation exercises—if you don't know how to do this ask your doctor or psychologist.
- Cognitive restructuring—with the help of a professional psychologist, a person can learn how to change the ways they think or perceive things.
- Problem solving—very important for reducing the overwhelmed feelings of inadequacy or powerlessness; this may need some professional intervention.
- Communication—talk to family, friends, or a professional about how you feel and what you are experiencing.
- Humor—develop and keep a sense of humor because it is an enormously helpful in maintaining our "normal" perspective on things.

It is also very important, when a mother is suffering from PPD, that she maintains the mother–baby bond. Such as:

- Nurse or feed the baby frequently.
- Provide a quiet place for the baby to rest, and rest when the baby does.
- Hold and talk softly to the infant often—keep baby warm, dry, and fed.
- Involve others in caring for the baby.
- Take time with the other children.
- Go outside with the baby when the weather permits.

Some things for mothers to do for herself:

- Talk to someone about your feelings.
- Set aside time to talk with your partner regarding what is going on and how you feel.
- Let people help you.

+ Do something for yourself every day; even if it is only for 15 minutes.
+ Rest when you can—every day.
+ Exercise—walking with the baby, going to the gym when your partner gets home, etc.
+ Practice good nutrition; avoid alcohol, nicotine, and caffeine.
+ Keep a journal of how you feel—this can be helpful and will probably be interesting later.
+ Set goals for yourself—keep them simple, but stick to them.
+ Give yourself permission to feel overwhelmed, and then do something about it.

Some things that the partner can do to help the new mother:

+ Listen to and validate the mother's feelings.
+ Avoid criticizing or judging.
+ Be patient.
+ Give the mother several breaks from child and home care daily.
+ Support the idea of getting some help in the house if needed.
+ Talk to a doctor or therapist about what you can do to help.

WHAT PATIENTS CAN DO TO DEAL WITH DEPRESSION

One of the worst things about being depressed is feeling so miserable that you can't stand it but being so immobilized by the disorder that you can't do anything about it. When people are depressed or can feel they are becoming depressed, or if you see someone you care about slipping into a depression, they often don't have any idea as to what they can do to improve the situation or who to turn to for help. Unfortunately, there are many things that people reach for first that will only make things worse. Turning to drugs or alcohol, socially isolating, eating too much, spending too much money, and getting involved in activities that will cause difficulties (e.g., gambling) are examples of what will only make a difficult situation even worse. So what *should* people do? Although the depressed patient will find reasons why any suggestion is either wrong or won't work, it is important that the depressed patient do something—anything positive that has a chance to help. For many people who don't know what to do, talking to their PCP is a good place to start. The PCP may recommend medication, but they will also be able to refer a patient to a psychologist, psychiatrist, or other mental health professional; perhaps the patient had prior contact with a mental health professional or knows someone who has. Patients can contact their health maintenance organization (HMO) or a managed care plan through their health insurance program to seek a recommendation of mental health professionals in their plan. Community mental health clinics, hospitals with mental health or psychiatric clinics, and clinics at a university or medical school may offer outpatient services to the public; state mental hospitals often provide outpatient clinics as well. If a person is feeling very distraught or suicidal, the local emergency room is the best place to go. Some hospitals have a psychiatric unit where people can receive inpatient care on a short-term basis. Most communities have family service agencies, social service agencies, church-sponsored counseling centers, private clinics, and facilities that provide services. If a person doesn't know where to turn for help, then a clergy person is someone who usually knows where to refer someone. Places of employment may also be a good reference source—many companies offer employee assistance programs (EAPs) that can provide brief counseling or can refer a person to clinics or to another professional. Finally, a person can look in the yellow pages of the phone book and call a local medical or psychological society for a referral to a licensed professional. It is important that the chosen professional is licensed to provide mental health services, which means that they have met the educational and professional standards in their field that qualifies them to offer these services.

In addition to reaching out for professional help, there are several things that people suffering from depression can do to help themselves. For example, when a person feels hopeless and begins to think dark thoughts, they can remind themselves that this is not reality—this is the depression. Seeing the world through the dark brown glasses of depression will make everything look bleak, and you need to remember that this is one of the tricks that depression can play. Depressed people have difficulty with motivating themselves to do anything, but if they sit around waiting for motivation to happen they may be waiting for a long time. It is important to move and do something. Set short-term, reasonable goals and hold yourself accountable for fulfilling them, but don't blame others, the weather, and so forth for not completing your goals—just do it.

When people are depressed, the small tasks in life seem so huge that they tend to be put off, get bigger, and multiply. Break large tasks into smaller ones, and set priorities. Don't try to do too many things at once, and take short breaks. Making even a little progress is better than not doing anything at all. Don't avoid people; find someone close to you who you can confide in. Stay active doing things you like to do. This may be difficult because you may not feel good at the time, but the activities will have a cumulative impact, and the more you do the sooner you will start to feel "normal" again. Get involved with mild exercise and some recreational and social events. If you don't feel like doing much, then do just a little; but do something. Don't look for quick fixes or rapid solutions—getting better takes time and persistence. People don't "snap out" of depression, but rather they gradually start to see progress and then begin to feel better. Very frequently, people suffering from depression want to *be* better, but they often don't want to do the work to *get* better—it just feels like too much.

It is important for people suffering from depression to realize that when depressed you do not think about things as you normally would, and therefore, it is best if you don't try to make major decisions unless you absolutely have to, and even then you should get advice from people you trust. Although positive thinking is challenging while depressed, it can start to produce some small changes in the way you think and feel. One piece of advice that is difficult for the depressed to accept is to let people help you. Depressed people feel helpless and hopeless and, most of all, feel like a burden to everyone else. It is difficult to ask for help, but this one step may be the single thing that actually spurs improvement. Typically, most people find it easier to give help than to ask for it, but as much as we may like to do the giving, it is especially important to give others the opportunity to feel good about helping us—the door swings both ways.

Another idea that can often help with depression is caring for a pet, such as a cat, dog, bird, or even fish or hermit crabs. Pets are a significant boon to mental health and can certainly help people with depression.[37] They can facilitate social interaction and exercise by taking the pet for a walk and seeing friends and neighbors, but the pet can be a source of a meaningful relationship itself. The responsibility of caring for a pet can also provide a much-needed and important activity. If keeping a pet is not realistic, it may be possible to borrow or care for the pets of others as a way to enjoy a pet with minimal commitment, inconvenience, or expense while helping someone else at the same time.

Considering the things that we can do to help people with depression, we must remember that the best form of treatment for any condition is *prevention*, and this is especially true of depression. Taking care of our physical and emotional health is a responsibility that cannot be taken too lightly, and yet, most of us neglect to do the most basic things to care for ourselves. Smoking, drinking alcohol, using recreational drugs, overeating, eating poorly, not seeking medical or psychological help when needed, and not exercising are all things that we have control over. To not exert that control is asking for trouble; it is important that we stay physically and socially active. Remember that when we talk about preventing and treating depression we typically mean "clinical depression," but we must keep in mind that subclinical depression also takes its toll and is often as costly and debilitating as clinical depression.[38]

PROBLEMS IN RECEIVING ADEQUATE TREATMENT FOR DEPRESSION

With rising health care costs and managed care companies controlling access to care, it is becoming more difficult to obtain appropriate mental health care for an adequate period of time. In fact, the current climate for mental health care has overturned more than a century of clinical wisdom and experience, which has demonstrated that given appropriate care in a timely fashion for an adequate length of time, the large majority of people with depression improve. Presently, for example, it is often difficult to have a suicidal patient admitted into the hospital, and it is even more difficult to keep them hospitalized long enough to be clinically stabilized or to receive adequate treatment, making most acute conditions very challenging to treat.[39]

It is inadequate access to care that is a primary constraint in the development of a reasonable national mental health system. Presently, our system is primarily crisis-oriented, and many conditions are not treated appropriately. The current mental health treatment system in the United States is an international embarrassment so woefully inadequate that there is no justification for how bad it has become. Some of the problems that exist regarding the access to adequate care are:

- The stigma that still remains regarding mental and emotional conditions/illnesses
- Inadequate public awareness and education about mental health issues and problems
- Inadequate funding and reimbursement for mental health services
- Inappropriate or unavailable opportunities for screening and early intervention
- Fragmentation of the mental health delivery system with PCPs providing most mental health care
- Inadequately trained or inaccessible providers
- Lack of resources to provide the care that we need, for example:
  - Inadequate health insurance, and insurance companies that deny or restrict appropriate access to care
  - Lack of income to afford private care
  - Locations for mental health services may be difficult to reach and many people don't have access to private or public transportation
  - The homeless who need mental health care rarely have access to that care
  - People with addiction problems who have additional mental health needs may not receive the care they need because of their addiction
  - The unemployed do not have resources to access care
  - Uneducated or misinformed people may not know that they need care or where to find it[40]

One of the true tragedies in American health care is that we, in many ways, have the best available health and mental health care in the world, but in terms of delivering services to those who need them, we are woefully inadequate. According to the statistics regarding the quality of health care delivery systems, the United States doesn't even rank in the top 20. What is developing in this country is a system where the rich can seek private care while the poor use public care.[41] On the surface, this may not seem to be a terrible situation, but it is misleading because there are millions of people (many of whom have full-time jobs) who are either uninsured or seriously underinsured. Being employed doesn't necessarily mean you have access to medical insurance and adequate treatment. According to the WHO, there are three main factors that highly protect against mental illnesses, especially depression:[42]

1.   Having sufficient money to be able to exercise some control in response to severe events
2.   Access to material resources that allow the possibility of making choices in the face of severe events
3.   Psychological support from family, friends, or health providers

Clearly, these three factors are not available to many people in society, and these are some of the reasons why a negative correlation exists between social class and mental illness.

According to the Depression and Bipolar Support Alliance (DBSA), there are some serious issues related to the quality of mental health care in the United States:[43]

+   There is a lack of prevention and long-term care management due to the crisis-oriented and reactionary structure of the mental health system.
+   There is a serious fragmentation of mental health services.
+   There is insufficient funding and reimbursement for mental health services.
+   Many providers are not adequately trained to offer the mental health services they are required to deliver (and this includes PCPs and many sub-doctoral level providers).
+   Good research using appropriate outcome measures is not as much a part of the picture as it needs to be.
+   For many patients there is inadequate follow-up and poor treatment adherence.
+   There is little attention paid to the consumers, and the ones that are ignored most are those without insurance or any way to get it.

These observations represent a serious indictment of our mental health care delivery system, but there are few who would dispute them. For those who claim that we are doing a good job, they need to look at the data more closely. So, what needs to be done? The DBSA has some suggestions:

+   In treating depression, don't just use medications; use psychosocial treatments as well.
+   There needs to be better case management and coordination of care.
+   Better screening and early detection of depression.

+ More use of peer support programs in the treatment of depression (similar to what is being done in Reach for Recovery for breast cancer survivors).
+ Train providers to offer more culturally competent treatment for depression.
+ Use a truly consumer-driven approach to mental health—don't just talk a good game.
+ Use recovery-oriented treatment approaches rather than just simply minimizing acute symptoms.

SUMMARY

The picture is clear:

+ Depression is a serious and common problem that affects people of all social and racial groups throughout the world.
+ Good and affordable treatment is available.
+ Most people who have depression do not receive adequate treatment.
+ We must do more and do it better.

It is not easy for any of us to tackle a problem of this magnitude, but by being responsible and taking care of our own health and mental health needs, we can also reach out to help others who are dealing with depression or other mental health issues by sharing information and pointing them in the direction to find the help they need. It is not your job to treat or even nag others into compliance, but don't avoid the issue. If your PCP doesn't perform depression screening, ask to see if they would consider adding that to their practice. You can also inform yourself and get involved politically and socially to try to get some attention focused on these issues.

There are no solutions to the problem of depression—it will always be with us in one form or another. However, by taking care of our own psychological needs and encouraging those we care about to do the same, we can make a dent. Being a good role model is important, but we should also be willing to advocate for mental health care needs with health providers, insurance companies, clinics, schools, and even politicians. All of us need to get involved—we are worth it.

Notes

CHAPTER 1

1. B.L.E. Hankin, & L.Y. Abramson. (2001). Development of gender differences in depression: An elaborated cognitive vulnerability-transactional stress theory. *Psychological Bulletin, 127*(6), 773–796.

2. R.J. Comer. (2004). *Abnormal psychology* (5th ed.). New York: Worth.

3. American Psychiatric Association. (2000). *Diagnostic and statistical manual of mental disorders* (4th ed., text revision). Washington, DC: Author.

4. A. Solomon. (2001). *The noonday demon: An atlas of depression.* New York: Scribner, p. 2.

5. National Institute of Mental Health. (2000). *Depression.* Retrieved January 14, 2007, from http://www.nimh.nih.gov/publicat/depression.cfm.

6. B.G. Druss, R.A. Rosenheck, & W.H. Sledge. (2000). Health and disability costs of depressive illness in a major U.S. corporation. *American Journal of Psychiatry, 157*(8), 1274–1278.

7. Medical News Today. (2005). Majority of people with depression are not adequately treated, USA. Retrieved May 2, 2008, from http://www.medicalnewstoday.com/articles/25266.php.

8. M.B. Glenn & S.B. Bergman. (1997). Cardiovascular changes following spinal cord injury. *Topics in Spinal Cord Injury Rehabilitation, 2,* 45–53.

9. B.W. Penning, S.W. Geerlings, D.J. Deeg, J.T. van Eijk, W. van Tilburg, & A.T. Beekman. (1999). Minor and major depression and the risk of death in older persons. *Archives of General Psychiatry, 56*(10), 889–895.

10. Depression and Bipolar Support Alliance. (2006). *The state of depression in America.* Retrieved January 15, 2007, from http://www.dbsalliance.org/pdfs/wpsearchable.pdf.

11. K.P. Ebmeier, C. Donaghey, & J.D. Steele. (2006). Recent developments and current controversies in depression. *Lancet, 367,* 153–167.

12. Ebmeier et al. (2006).

13. Helpguide. (2006). *Depression in older adults and the elderly: Signs, symptoms, causes and treatments.* Retrieved May 2, 2006, from http://www.helpguide.org/mental/depression_elderly.htm.

14. J. Barth. (1967). *End of the road.* New York: Doubleday and Company.

15. Suicide and Crisis Center. (2005). *Suicide facts and statistics.* Retrieved January 16, 2007, from http://www.sccenter.org/facts.html.

16. K.L. Swartz. (2007). *Depression and anxiety: The Johns Hopkins white papers.* Baltimore, MD: Johns Hopkins Medicine.

17. Swartz (2007).

18. Cross-National Collaborative Group. (1992). The changing rate of major depression: Cross national comparisons. *Journal of the American Medical Association, 268,* 3098–3105.

19. H.E. Morselli. (1882). *An essay on comparative moral statistics.* New York: D. Appleton & Company.

20. J.L. McIntosh. (1991). Epidemiology of suicide in the U.S. In A.A. Leenaars (Ed.), *Lifespan perspectives of suicide,* pp. 55–70. New York: Plenum Press.

21. E.S. Shneidman. (2001). *Comprehending suicide: Landmarks in 20th century suicidology.* Washington, DC: American Psychological Association.

22. Shneidman (2001).

23. K. Menninger. (1938). *Man against himself.* New York: Harcourt.

24. A.T. Beck. (1986). Hopelessness as a predictor of eventual suicide. In J.J. Mann & M. Stanley (Eds.), *Psychobiology of suicidal behavior* (pp. 90–96). New York: Academy of Sciences.

25. L.Y. Abramson, M.E. Seligman, & J.D. Teasdale. (1978). Learned helplessness in humans: Critique and reformulation. *Journal of Abnormal Psychology, 87*(1), 49–74.

26. Beck (1986).

27. P.M. Salkovskis. (2002). Empirically grounded clinical interventions: Cognitive-behavioral therapy progresses through a multi-dimensional approach to clinical science. *Behavioral and Cognitive Psychotherapy, 30,* 3–9.

28. Swartz (2007).

CHAPTER 2

1. M.E.P. Seligman & S.F. Maier. (1967). Failure to escape traumatic shock. *Journal of Experimental Psychology, 74,* 1–9.

2. G.M. Williamson. (2000). Pain, functional disability and depressed affect. In G.M. Williamson & D.R. Schaffer (Eds.), *Physical illness and depression in older adults: A handbook of theory, research and practice* (pp. 51–64). New York: Plenum Publishers.

3. M.L. Drew. K.S. Dobson. & H.J. Stam. (1999). The negative self-concept in clinical depression: A discourse analysis. *Canadian Psychology, 40*(2), 192–204.

CHAPTER 3

1. National Institute of Mental Health. (2003). *Depression: A treatable illness.* Retrieved January 5, 2007, from http://menanddepression.nimh.nih.gov/inforpage.asp?jd=15.

2. W. E. Narrow. One-year prevalence of depressive disorders among adults 18 and over on July 1, 1998. Unpublished table.

3. D. G. Blazer, R. C. Kessler, K. A. McGonagle, & M. S. Swartz. (1994). The prevalence and distribution of major depression in a national community sample: The National Comorbidity Survey. *American Journal of Psychiatry, 151,* 979–986.

4. R. C. Harrington, H. Fudge, M. L. Rutter, D. Bredinkamp, C. Groothues, & J. Pridham. (1993). Child and adult depression: A test of continuities with data from a family study. *British Journal of Psychiatry, 162,* 627–633.

5. C. M. Callahan, S. L. Hui, N. A. Neinaber, B. S. Musick, & W. M. Tierny. (1994). Longitudinal study of depression and health services use among elderly primary care patients. *Journal of the American Geriatrics Society, 42,* 833–838.

6. D. C. Speer & M. G. Schneider. (2003). Mental health needs of older adults and primary care: Opportunity for interdisciplinary geriatric team practice. *Clinical Psychology: Science and Practice, 2,* 85–101.

7. A. M. Ludwig. (1995). *The price of greatness: Resolving the creativity and madness controversy.* New York: Guilford.

8. K. L. Swartz. (2007). *Depression and anxiety: The Johns Hopkins white papers.* Baltimore, MD: Johns Hopkins Medicine.

9. G. L. Klerman & M. Weissman. (1989). Increasing rates of depression. *Journal of the American Medical Association, 261,* 2229–2235.

10. H. Z. Reinherz, R. M. Giaconia, B. Pakiz, A. B. Siverman, A. K. Frost, & E. S. Lefkowitz. (1993). Psychosocial risks for major depression in late adolescence: A longitudinal community study. *Journal of the American Academy of Child and Adolescent Psychiatry, 32*(6), 1155–1163.

11. M. M. Ohayon. (2007). Epidemiology of depression and its treatment in the general population. *Journal of Psychiatric Research, 41*(3–4), 207–213.

12. R. R. DeMarco. (2000). The epidemiology of major depression: Implications of occurrence, recurrence, and stress in a Canadian community sample. *Canadian Journal of Psychiatry, 45*(1), 67–74.

13. A. MacLean & R. M. Hauser. (2000). *Socioeconomic status and depression among adult siblings.* Paper presented at the 2000 Meetings of the Population Association of America, Los Angeles, CA.

14. R. C. Kessler. (1982). A disaggregation of the relationship between socioeconomic status and psychological distress. *American Sociological Review, 47*(2), 752–764.

15. C. E. Ross & J. Mirowsky. (1989). Explaining the social patterns of depression: Control and problem solving—or support and talking. *Journal of Health and Social Behavior, 30*(2), 206–219.

16. MacLean & Hauser (2000).

17. C.J.L. Murray & A. D. Lopez. (1996). *The global burden of disease.* Boston, MA: Harvard University Press.

18. R. J. Comer. (2004). *Abnormal psychology.* New York: Worth.

19. V. Patel. (2002). Gender and mental health research in developing countries. *Global Forum for Health Research, Arush,* 1–10.

20. World Health Organization. (1969–1989). *World statistics annual* (annual volumes, vol. 1). Geneva: Author.

21. N. Sartorius. (1979). Research on affective disorders within the framework of the WHO programme. In M. Shou & E. Stromgren (Eds.), *Aarhus symposia: Origin, prevention, and treatment of affective disorders* (pp. 207–231). London: Academic Press.

22. R. L. Fishback & B. Herbert. (1997). Domestic violence and mental health: Correlates and conundrums within and across cultures. *Social Science and Medicine, 45,* 1161–1170.

23. L. Dennerstein, J. Astbury, & C. Morse. (1993). *Psychological and mental health aspects of women's health.* [Brochure].Geneva: World Health Organization.

24. V. Patel, R. Araya, G. Lewis, & L. Swartz. (2000). Socio-economic factors and mental health. *Mental health: A call for action by world health ministers.* Geneva: World Health Organization.

25. WHO (1969–1989).

26. J. Broadhead & M. Abas. (1998). Life events and difficulties and the onset of depression among women in low-income urban settings in Zimbabwe. *Psychological Medicine, 29,* 29–38.

27. J. L. Ayaso-Mateos & J. L. Vázquez-Barquero. (2001). Depressive disorders in Europe: Prevalence figures from the ODIN study. *The British Journal of Psychiatry, 179,* 308–316.

28. T. Stompe, G. Ortwein-Swoboda, H. R. Chaudhry, A. Friedmann, T. Wenzel, & H. Schanda. (2001). Guilt and depression: A cross-cultural comparative study. *Psychopathology, 34*(6), 289–298.

29. P. F. Sullivan, M. C. Neale, & K. S. Kendler. (2000). Genetic epidemiology of major depression: Review and meta-analysis. *American Journal of Psychiatry, 157*(10), 1552–1562.

30. MacLean & Hauser (2000).

31. MacLean & Hauser (2000).

32. MacLean & Hauser (2000).

33. Helpguide. (2006). *Depression in older adults and the elderly: Signs, symptoms, causes and treatments.* Retrieved May 2, 2006, from http://www.helpguide.org/mental/depression_elderly.htm.

34. National Institute of Mental Health (2003).

35. A. J. Cleave. (2004). Biological models of unipolar depression. In M. Power, (Ed.), *Mood disorders: A handbook of science and practice.* Chichester, UK: John Wiley.

36. Swartz (2007).

37. Swartz (2007).

38. F. Holsboer. (2001). Stress, hypercorticolism, and corticosteroid receptors in depression: Implications for therapy. *Journal of Affective Disorders, 62*(1–2), 77–91.

39. H. G. Pope, Jr., G. H. Cohane, G. Kanayama, A. J. Siegel, & J. I. Hudson. (2003). Testosterone gel supplementation for men with refractory depression: A randomized placebo-controlled trial. *American Journal of Psychiatry, 160,* 105–111.

40. Pope, et al., 2003.

41. U. Schweiger, M. Deuschle, B. Weber, A. Körner, C-H. Lammers, J. Schmider, et al. (1999). Testosterone, gonadotropin, and cortisol secretion in male patients with major depression. *Psychosomatic Medicine, 61,* 292–296.

42. W. E. Bunney & B. G. Bunney. (2000). Molecular clock genes in man and lower animals: Possible implications for circadian abnormalities in depression. *Neuropsychopharmacology, 22*(4), 335–345.

43. M. E. Thase, R. Jindal, & R. H. Howland. (2002). Biological aspects of depression. In I. H. Gotlib & C. L. Hammen (Eds.), *Handbook of depression* (pp. 192–218). New York: Guilford.

44. A. Wichniak, D. Reimann, A. Kieman, U. Voderholzer, & W. Jernajczyk. (2000). Comparison between eye movement latency and REM sleep parameters in major depression. *European Archives of Psychiatric Clinical Neuroscience, 250*(1), 48–52.

45. P. L. Delgado & F. A. Moreno. (2000). Role of norepinephrine in depression. *Journal of Clinical Psychiatry, 61*(Suppl.), 5–12.

46. Thase, et al. (2002).

47. Comer (2004).

48. Swartz (2007).

49. P. H. Wender, S. S. Kety, D. Rosenthal, F. Schulsinger, J. Ortmann, & I. Lunde. (1986). Psychiatric disorders in the biological and adoptive families of adopted individuals with affective disorders. *Archives of General Psychology, 43,* 923–929.

50. Swartz (2007).

51. N. Craddock & I. Jones. (1999). Genetics of bipolar disorder. *Journal of Medical Genetics, 36*(8), 585–594.

52. Sullivan, et al. (2000).

53. K. R. Merikangas, M. M. Weissman, & D. L. Pauls. (1985). Genetic factors in the sex ratio of major depression. *Psychological Review, 80,* 252–283.

54. P. Bebbington. (2004). The classification and epidemiology of unipolar depression. In M. Power (Ed.), *Mood disorders: A handbook of science and practice.* Chichester, UK: John Wiley.

55. B. D. Kennard, G. J. Emslie, T. L. Mayes, & J. L. Hughes. (2006). Relapse and recurrence in pediatric depression. *Child and Adolescent Psychiatric Clinics of North America, 15*(4), 1057–1079.

56. S. Lindeman, J. Hamalainen, E. Isometsa, J. Kaprio, K. Poikolainen, A. Heikkenin, et al. (2000). The 12-month prevalence and risk factors for major depressive episode in Finland: Representative sample of 5993 adults. *Acta Psychiatrica Scandinavica, 102,* 178–184.

57. S. Targosz, P. Bebbington, G. Lewis, R. Brugha, R. Jenkins, M. Farrell, et al. (2003). Lone mothers social exclusion and depression. *Psychological Medicine*, 33, 715–722.

58. Swartz (2007).

59. R. C. Kessler & W. J. McGee. (1993). Childhood adversities and adult depression: Basic patterns of association in a U.S. national survey. *Psychological Medicine*, 23, 679–690.

60. Reinherz et al. (1993).

61. N. Krause, G. Jay, & J. Liang. (1991). Financial strain and psychological well-being among the American and Japanese elderly. *Psychology and Aging*, 6, 170–181.

62. G. M. Williamson & R. Schultz. (1992). Physical illness and symptoms of depression among elderly outpatients. *Psychology of Aging*, 7(3), 343–351.

63. D. G. Myers. (2000). *The American paradox: Spiritual hunger in an age of plenty.* New Haven, CT: Yale University Press.

64. Myers (2000).

65. V. G. Maureas, A. Beis, A. Mouyias, F. Rigoni, & G. C. Lyketsos. (1986). Prevalence of psychiatric disorders in Athens: A community study. *Social Psychiatry*, 21, 172–181.

66. S. E. Romans-Clarkson, V. A. Walton, G. P. Herbison, & P. E. Mullen. (1988). Marriage, motherhood, and psychiatric morbidity in New Zealand. *Psychological Medicine*, 18(4), 983–990.

67. K. Lowenthal, V. Goldblatt, T. Gorton, G. Lubitsch, H. Bicknell, D. Fellowes, & A. Sowden. (1995). Gender and depression in Anglo-Jewry. *Psychological Medicine*, 25, 1051–1064.

68. Myers (2000).

69. MacLean & Hauser (2000).

70. J. Rottenberg & I. H. Gotlib. (2004). Socioemotional functioning in depression. In M. Power (Ed.), *Mood disorders: A handbook of science and practice.* Chichester, UK: John Wiley.

71. S. M. Monroe & K. Hadjiyannakis. (2002). The social environment and depression: Focusing severe life stress. In I. H. Gotlib & C. L. Hammen (Eds.), *Handbook of depression: Research and treatment* (pp. 314–340). New York: Guilford Press.

72. O. F. Kernberg. (1976). *Objects-relations theory and clinical psychoanalysis.* New York: Jason Aronson.

73. O. F. Kernberg. (1997). Convergences and divergences in contemporary psychoanalytic techniques and psychoanalytic psychotherapy. In J. K. Zeig (Ed.), *The evolution of psychotherapy: The third conference.* New York: Brunner/Mazel.

74. P. J. Bieling & Z. V. Segal. (2004). Cognitive models and issues in depression. In M. Power (Ed.), *Mood disorders: A handbook of science and practice.* Chichester, UK: John Wiley.

75. A. Beck. (2002). Cognitive models of depression. In R. L. Leahy & E. T. Dowds (Eds.), *Clinical advances in cognitive psychotherapy: Theory and application* (pp. 29–61). New York: Springer.

76. A. Beck, A. J. Rush, B. F. Shaw, & G. Emery. (1979). *Cognitive theory of depression*. New York: Guilford Press.

77. Beck et al. (1979).

78. G. I. Metalsky & T. E. Joiner. (1992). Vulnerability to depressive symptomatology: A prospective test of the diathesis-stress and causal mediation components of the hopelessness theory of depression. *Journal of Personality and Social Psychology, 63*(4), 667–675.

79. P. M. Lewinsohn, G. N. Clarke, H. Hops, & J. Andrews. (1990). Cognitive-behavioral treatment for depressed adolescents. *Behavioral Therapy, 21,* 385–401.

80. C. Peterson. (1993). Helpless behavior. *Behavior Research and Therapy, 31*(3), 289–295.

81. M.E.P. Seligman. (1975). *Helplessness*. San Francisco: Freeman.

82. Swartz (2007).

83. Bebbington (2004).

84. M. Power (Ed.). (2004). *Mood disorders: A handbook of science and practice.* Chichester, UK: John Wiley.

CHAPTER 4

1. M. Fava & K. Kendler. (2000). Major depressive disorder. *Neuron, 28*(2), 335–341.

2. L. L. Judd, H. S. Akiskal, J. D. Maser, P. J. Seiler, J. Endicott, W. Coryell, et al. (1998). A prospective 12-year study of subsyndromal depressive symptoms in unipolar major depressive disorders. *Archives of General Psychiatry, 55,* 694–700.

3. T. I. Mueller & A. C. Leon. (1996). Recovery, chronicity, and levels of psychopathology in major depression. *Psychiatric Clinics of North America, 19*(1), 85–102.

4. M. B. First & A. Tasman (Eds.). (2004). *DSM-IV-TR*™ *mental disorders: Diagnosis, etiology, and treatment.* Chichester, UK: John Wiley & Sons, Ltd.

5. NIMH Fact Sheets on Depression and Other Illnesses. (2002). Retrieved February 12, 2007, from http://www.nimh.nih.gov/publicat/coocurmenu.cfm.

6. First & Tasman (Eds.) (2004).

7. K. Swartz. (2007). *Depression and anxiety: The Johns Hopkins white papers.* Baltimore, MD: Johns Hopkins Medicine.

8. American Psychiatric Association. (2000). *Diagnostic and statistical manual of mental disorders* (4th ed., text revision). Washington, DC: Author.

9. American Psychiatric Association (2000).

10. First & Tasman (Eds.) (2004).

11. N. E. Rosenthal & M. C. Blehar (Eds.). (1989). *Seasonal affective disorders and phototherapy.* New York: The Guildford Press.

12. American Psychiatric Association. (1994). *Diagnostic and statistical manual of mental disorders* (4th ed.). Washington, DC: Author.

13. R. Nydegger. (2006). Postpartum depression: More than the "baby blues?" In T. G. Plante (Ed.), *Mental disorders of the new millennium* (vol. 3). Westport, CT: Praeger.

14. First & Tasman (Eds.) (2004).

15. D. A. Regier, D. S. Rae, W. E. Narrow, C. T. Kaelber, & A. F. Schatzberg. (1998). Prevalence of anxiety disorders and their co-morbidity with mood and addictive disorders. *British Journal of Psychiatry, 173*(Suppl. 34), 24–28.

16. M. Fava, M. A. Rankin, E. C. Wright, J. E. Alpert, A. A. Niernberg, J. Fava, et al. (2000). Anxiety disorders in major depression. *Comprehensive Psychiatry, 41*(2), 97–102.

17. Fava et al. (2000).

18. D. Bakish. (1999). The patient with co-morbid depression and anxiety. *Journal of Clinical Psychiatry, 60*(Suppl. 6), 20–24.

19. Regier et al. (1998).

20. R. J. Comer. (2004). *Abnormal psychology* (5th ed.). New York: Worth.

21. R. B. Lydriara & O. Brawman-Mintzer. (1998). Anxious depression. *Journal of Clinical Psychiatry, 59*(Suppl. 18), 10–17.

22. B. N. Gaynes, K. M. Magruder, B. J. Burns, H. R. Wagner, K.S.H. Yarnall, & W. E. Broadhead. (1999). Does a coexisting anxiety disorder predict persistence of depressive illness in primary care patients with major depression? *General Hospital Psychiatry, 21*(3), 158–167.

23. Comer (2004).

24. Swartz (2007).

25. First & Tasman (Eds.) (2004).

26. M. D. Eisner, P. P. Katz, G. Lactao, & C. Iribarren. (2005). Impact of depressive symptoms on adult asthma outcomes. *Annals of Allergy, Asthma, and Immunology, 94*(5), 566–574.

27. C. G. Simpson. (1996, January 17). Cited in W. Leary, As fellow traveler of other illnesses, depression often goes in disguise. *New York Times*, p. C-9.

28. D. Polsky, J. A. Doshi, S. Marcus, D. Olsin, A. Rothband, N. Thomas, et al. (2005). Long-term risk for depressive symptoms after a medical diagnosis. *Archives of Internal Medicine, 165*, 1260–1266.

29. Polsky et al. (2005).

30. Swartz (2007).

31. A. M. Ziess, P. M. Lewinshoh, P. Rohde, & J. R. Seeley. (1996). Relationship of physical disease and functional impairment of depression in older people. *Psychology and Aging, 11*, 572–581.

32. NIMH Fact Sheets on Depression and Other Illnesses (2002).

33. W. Katon. (1996). The impact of major depression on chronic medical illness. *General Hospital Psychiatry, 18*, 215–219.

34. J. S. Kahan, J. M. Mitchell, B. J. Kemp, & R. H. Adkins. (2006). The results of a 6-month treatment for depression on symptoms, life satisfaction, and community activities among individuals aging with a disability. *Rehabilitation Psychology, 51*(1), 13–22.

35. G. E. Simon, M. Von Korff, K. Saunders, D. L. Miglioretti, P. K. Crane, G. van Belle, et al. (2006). Association between obesity and psychiatric disorders in the U.S. adult population. *Archives of General Psychiatry, 63*(7), 824–830.

36. A. A. Ariyo, M. Haan, C. M. Tangen, J. C. Rutledge, M. Cushman, A. Dobs, & C. D. Furberg. (2000). Depressive symptoms and risks of coronary heart disease and mortality in elderly Americans. *Circulation, 102*, 1773–1779.

37. R. A. Schoevers, A.T.F. Beekman, W. van Tilburg, D.J.H. Deeg, C. Joncker, M. I. Geerlings, et al. (2000). Association of depression and gender with mortality in old age. *The British Journal of Psychiatry, 117*, 336–342.

38. K. Swartz. (2006). *Depression and anxiety: The Johns Hopkins white papers.* Baltimore, MD: Johns Hopkins Medicine.

39. B. J. Kemp & L. Mosqueda (Eds.). (2004). *Aging with a disability: What the clinician needs to know.* Baltimore, MD: Johns Hopkins University Press.

40. S. J. Blumberg, P. M. West, & F. W. Ellis. (1954). A possible relationship between psychological factors and human cancer. *Psychosomatic Medicine, 16*, 227–287.

41. L. R. Derogatis, M. D. Abeloff, & C. D. McBeth. (1976). Cancer patients and their physicians in the perception of psychological symptoms. *Psychosomatics, 17*, 197–201.

42. K. M. Stavraky, C. N. Buck, & J. M. Worklin. (1968). Psychological factors in the outcomes of human cancer. *Journal of Psychosomatic Research, 12*, 251–259.

43. B. Klopfer. (1957). Psychological variables in human cancer. *Journal of Projective Techniques, 21*, 331–340.

44. F. I. Fawzy, N. W. Fawzy, C. S. Hyun, R. Elashoff, D. Guthrie, J. L. Fahey, et al. (1993). Malignant melanoma: Effects of an early structured psychiatric intervention, coping, and affective state on recurrence and survival six years later. *Archives of General Psychiatry, 50*(9), 681–689.

45. D. Speigel, J. R. Bloom, H. C. Kraemer, & E. Gottheil. (1989). Effect of psychosocial treatment on survival of patients with metastatic breast cancer. *Lancet, 2*, 888–891.

46. M. L. Schrifte. (1962). Toward identification of a psychological variable in host resistance to cancer. *Psychosomatic Medicine, 24*, 390–397.

47. R. W. Linkins & G. W. Comstock. (1990). Depressed mood and development of cancer. *American Journal of Epidemiology, 132*, 962–972.

48. R. C. Hahn & D. B. Petitti. (1988). Minnesota Multiphasic Personality Inventory-rated depression and the incidence of breast cancer. *Cancer, 61*, 845–848.

49. G. A. Kaplan & P. Reynolds. (1988). Depression and cancer mortality and morbidity: Prospective evidence from the Almeda County Study. *Journal of Behavioral Medicine, 11*(1), 1–13.

50. N. Frasure-Smith, F. Lespérance, M. Juneau, M. Tulajic, & M. G. Bourassa. (1999). Gender, depression, and one-year prognosis after myocardial infarction. *Psychosomatic Medicine, 61*, 26–37.

51. H. D. Sesso, I. Kawachi, P. S. Voconas, & S. Sparrow. (1998). Depression and the risk of coronary heart disease in the Normative Aging Study. *American Journal of Cardiology, 82*(7), 851–856.

52. Swartz (2007).

53. Swartz (2007).

54. Swartz (2007).

55. Swartz (2007).

56. P. Bebbington. (2004). The classification and epidemiology of unipolar depression. In M. Power (Ed.), *Mood disorders: A handbook of science and practice*. Chichester, UK: John Wiley and Sons, Ltd.

57. E. F. Torrey & M. B. Knable. (2002). *Surviving manic depression: A manual on bipolar disorder for patients, families, and providers*. New York: Basic Books.

58. Swartz (2007).

59. Swartz (2007).

60. NIMH Fact Sheets on Depression and Other Illnesses (2002).

61. J. Angst. (1998). The emerging epidemiology of hypomania and bipolar II disorder. *Journal of Affective Disorders, 50*, 143–151.

62. K. R. Jamison. (1995, February). Manic-depressive illness and creativity. *Scientific American, 272*(2) 63–67.

63. American Psychiatric Association (1994).

64. M. Power (Ed.). (2004). *Mood disorders: A handbook of science and practice*. Chichester, UK: John Wiley and Sons, Ltd.

65. Power, 2004.

66. American Psychiatric Association (2000).

67. First & Tasman (Eds.) (2004).

CHAPTER 5

1. T. Field. (1995). Infants of depressed mothers. *Infant Behavior and Development, 18*, 1–13.

2. D. A. Regier, W. E. Narrow, D. S. Rae, R. W. Manderscheid, B. Z. Locke, & F. K. Goodwin. (1993). The de-facto mental and addictive disorders service system: Epidemiological Catchment Area perspective 1-year prevalence rates of disorders and services. *Archives of General Psychiatry, 50*(2), 85–94.

3. S. Nolen-Hoeksema & J. S. Girgus. (1994). The emergence of gender differences in depression during adolescence. *Psychological Bulletin, 115*, 424–443.

4. F. M. Culbertson. (1997). Depression and gender: An international review. *American Psychologist, 52*(1), 25–31.

5. Culbertson (1997).

6. World Health Organization. (2003). *Gender and women's health*. Retrieved December 14, 2006, from http://www.who.int/mental_health/prevention/gender women/en/.

7. P. E. Bebbington, G. Dunn, R. Jenkins, G. Lewis, T. Brugha, M. Farrell, et al. (2003). The influence of age and sex on the prevalence of depressive conditions: Report from the National Survey of Psychiatric Morbidity. *Psychological Medicine, 28*, 9–19.

8. D. L. Spangler, A. D. Simons, S. M. Monroe, & M. E. Thase. (1996). Gender differences in cognitive diathesis-stress domain match implications for differential pathways to depression. *Journal of Abnormal Psychology, 105*(4), 653–657.

9. A. A. Khan, C. O. Gardner, C. A. Prescott, & K. S. Kendler. (2002). Gender differences in the symptoms of major depression in opposite-sex dyzigotic twin pairs. *American Journal of Psychiatry, 159,* 1427–1429.

10. J. Mirowsky & C. E. Ross. (1995). Sex differences in distress: Real or artifact? *American Sociological Review, 60*(3), 449–468.

11. S. Nolen-Hoeksema. (1990). *Sex differences in depression.* Stanford, CA: Stanford University Press.

12. E. F. Dunn & M. Steiner. (2000). The functional neurochemistry of mood disorders in women. In M. Steiner, K. A. Yonkers, & E. Erikson (Eds.), *Mood disorders in women* (pp. 71–82). London: Martin Dunitz.

13. S. Nolen-Hoeksema. (2002). Gender differences in depression. In I. H. Gottlib & C. L. Hammen (Eds.), *Handbook of depression* (pp. 492–509). New York: Guilford.

14. Nolen-Hoeksema (2002).

15. C. A. Patten, J. C. Gillin, A. J. Farkas, E. A. Gilpin, C. C. Berry, & J. P. Pierce. (1997). Depressive symptoms in California adolescents: Family structure and parental support. *Journal of Adolescent Health, 20,* 271–278.

16. A. D. Leunes, J. R. Nation, & N. M. Turley. (1980). Male-female performance in learned helplessness. *Journal of Psychology, 104,* 255–258.

17. Nolen-Hoeksema (2002).

18. L. Y. Abramson, M. E. Seligman, & J. D. Teasdale. (1978). Learned helplessness in humans: Critique and reformulation. *Journal of Abnormal Psychology, 87*(1), 49–74.

19. J. M. Cyranowski, E. Frank, E. Young, & M. K. Shear. (2000). Adolescent onset of the gender difference in the onset of the gender difference in the lifetime rates of major depression. *Archives of General Psychiatry, 57,* 21–27.

20. K. C. Kling, J. S. Hyde, C. J. Showers, & B. N. Buswell. (1999). Gender differences in self-esteem: A meta-analysis. *Psychological Bulletin, 125*(4), 470–500.

21. Nolen-Hoeksema (2002).

22. V. Patel & N. M. Oomman. (1999). Mental health matters too: Gynecological morbidity and depression in South Asia. *Reproductive Health Matters, 7,* 30–38.

23. World Health Organization (2003).

24. World Health Organization (2003), p. 1.

25. E. F. Torrey & M. B. Knable. (2002). *Surviving manic depression: A manual on bipolar disorder for patients, families, and providers.* New York: Basic Books.

26. W. M. Ensel. (1982). The role of age in the relationship of gender and marital status to depression. *Journal of Nervous and Mental Disease, 170,* 536–543.

27. B. Davar. (1999). *The mental health of Indian women: A feminist agenda.* New Delhi: Sage.

28. Davar (1999).

29. World Health Organization. (2000). *Women's mental health: An evidence-based review.* WHO/MSD/MHP00.1. Geneva: World Health Organization.

30. World Health Organization (2003).

31. V. Patel, M. Rodriques, & N. DeSouza. (2002). Gender, poverty & post-natal depression: A cohort study from Goa, India. *American Journal of Psychiatry, 159,* 43–47.

32. World Health Organization (2003).

33. World Health Organization (2003).

34. World Health Organization (2003).

35. R. Nydegger, M. Paludi, E. DeSouza, & C. Paludi. (2006). Incivility, sexual harassment and violence in the workplace. In M. Karsten (Ed.), *Gender, race and ethnicity in the workplace: Issues and challenges for today's organizations.* Westport, CT: Praeger.

36. K. A. Yonkers & S. J. Chantilis. (1995). Recognition of depression in obstetric/gynecology practices. *American Journal of Obstetrics and Gynecology, 173*(2), 632–638.

37. A. D. Rivera-Tovar & E. Frank. (1990). Late luteal phase dysphoric disorder in young women. *American Journal of Psychiatry, 147*(12), 403–411.

38. M. B. First & A. Tasman (Eds.). (2004). *DSM-IV-TR™ mental disorders: Diagnosis, etiology, and treatment.* Chichester, UK: John Wiley & Sons, Ltd.

39. P. J. Schmidt, L. K. Nieman, M. A. Danaceau, B. A. Adams, & D. R. Rubinow. (1998). Differential effects of gonadal steroids in women with and those without premenstrual syndrome. *New England Journal of Medicine, 338*(4), 209–216.

40. Schmidt et al. (1998).

41. Patel et al. (2002).

42. World Health Organization (2003).

43. R. Nydegger. (2006). Postpartum depression: More than the "baby blues?" In T. G. Plante (Ed.), *Mental disorders of the new millennium* (vol. 3). Westport, CT: Praeger.

44. M. W. O'Hara & A. M. Swain. (1996). Rates and risk of postpartum depression—a meta-analysis. *International Review of Psychiatry, 8,* 37–54.

45. Patel et al. (2002).

46. A. J. Gregoire, R. Kumar, and B. Everitt. (1996). Transdermal oestragen for treatment of severe postnatal depression [see comments]. *Lancet, 347*(9006), 930–933.

47. K. A. Leopold & L. B. Zoschnick. (2005). *Postpartum depression.* Retrieved March 3, 2007, from http://www.obgyn.het/femalepatient/default.asp?page=leopold.

48. D. Ryan & X. Kosturas. (2005). Psychiatric disorders in the postpartum period. *BC Medical Journal, 47*(2), 100–103.

49. Ryan & Kosturas (1995).

50. J. A. Hamilton. (1989). Postpartum psychiatric syndromes. *Psychiatric Clinics of North American, 12,* 89–103.

51. R. M. Nonacs & L. S. Cohen. (1998). Postpartum mood disorders: Diagnosis and treatment guidelines. *Journal of Clinical Psychiatry, 59*(Suppl. 2), 34–40.

52. Leopold & Zoschnick (2005).

53. M. W. O'Hara, D. J. Neunaber, & E. M. Zekoski. (1984). A prospective study of postpartum depression, prevalence, course, and predictive factors. *Journal of Abnormal Psychology, 91,* 158–171.

54. B. R. Troutman & C. E. Cutrona. (1990). Non-psychotic postpartum depression among adolescent mothers. *Journal of Abnormal Psychology, 99*(1), 69–78.

55. Womanshealth.gov. (2005). *Depression during and after pregnancy.* Retrieved April 3, 2007, from http://www.4women.gov/faq/postpartum.htm.

56. M. W. O'Hara. (1986). Social support, life events, and depression during pregnancy and the puerperium. *Archives of General Psychiatry, 43,* 569–573.

57. Yonkers & Chantilis (1995).

58. Womanshealth.gov (2005).

59. M. Altemus & K. Brogan. (2004). *Women and anxiety disorders: Implications for diagnosis.* Retrieved February 13, 2007, from http://www.touchbriefings.com/pdf/992/Altemus-Brogan_edit.pdf.

60. Z. N. Stowe & C. B. Nemeroff. (1995). Women at risk for postpartum onset of major depression. *American Journal of Obstetrics and Gynecology, 173,* 639–645.

61. Leopold & Zoschnick (2005), p. 1.

62. J. Prior. (1999). *Gender and mental health.* New York: New York University Press.

63. World Health Organization (2003).

64. National Institute of Mental Health. (2005). *Men and depression.* NIMH Publication No. 05-4972. Retrieved February 23, 2007, from http://www.menanddepression.nimh.nih.gov/infopage.asp?id=10.

65. M. X. Zamparripa, B. E. Wampold, & E. Gregory. (2003). *Journal of Counseling Psychology, 50*(3), 333–338.

66. T. Real. (1997). *I don't want to talk about it: Overcoming the secret legacy of male depression.* New York: Fireside.

67. Harvard Medical School. (November, 2006). Men and depression. *Harvard Mental Health Letter, 23*(5), 1–3.

68. National Institute of Mental Health (2005).

69. D. E. Ford, L. A. Mead, P. P. Chang, L. Cooper-Patrick, N. Y. Wang, & M. J. Klag. (1998). Depression is a risk factor for coronary artery disease in men: The precursors study. *Archives of Internal Medicine, 158*(13), 1422–1426.

70. R. A. Schoevers, A.T.F. Beekman, W. van Tilburg, D.J.H. Deeg, C. Joncker, M. I. Geerlings, et al. (2000). Association of depression and gender with mortality in old age. *The British Journal of Psychiatry, 177,* 336–342.

71. National Institute of Mental Health (2005).

72. A. M. Moller-Leimkuhler. (2000). Men and depression: Gender-related help-seeking behavior. *Fortschritte der Neurologie, Psychiatrie und ihrer Grenzgebiete, 68*(11), 489–495.

73. E. Pamuk, D. Makuc, K. Heck, C. E. Reuben, & K. Lochner. (1998). *Health, United States, 1998 with socioeconomic status and health chartbook.* DHHS Publication No: PHS 98-1232. Hyattsville, MD: National Center for Health Statistics.

74. T. E. Joiner, M. S. Alfano, & G. I. Metalsky. (1992). When depression breeds contempt: Reassurance seeking, self-esteem, and rejection of depressed college students by their roommates. *Journal of Abnormal Psychology, 10,* 171.

75. M. Magovcevic & M. E. Addis. (2005). Linking gender-role conflict to non-normative and self-stigmatizing perceptions of alcohol abuse and depression. *Psychology of Men & Masculinity, 6*(2), 127–136.

76. J. Pleck. (1981). *The myth of masculinity.* Cambridge, MA: MIT Press.

77. Life Positive. (2006). *Female and male depression and stress.* Retrieved February 14, 2006, from http://www.lifepositive.com/Mind/psychology/stress/male-depression. asp.

78. Harvard Medical School (2006).

79. M. M. Weissman, R. C. Bland, G. J. Canino, S. Greenwald, B.-G. Hwu, P. R. Joyce, et al. (1999). Prevalence of suicide ideation and suicidal attempts in nine countries. *Psychological Medicine, 29*(1), 9–17.

80. C.J.L. Murray & A. D. Lopez. (1996). *The global burden of disease.* Boston, MA: Harvard University Press.

81. D. L. Hoyert, K. D. Kochanek, & S. L. Murphy. (1999). Deaths: Final data for 1997. *National Vital Statistics Report, 47*(9). DHHS Publication No. 99–1120. Hyattsville, MD: National Center for Health Statistics.

82. World Health Organization (2003).

83. National Institute of Mental Health. (2000). *Depression.* Retrieved January 14, 2007, from http://www.nimh.nih.gov/publicat/depression.cfm.

84. Health Centers: Depression. (2007). *Depression in women: Understanding the gender gap.* Retrieved January 14, 2007, from http://health msn.com/centes/depres sion/articlepage.aspz?cp-documented=100050707.

85. E. Leibenluft. (2001). "Why are so many women depressed?" *Scientific American.* Retrieved March 21, 2007, from http://www.sciam.com/specalissues/0698leibenluft. html.

86. T. A. Roesler & N. McKenzie. (1994). Effects of childhood trauma on psychological functioning of adults sexually abused as children. *The Journal of Nervous and Mental Diseases, 182*(3), 145–150.

87. Nolen-Hoeksema (1990).

88. Nolen-Hoeksema & Girgus (1994).

89. BYU. (2006). *Gender and depression research. [On line].* Retrieved October 12, 2006, from http://archives.his.com/smartmarriages/2000-October/msg00023.html.

90. R. L. Kessler, K. A. McGonagle, M. Swartz, D. G. Blazer, & C. B. Nelson. (1993). Sex and depression in the National Comorbidity Survey I: Lifetime prevalence, chronicity, and recurrence. *Journal of Affective Disorders, 29*(2–3), 85–96.

91. Nolen-Hoeksema & Girgus (1994).

92. D. L. Spangler, A. D. Simons, S. M. Monroe, & M. E. Thase. (1996). Gender differences in cognitive diathesis-stress domain match implications for differential pathways to depression. *Journal of Abnormal Psychology, 105*(4), 653–657.

93. Nolen-Hoeksema (1990).

94. L. J. Bierut, A. C. Heath, K. K. Bucholz, S. H. Dinurddie, P. A. Madden, D. J. Stratham, et al. (1999). Major depressive disorder in a community-based twin sample: Are there different genetic and environmental contributions for men and women? *Archives of General Psychiatry, 56*(6), 557–563.

95. World Health Organization (2003).

96. J. V. Nazroo. (2001). Exploring gender differences in depression. *Psychiatric Times, 17*(3), 1–4.

97. Health Central. (2003). *Depression and gender stereotypes.* Retrieved February 28, 2006, from http://www.healthcentral.com/PrinterFriendly_hc/drdean/408/60603.html.

98. Prior (1999).

99. Prior (1999).

100. J. Uscher. (1991). *Women's madness: Mysogyny or mental illness?* London: Harvester Wheatsheaf.

101. T. Szasz. (1961). *Myth of mental illness.* New York: Harper & Row.

102. E. McGrath, G. P. Keita, B. Strickland, & N. F. Russo. (1990). *Women and depression: Risk factors and treatment issues.* Washington, DC: American Psychological Association, p. xii.

CHAPTER 6

1. P. Hazell. (2005). Depression in children and adolescents. *Clinical Evidence 14,* 1–16 (quote on p. 3).

2. Hazell. (2005).

3. R. C. Kessler, S. Avenevoli, & R. Merikangus. (2001). Mood disorders in children and adolescents: An epidemiologic perspective. *Biological Psychiatry, 49,* 1002–1014.

4. B. Birmaher, N. D. Ryan, D. E. Williamson, D. A. Brent, J. Kaufman, R. E. Dahl, et al. (1996). Childhood and adolescent depression: Part I. A review of the past 10 years. *Journal of the American Academy of child and Adolescent Psychiatry, 35,* 1427–1439.

5. M. M. Weissman, R. C. Bland, G. J. Canino, S. Greenwald, B.-G. Hwu, P. R. Joyce, et al. (1999). Prevalence of suicide ideation and suicidal attempts in nine countries. *Psychological Medicine, 29*(1), 9–17.

6. Hazell (2005).

7. J. H. Kashani, D. P. Cantwell, W. O. Shekim, & J. C. Reid. (1982). Major depressive disorder, in children admitted to an inpatient community mental health center. *American Journal of Psychiatry, 139,* 671–672.

8. Hazell (2005).

9. Birmaher et al. (1996).

10. B. L. Hankin, L. Y. Abramson, T. E. Moffitt, P. A. Silva, R. McGee, & K. E. Angell. (1998). Development of depression from preadolescence to young adulthood: Emerging gender differences on a ten-year longitudinal study. *Journal of Abnormal Psychology, 107*(1), 128–140.

11. Substance Abuse and Mental Health Services Administration. (2005). *Results from the 2004 National Survey on Drug Use and Health: National Findings* (Office of Applied Studies, NSDUH Series H-27, DHHS Publication No. SMA 05–4061). Rockville, MD: Author.

12. A. Angold, M. M. Weissman, K. R. Merikangas, B. A. Prusoff, P. Wickramaratne, G. D. Gammon, et al. (1987). Parent and child reports of depressive symptoms

in children at low and high risk of depression. *Journal of Child Psychology and Psychiatry, 28*(6), 901–915.

13. N. D. Ryan, J. Puig-Atich, H. Abrosini, H. Rabinovich, D. Robinson, B. Nelson, et al. (1987). The clinical pattern of major depression in children and adolescents. *Archives of General Psychiatry, 44*(10), 854–861.

14. World Health Organization. (2003). *Gender and women's health.* Retrieved December 14, 2006, from http://www.who.int/mental_health/prevention/gender women/en/.

15. American Academy of Child and Adolescent Psychiatry. (2007). Practice parameter for the assessment and treatment of children and adolescents with bipolar disorder. *Journal of the American Academy of Child and Adolescent Psychiatry, 46*(1), 107–125.

16. Neighborhoods and gendered child development. (2002). *Gender and depression. Towson University.* Retrieved February 14, 2006, from http://pages.towson.edu/ itrow/research/current%20research%20projects/gender&depression.

17. H. Z. Reinherz, R. M. Giaconia, A.M.C. Hauf, M. S. Wasserman, & A. B. Silverman. (1999). Major depression in the transition to adulthood: Risks and impairments. *Journal of Abnormal Psychology, 108*(3), 500–510.

18. H. Z. Reinherz, R. M. Giaconia, B. Pakiz, A. B. Siverman, A. K. Frost, & E. S. Lefkowitz. (1993). Psychosocial risks for major depression in late adolescence: A longitudinal community study. *Journal of the American Academy of Child and Adolescent Psychiatry, 32*(6), 1155–1163.

19. Reinherz et al. (1999).

20. A. H. Mezalis, J. S. Hyde, & L. Y. Abramson. (2006). The developmental origins of cognitive vulnerability to depression: Temperament, parenting, and negative life events in childhood as contributors to negative cognitive style. *Developmental Psychology, 42*(6), 1012–1025.

21. P. Cohen, C. N. Velaz, J. Brook, & J. Smith. (1989). Mechanisms of the relation between perinatal problems, early childhood illness and psychopathology in late childhood and adolescence. *Child Development, 60*, 701–709.

22. Reinherz et al. (1999).

23. S. M. Stewart, B. D. Kennard, P.W.H. Lee, C. W. Hughes, T. Mayes, G. J. Emslie, et al. (2004). A cross-cultural investigation of cognitions and depressive symptoms in adolescents. *Journal of Abnormal Psychology, 113*, 248–257.

24. Reinherz et al. (1999).

25. P. P. Chang, D. E. Ford, L. A. Mead, L. Cooper-Patrick, & M. J. Klag. (1997). Insomnia in young men and subsequent depression: The Johns Hopkins precursors study. *American Journal of Epidemiology, 146*(2), 105–114.

26. D. Blazer, L. George, & R. Landerman. (1986). The phenomenology of late life depression. In P. E. Bebbington & R. Jacoby (Eds.), *Psychiatric disorders in the elderly* (pp. 143–152). London: Mental Health Foundation.

27. G. Downey & J. C. Coyne. (1990). Children of depressed parents: An integrative review. *Psychological Bulletin, 108*, 50–76.

28. M. M. Weissman, P. Wickramaratne, Y. Nomura, V. Warner, D. Pilowsky, & H. Verdeli.(2005). Offspring of depressed parents: 20 years later. *American Journal of Psychiatry, 163*(6), 1001–1008.

29. H. Finkelstein. (1988). The long-term effects of early parental death: A review. *Journal of Clinical Psychology, 44,* 3–9.

30. Reinherz et al. (1993).

31. Reinherz et al. (1999).

32. R. H. Bradley & R. F. Corwyn. (2000). Moderating effect of perceived amount of family conflict on the relation between home environmental processes and the well-being of adolescents. *Journal of Family Psychology, 14,* 349–364.

33. D. Formoso, N. A. Gonzales, & L. S. Aiken. (2000). Family conflict and children's internalizing and externalizing behavior: Protective factors. *American Journal of Community Psychology, 28,* 175–199.

34. Kashani et al. (1982).

35. American Psychiatric Association Work Group on Eating Disorders. (2000). Practice guidelines for the treatment of patients with eating disorders (revision). *American Journal of Psychiatry, 157*(1 Suppl.), 671–675.

36. L. J. Heinberg & J. K. Thompson. (1995). Body image and televised images of thinness and attractiveness: A controlled laboratory investigation. *Journal of Social and Clinical Psychology, 14*(4), 325–338.

37. World Health Organization (2003).

38. D. H. Lam, C. R. Brewin, R. T. Woods, & P. E. Bebbington. (1987). Cognition and social adversity in the depressed elderly. *Journal of Abnormal Psychology, 96*(1), 23–26.

39. K. L. Swartz. (2007). *Depression and anxiety: The Johns Hopkins white papers.* Baltimore, MD: Johns Hopkins Medicine.

40. J. M. Lyness, E. D. Caine, D. A. King, Y. Conwell, P. R. Duberstein, & C. Cox. (2002). Depressive disorders and symptoms in older primary care patients: One year outcomes. *American Journal of geriatric Psychiatry, 10,* 275–282.

41. K. Jorgenelis, A. M. Pot, A.M.H. Eisses, A.T.F. Beekman, H. Klister, & M. W. Ribbe. (2004). Prevalence and risk indicators of depression in elderly nursing home patients: the AGED study. *Journal of Affective Disorders, 83,* 135–142.

42. B. A. Teachman. (2006). Aging and negative affect: The rise and fall and rise of anxiety and depression symptoms. *Psychology and Aging, 21*(1), 201–207.

43. Y. Conwell, J. M. Lyness, P. Duberstein, C. Cox, L. Seidlitz, A. DiGiorgio, et al. (2000). Completed suicide among older patients in primary care practices: A controlled study. *Journal of American Geriatrics Society, 48*(1), 23–29.

44. B. D. Lebowitz, J. L. Pearson, L. S. Schneider, C. F. Reynolds, G. S. Alexopoulos, M. I. Bruce, et al. (1997). Diagnosis and treatment of depression in later life: consensus statement update. *Journal of the American Medical Association, 278*(14), 1186–1190.

45. National Institute of Mental Health. (2000). *Depression.* Retrieved January 14, 2007, from http://www.nimh.nih.gov/publicat/depression.cfm.

46. National Institute of Mental Health (2000).

47. C. F. Reynolds, III, M. A. Dew, B. G. Pollock, B. H. Mulsant, E. Frank, M. D. Miller, et al. (2006). Maintenance treatment of major depression in old age. *New England Journal of Medicine, 354*, 1130–1138.

48. S. Meeks. (1990). Age bias in the diagnostic decision-making behavior of clinicians. *Professional Psychology: Research & Practice, 21*(4), 279–284.

49. L. S. Cohen, C. N. Soares, A. F. Vitonis, M. W. Otto, & B. L. Harlow. (2006). Risk for new onset of depression during the menopausal transition: The Harvard study of moods and cycles. *Archives of General Psychiatry, 63*(4), 385–90.

50. R. Zemore & N. Eames. (1979). Psychic and somatic symptoms of depression among young adults, institutionalized aged and non-institutionalized aged. *Journal of Gerontology, 34*(5), 716–722.

51. Blazer et al. (1986).

52. Helpguide. (2006). *Depression in older adults and the elderly: Signs, symptoms, causes and treatments.* Retrieved May 2, 2006, from http://www.helpguide.org/mental/depression_elderly.htm.

53. D. A. King, C. Cox, J. M. Lyness, & E. D. Caine. (1995). Neuropsychological effects of depression and age in an elderly sample: A confirmatory study. *Neuropsychology, 9*(3), 399–428.

54. King et al. (1995).

55. World Health Organization. (2000). *Women's mental health: An evidence-based review* (WHO/MSD/MHP00.1). Geneva: World Health Organization.

56. National Institute on Aging. (1999). *Progress report on Alzheimer's disease* (NIH Publication No. 99–4664). Bethesda, MD: National Institute on Aging.

57. World Health Organization (2000).

58. National Institute of Mental Health. (2005). *Men and depression* (NIMH Publication No. 05–4972). Retrieved February 23, 2007, from http://www.menanddepression.nimh.nih.gov/infopage.asp?id=10.

59. National Institute of Mental Health (2005).

60. Conwell et al. (2000).

61. S. E. Barnow & M. Linden. (2000). Epidemiology and psychiatric morbidity of suicidal ideation among the elderly. *The Journal of Crisis Intervention and Suicide Prevention, 21*(4), 171–180.

62. Barnow & Linden (2000).

63. J. J. Gallo & P. V. Rubins. (1999). Depression without sadness: Alternative presentations of depression in later life. *American Family Physician, 278*(14), 1186–1190.

64. G. M. Williamson & R. Schulz. (1992). Physical illness and symptoms of depression among elderly outpatients. *Psychology and Aging, 7*(3), 343–351.

65. H. T. Nguyen & A. B. Zonderman. (2006). Relationship between age and aspects of depression: Consistency and reliability across the longitudinal studies. *Psychology and Aging, 21*(1), 119–126.

66. Williamson & Schulz (1992).

67. Williamson & Schulz (1992).

68. Helpguide (2006).

69. Helpguide (2006).

CHAPTER 7

1. J. R. Castro & K. G. Rice. (2003). Perfectionism and ethnicity: Implications for depressive symptoms and self-reported academic achievement. *Cultural Diversity and Ethnic Minority Psychology, 9*(1), 64–78.

2. N. A. Fouad & P. Arredondo. (2007). *Becoming culturally oriented: Practical advice for psychologists and educators.* Washington, DC: American Psychological Association.

3. A. Weisman, G. Feldman, C. Gruman, R. Rosenberg, R. Chummaro, & I. Belozersky. (2005). Improving mental health services for Latino and Asian immigrant elders. *Professional Psychology: Research & Practice, 36*(6), 642–648.

4. Mental Health: A Report of the Surgeon General. (1999). *Mental health: culture, race and ethnicity—Supplement.* Retrieved May 2, 2006, from http://mental health.samhsa.gov/cre/toc.asp.

5. F. K. Cheung & L. R. Snowden. (1990). Community mental health and ethnic minority population. *Community Mental Health Journal, 26,* 89–102.

6. Mental Health: A Report of the Surgeon General (1999).

7. M. A. Oquendo, S. P. Ellis, S. Greenwald, K. M. Malone, M. M. Weissman, & J. J. Mann. (2001). *American Journal of Psychiatry, 158,* 1652–1658.

8. B. D. Kennard, S. M. Stewart, J. L. Hughes, P. G. Patel, & G. J. Emslie. (2006). Cognitions and depressive symptoms among ethnic minority adolescents. *Cultural Diversity and Ethnic Minority Psychology, 12*(3), 578–591.

9. K.A.S. Wickrama, S. Noh, & C. M. Bryant. (2005). Racial differences in adolescent distress: Differential effects of the family and community for Blacks and Whites. *Journal of Community Psychology, 33,* 261–282.

10. Kennard et al. (2006).

11. M. P. Beaudet. (1996). Depression. *Health Reports, 7,* 11–15.

12. J. J. Dowd & V. L. Bengtson. (1978). Aging in minority populations: an examination of the double jeopardy hypotheses. *Journal of Gerontological Social Work, 5,* 127–145.

13. D. R. Williams & A.-M. Chung. (1997). *Racism and health.* Unpublished manuscript.

14. McMan's Depression and Bipolar Webpage. (2006). *Ethnopolar—Ethnicity and depression and bipolar.* Retrieved May 2, 2006, from http://www.mcmanweb.com/artile-151.htm.

15. A. Y. Zhang & L. R. Snowden. (1999). Ethnic characteristics of mental disorders in five U.S. communities. *Cultural Diversity and Ethnic Minority Psychology, 5*(2), 134–146.

16. R. G. Wight, C. S. Aneshensel, A. L. Botticello, & J. E. Sepúlveda. (2005). A multilevel analysis of ethnic variation in depressive symptoms among adolescents in the United States. *Social Science & Medicine, 60,* 2073–2084.

17. M. G. Constatntine. (2006). Perceived family conflict, parental attachment, and depression in African American female adolescents. *Cultural Diversity and Ethnic Minority Psychology, 12*(4), 697–709.

18. K. L. Pottick, S. A. Kirk, D. K. Hsieh, & X. Tian. (2007). Judging mental disorder in youths: Effects of client, clinician, and contextual differences. *Journal of Consulting and Clinical Psychology, 75*(1), 1–8.

19. Pottick et al. (2007).

20. J. Miranda, G. Bernal, A. Lau, L. Kohn, W. Hwang, & T. LaFromboise. (2005). State of science on psychosocial interventions for ethnic minorities. *Annual Review of Clinical Psychology, 1*, 113–142.

21. A. K. Mansfield, M. F. Addis, & W. Courtenay. (2005). Measurement of men's help seeking: Development and evaluation of the barriers to help seeking scale. *Psychology of Men & Masculinity, 6*(2), 95–108.

22. McMan's Depression and Bipolar Webpage (2006).

23. U.S. Census Bureau. (2004). *U.S. Census 2004*. Retrieved February 13, 2007, from http://www.census.gov

24. H. Hiott, J. G. Grzywacz, T. A. Arcury, & S. A. Quandt. (2006). Gender differences in anxiety and depression among immigrant Latinos. *Families, Systems, & Health, 24*(2), 137–146.

25. Kennard et al. (2006).

26. Hiott et al. (2006).

27. J. M. Fragoso & S. Kashubeck. (2000). Machismo, gender role conflict, and mental health in Mexican American men. *Psychology of Men and Masculinity, 1*(2), 87–97.

28. B. Moradi & C. Risco. (2006). Perceived discrimination experiences and mental health of Latina/o American persons. *Journal of Counseling Psychology, 53*(4), 411–421.

29. Mental Health: A Report of the Surgeon General (1999).

30. Cheung & Snowden (1990).

31. A. S. Young, R. Klap, C. D. Sherbourne, & K. B. Wells. (2001). The quality of care for depressive and anxiety disorders in the United States. *Archives of General Psychiatry, 58*, 55–61.

32. K. Fiscella, P. Franks, M. Doescher, & B. Saver. (2002). Disparities in health care by race, ethnicity, and language among the insured: Findings from a national sample. *Medical Care, 40*, 52–59.

33. R. Lewis-Fernández, A. K. Das, C. Alfonso, M. M. Weissman, & M. Olfson. (2005). Depression in US Hispanics: Diagnostic and management considerations in family practice. *Journal of the American Board of Family Practice, 18*, 282–296.

34. R. G. Malgady, L. H. Rogler, & G. Constantino. (1987). Ethnocultural and linguistic bias in mental health evaluation of Hispanics. *American Psychologist, 42*(3), 228–234.

35. Mental Health: A Report of the Surgeon General (1999).

36. McMan's Depression and Bipolar Webpage (2006).

37. S. Okazaki. (1997). Sources of ethnic differences between Asian American and Whit American college students on measures of depression and social anxiety. *Journal of Abnormal Psychology, 106*(1), 52–60.

38. P. D. Akutsu & J. P. Chu. (2006). Clinical problems that initiate professional help-seeking behaviors from Asian Americans. *Professional Psychology: Research & Practice, 37*(4), 407–415.

39. U.S. Department of Health and Human Services. (2001). *Mental health: Culture, race and ethnicity—A supplement to, Mental health: A report to the Surgeon General.* Rockville, MD: U.S. Department of Health and Human Services, Public Health Service, Office of the Surgeon General.

40. J. L. Chin. (1998). Mental health services and treatment. In L. C. Lee & N.W.S. Zane (Eds.), *Handbook of Asian American psychology* (pp. 485–504). Thousand Oaks, CA: Sage.

41. R. G. Blair. (2000). Risk factors associated with PTSD and major depression among Cambodian refugees. *Health and Social Work, 25,* 23–30.

42. U.S. Department of Health and Human Services (2001).

43. B. Greene. (2007). Delivering ethical psychological services to lesbian, gay, and bisexual clients. In *Handbook of counseling and psychotherapy with lesbian, gay, bisexual, and transgender clients* (2nd ed.). Washington, DC: American Psychological Association.

44. C. Matthews. (2007). Affirmative lesbian, gay, and bisexual counseling with all clients. In *Handbook of counseling and psychotherapy with lesbian, gay, bisexual, and transgender clients* (2nd ed.). Washington, DC: American Psychological Association.

45. R. A. Zakalik & M. Wei. (2006). Adult attachment, perceived discrimination based on sexual orientation, and depression in gay males: Examining the mediation and moderation effects. *Journal of Counseling Psychology, 53*(3), 302–313.

46. K. A. Brennan, C. L. Clark, & P. R. Shaver. (1998). Self-report measurement of adult attachment: an integrative overview. In J. A. Simpson & W. S. Rholes (Eds.), *Attachment theory and close relationships* (pp. 46–76). New York: Guilford Press.

47. R. M. Diaz, G. Ayala, E. Bein, J. Henne, & B. Marin. (2001). The impact of homophobia, poverty, and racism on the mental health of gay and bisexual Latino men: findings from three U.S. cities. *American Journal of Public Health, 91,* 927–932.

48. A. R. D'Augelli. (1992). Lesbian and gay male undergraduate's experiences of harassment and fear on campus. *Journal of Interpersonal Violence, 7,* 383–395.

49. S. D. Cochran, J. G. Sullivan, & V. M. Mays. (2003). Prevalence of mental disorders, psychological distress, and mental health services use among lesbian, gay, and bisexual adults in the United States. *Journal of Consulting and Clinical Psychology, 71*(1), 53–61.

50. P. Gibson. (2006). *Gay male and lesbian suicide.* Retrieved May 2, 2006, from http://lambda.org/youth_suicide.htm.

51. Gibson (2006).

52. A. Bell & M. Weinberg. (1978). *Homosexualities: A study of diversity among men and women.* New York: Simon & Shuster.

53. Bell & Weinberg (1978).

54. K. Jay & A. Young. (1977). *The gay report: Lesbians and gay men speak out about their sexual experiences and lifestyles.* New York: Summit.

55. N. L. Thompson, B. R. McCandless, & B. R. Strickland. (1971). Personal adjustment of male and female homosexuals and heterosexuals. *Journal of Abnormal Psychology, 78,* 237–240.

56. M. C. Zea, C. A. Reisen, & P. J. Poppen. (1999). Psychological well-being among Latino lesbians and gay men. *Cultural Diversity and Ethnic Minority Psychology, 5*(4), 371–379.

57. Zea et al. (1999).

CHAPTER 8

1. R. J. Comer. (2004). *Abnormal psychology* (5th ed.). New York: Worth.

2. American Psychological Association. (1993). *Practice guideline for major depressive disorder in adults.* Washington, DC: Author.

3. D. Widloecher. (2001). The treatment of affects: An interdisciplinary issue. *Psychoanalytic Quarterly, 70*(1), 243–264.

4. Comer (2004).

5. F. Leichseuring. (2001). Comparative effects of short-term psychodynamic psychotherapy and cognitive-behavioral therapy in depression: A meta-analytic approach. *Clinical Psychology Review, 21*(3), 401–419.

6. S. Junger. (1997). *The perfect storm: A true story of men against the sea.* New York: W. W. Norton & Company.

7. T. Szasz. (1960). The myth of mental illness. *American Psychologist, 15,* 113–118.

8. A. Ellis. (1961). *A guide to rational living.* Englewood Cliffs, NJ: Prentice-Hall.

9. A. Beck, A. (2002). Cognitive models of depression. In R. L. Leahy & E. T. Dowds (Eds.), *Clinical advances in cognitive psychotherapy: Theory and application* (pp. 29–61). New York: Springer.

10. P. Rohde, J. R. Seeley, N. K. Kaufman, G. N. Clarke, & E. Stice. (2006). Predicting time to recovery among depressed adolescents treated in two psychosocial group interventions. *Journal of Consulting and Clinical Psychology, 74*(1), 80–88.

11. Z. V. Segal, S. Kennedy, M. Gemar, K. Hood, R. Pedersen, & T. Buis. (2006). Cognitive reactivity to sad mood provocation and the prediction of depressive relapse. *Archives of general psychiatry, 63,* 749–755.

12. R. J. DeRubeis, S. D. Hollon, J. D. Amsterdam, R. C. Shelton, P. R. Young, R. M. Salomon, et al. (2001). Cognitive therapy vs. medications in treatment of moderate to severe depression. *Archives of General Psychiatry, 62,* 397–408.

13. D. R. Hopko, C. W. Lejuez, K. J. Ruggiero, & G. H. Eifert. (2003). Contemporary behavioral activation treatments for depression: Procedures, principles, and progress. *Clinical Psychology Review, 23,* 699–717.

14. L. P. Rehm. (1995). Psychotherapies for depression. In K. D. Craig & K. S. Dobson (Eds.), *Anxiety and depression in adults and children* (pp. 183–208). Thousand Oaks, CA: Sage, p. 202.

15. B. F. Skinner. (1953). *Science and human behavior.* New York: Free Press.

16. C. B. Ferster. (1973). A functional analysis of depression. *American Psychologist, 28,* 857–870.

17. Ferster (1973).

18. P. M. Lewinsohn, J. M. Sullivan, & S. J. Grosscup. (1980). Changing reinforcing events: An approach to the treatment of depression. *Psychotherapy: Theory, Research and Practice, 47,* 322–334.

19. N. S. Jacobson, K. S. Dobson, P. A. Truax, M. E. Addis, K. Koerner, J. K. Gollan, et al. (1996). A component analysis of cognitive-behavioral treatment for depression. *Journal of Consulting and Clinical Psychology, 64,* 295–304.

20. S.R.H. Black & D. Jones. (2002). Marital and family therapy for depression in adults. In I. H. Gotlib & C. L. Hammen (Eds.), *Handbook of depression* (pp. 422–440). New York: Guilford.

21. A. M. Zeiss, P. M. Lewinsohn, & R. F. Munoz. (1979). Nonspecific improvement effects in depression using interpersonal cognitive, and pleasant events focused treatments. *Journal of Consulting and Clinical Psychology, 47,* 427–439.

22. Jacobson et al. (1996).

23. M. W. Otto, J. A. Pava, & S. Sprich-Buckminster. (1996). Treatment of major depression: Application and efficacy of cognitive-behavioral therapy. In M. H. Pollack & M. W. Otto (Eds.), *Challenges in clinical practice: Pharmacologic and psychosocial strategies* (pp. 31–52). New York: Guilford Press.

24. C. W. Lejuez, D. R. Hopko, & S. D. Hopko. (2001). A brief behavioral activation treatment for depression: Treatment manual. *Behavior Modification, 25,* 255–286.

25. Hopko et al. (2003).

26. M. M. Weissman, J. C. Markowitz, & G. L. Klerman. (2000). *Comprehensive guide to interpersonal psychotherapy.* New York, Basic Books.

27. M. L. Bruce & K. M. Kim. (1992). Differences in the effects of divorce on major depression in men and women. *American Journal of Psychiatry, 149,* 914–917.

28. Black & Jones. (2002).

29. G. S. Diamond, B. F. Reis, G. M. Diamond, L. E. Siqueland, & L. Isaacs. (2002). Attachment-based family therapy for depressed adolescents: A treatment development study. *Journal of the American Academy of Child and Adolescent Psychiatry, 41,* 1190–1196.

30. D. A. Brent, D. Holder, D. Kolko, B. Birmaher, M. Baugher, C. Roth, et al. (1997). A clinical psychotherapy trial for adolescent depression comparing cognitive, family, and supportive therapy. *Archives of General Psychiatry, 54*(9), 877–885.

CHAPTER 9

1. M. Sandler. (1990). Monoamine oxidase inhibitors in depression: History and mythology. *Journal of Psychopharmacology, 4,* 136–139.

2. H. P. Loomer, J. C. Saunders, & N. S. Klein. (1957). A clinical and pharmacodynamic evaluation of iproniazid as a psychic energizer. *Psychiatric Research Reports of the American Psychiatric Association, 135*(8), 129–141.

3. J. Rosack. (2006). MAOI skin patch wins FDA approval for depression. *Psychiatric News, 41*(7), 31.

4. R. Kuhn. (1958). The treatment of depressive states with G22355 (imipramine hydrochloride). *American Journal of Psychiatry, 115*(5), 459–464.

5. M. J. Gitlin, R. Suri, L. Altshuler, J. Zuckerbrow-Miller, & L. Fairbanks. (2002). Bupropion-sustained release as a treatment for SSRI-induced sexual side effects. *Sex & Marital Therapy, 28*(2), 131–138.

6. Federal Drug Administration. (2006). *FDA approves first drug for seasonal depression.* Retrieved June 12, 2007, from http://www.fad.gov.bbs.topics/NEWS/2006/NEWo1388.html.

7. K. L. Swartz. (2007). *Depression and anxiety: Johns Hopkins white papers.* Baltimore, MD: Johns Hopkins Medicine.

8. FDA (2006).

9. FDA (2006).

10. K. Swartz. (2006). *Depression and anxiety: Johns Hopkins white papers.* Baltimore, MD: Johns Hopkins Medicine.

11. M. S. Milane, M. A. Suchard, M. L. Wong, & J. Licinio. (2006). Modeling of the temporal patterns of fluoxetine prescriptions and suicide rates in the United States. *Public Library of Science Medicine, 3,* 816.

12. FDA (2006).

13. A. L. Berman, D. A. Jobes, & M. M. Silverman. (2006). *Adolescent suicide: Assessment and intervention* (2nd ed.). Washington, DC: American Psychological Association.

14. FDA (2006).

15. FDA (2006).

16. FDA (2006).

17. Harvard Medical School. (Sept. 2006). Improving care for depression. *Harvard Mental Health Letter, 23*(3), 1–3.

18. Depression and Bipolar Support Alliance. (2006). *The state of depression in America.* Retrieved March 3, 2007, from http://www.dbsalliance.org/site/PageServer?pagename=about_initiatives_stateofdepression.

19. Berman et al. (2006).

20. B. N. Gaynes, A. J. Rush, M. Trivedi, S. R. Wisniewski, G. K. Galasubramani, D. C. Spencer, et al. (2005). A direct comparison of presenting characteristics of depressed outpatients from primary vs. specialty care settings: preliminary findings from the STAR*D clinical trial. *General Hospital Psychiatry, 25*(1), 119–142.

21. American Psychological Association. (1993). *Practice guideline for major depressive disorder in adults.* Washington, DC: Author.

22. FDA (2006).

23. Harvard Medical School. (February, 2007). Electroconvulsive therapy. *Harvard Mental Health Letter, 23*(8), 1–4.

24. K. Dukakis & L. Tye, L. (2006). *Shock: The healing power of electroconvulsive therapy.* New York: Penguin.

25. FDA (2006).

26. FDA (2006).

27. Swartz (2007).

28. B. D. Goldman. (1999). The circadian time system and reproduction in mammals. *Steroids, 64*(9), 679–685.

29. N. E. Rosenthal & M. C. Blehar. (Eds.). (1989). *Seasonal affective disorder & phototherapy.* New York: Guilford.

30. C. T. Teng, D. Akerman, T. A. Cordás, S. Kaspar, & A.H.G. Vierira. (1995). Seasonal affective disorder in a tropical country: A case report. *Psychiatry Research, 56*(1), 11–15.

31. K. P. Ebmeier, A. Berge, D. Semple, P. Shah, & D. Steele. (2004). Biological treatments in mood disorders. In M. Power (Ed.), *Mood disorders: A handbook of science and practice.* Chichester, UK: John Wiley and Sons, Ltd.

32. J. K. McNeil, E. M. LeBlanc, & M. Joyner. (1991). The effect of exercise on depressive symptoms in the moderately depressed elderly. *Psychology and Aging, 6*(3), 487–488.

33. FDA (2006).

34. P. Wu, C. Fuller, X. Liu, H.-C. Lee, B. Fan, C. W. Hoven, et al. (2007). Use of complementary and alternative medicine among women with depression: Results of a national survey. *Psychiatric Services, 58*(3), 349–356.

35. McNeil et al. (1991).

36. K. Linde, G. Ramirez, C. D. Mulrow, A. Pauls, W. Weidenhammer, & D. Melchart. (1996). St. John's Wort for depression—an overview and meta-analysis of randomized clinical trials. *British Medical Journal, 313,* 253–258.

37. A. A. Nierenberg & D. Mischoulon. (2005). St. John's Wort for depression: What's next? Paper read at *Natural Remedies for Psychiatric Disorders: Considering the Alternatives.* Harvard University School of Medicine and Massachusetts General Hospital, Boston, MA, June 24–26, 2005.

38. Linde et al. (1996).

39. A. L. Stoll. (2005). Omega-3 fatty acids in mood disorders. Paper read at, *Natural Remedies for Psychiatric Disorders: Considering the Alternatives.* Harvard Medical School and Massachusetts General Hospital, Boston, MA, June 24–26, 2005.

40. J. R. Hibbeln. (1998). Seafood consumption, the DHA content of mothers' milk, and prevalence rates of postpartum depression: A cross-national, ecological analysis. *Journal of Affective Disorders, 69,* 15–29.

41. Nierenberg & Mischoulon (2005).

42. B. D. Goldman. (1999). The circadian timing system and reproduction in mammals. *Steroids, 64*(9), 679–685.

43. FDA (2006).

44. A. Wirz-Justice & R. H. Van den Hoofdakker. (1999). Sleep deprivation in depression: What do we know where do we go? *Biological Psychiatry, 46*(4), 445–453.

45. J. E. Alpert. (2005). SAM-e, folate & B12: One carbon metabolism and depression. Paper presented at *Natural Remedies for Psychiatric Disorders: Considering*

the Alternatives. Harvard Medical School and Massachusetts General Hospital, June 24–26, 2005, Boston, MA.

46. M. J. Taylor, S. M. Carney, G. M. Goodwin, & J. R. Geddes. (2004). Folate for depressive disorders: Systematic review and meta-analysis of randomized controlled trials. *Journal of Psychopharmocology, 18*(2), 251–256.

CHAPTER 10

1. National Institute of Mental Health. (2003). *Depression: A treatable illness.* Retrieved January 5, 2007, from http://menanddepression.nimh.nih.gov/inforpage.asp?jd=15.

2. I. Elkin, M. T. Shea, J. T. Watkins, S. D. Imber, S. M. Sotsky, J. F. Collins, et al. (1989). National Institute of Mental Health Treatment of Depression Collaborative Research Program: General effectiveness of treatments. *Archives of General Psychiatry, 46,* 971–982.

3. K. Swartz. (2007). *Depression and anxiety: The Johns Hopkins white papers.* Baltimore, MD: Johns Hopkins Medicine.

4. Swartz. (2007).

5. M. Olfson & G. L. Klerman. (1993). Trends in the prescription of antidepressants by office-based psychiatrists. *American Journal of Psychiatry, 150,* 571–577.

6. CNN. (2007). *CDC: Antidepressants most prescribed drugs in US.* Retrieved April 3, 2007, from http://www.cnn.com/2007/HEALTH/07/09/antidepressants/index.html?eref=rss_topstories.

7. M. J. Gitlin, R. Suri, L. Altshuler, J. Zuckerbrow-Miller, & L. Fairbanks. (2002). Bupropion-sustained release as a treatment for SSRI-induced sexual side effects. *Sex & Marital Therapy, 28*(2), 131–138.

8. Swartz. (2007).

9. S. D. Hollon, R. J. DeRubeis, R. C. Shelton, & B. Weiss. (2002). The emperor's new drugs: effect size and moderation effects. *Prevention & Treatment* 5:Article 28. Retrieved August 2, 2007, from http://www.journals.apa.org/prevention/volume5/toc-jul15–02.html.

10. M. M. Weissman, J. C. Markowitz, & G. L. Klerman. (2000). *Comprehensive guide to interpersonal psychotherapy.* New York, Basic Books.

11. Swartz. (2007).

12. Hollon et al. (2002).

13. J. Scott. (2007). Bipolar disorders. In C. Freeman & M. Powers (Eds.), *Handbook of evidence-based psychotherapies: A guide for research and practice* (pp. 301–313). West Sussex, England: John Wiley & Sons, Ltd.

14. G. Emslie, C. Kratochvil, B. Vitello, S. Silva, T. Mayes, S. McNulty, et al. (2006). Treatment for adolescents with depression study (TADS): Safety results. *Journal of the American Academy of Child and Adolescent Psychiatry, 45*(12), 1440–1445.

15. R. F. Farmer & R. O. Nelson-Gray. (2005). *Personality-guided behavior therapy.* Washington, DC: American Psychological Association.

16. Harvard Medical School. (Sept. 2006). Improving care for depression. *Harvard Mental Health Letter, 23*(3), 1–3.

17. J. S. Kahan, J. M. Mitchell, B. J. Kemp, & R. H. Adkins. (2006). *Rehabilitation Psychology, 51*(1), 13–22.

18. D. J. Miklowitz, M. W. Otto, E. Frank, N. A. Reilly-Harrington, S. R. Wisniewski, J. N. Kogan, et al. (2007). Psychosocial treatments for bipolar depression. *Archives of General Psychiatry, 64,* 419–427.

19. Scott. (2007).

20. M. E. Lickey & B. Gordon. (1991). *Medicine and mental illness: The use of drugs in psychiatry.* New York: W. H. Freeman.

21. R. F. Prien, E. M. Caffey, & C. J. Klett. (1974). Factors associated with treatment success in lithium carbonate prophylaxis. *Archives of General Psychiatry, 31,* 189–192.

22. C. L. Bowden. (2001). Strategies to reduce misdiagnosis of bipolar depression. *Psychiatric Services, 52*(1), 51–55.

23. J. W. Jefferson & J. H. Greist. (1994). Mood disorders. In R. E. Hales, S. C. Yudofsky, & J. A. Talbott (Eds.), *The American Psychiatric Press textbook of psychiatry* (2nd ed.). Washington, DC: American Psychiatric Press.

24. Scott. (2007).

25. Scott. (2007).

26. Scott. (2007).

27. Swartz. (2007).

28. American Academy of Child & Adolescent Psychiatry. (2004). *Facts for families: Bipolar disorder in children and teens,* No. 38, June, 2004. Retrieved May 4, 2007, from http://www.aacap.org/cs/root/facts_for_families/bipolar_disorder_in_children_and_teens.

29. World Health Organization. (2000). *Women's mental health: An evidence-based review* (WHO/MSD/MHP00.1). Geneva: World Health Organization.

30. R. M. Nonacs & L. S. Cohen. (1998). Postpartum mood disorders: Diagnosis and treatment guidelines. *Journal of Clinical Psychiatry, 59*(Suppl. 2), 34–40.

31. Alaska Federal Health Care Agreement. (1993). *Depression in primary care: Detection, diagnosis, and treatment.* Rockville, MD: U.S. Department of Health and Human Services.

32. M. W. O'Hara, S. Scott, L. L. Gorman, & A. Wenzel. (2000). Efficacy of interpersonal psychotherapy for postpartum depression. *Archives of General Psychiatry, 57,* 1039–1045.

33. R. Nonacs, A. C. Viguera, & L. S. Cohen. (2005). Psychiatric aspects of pregnancy. In S. G. Kornstein & A. H. Clayton (Eds.), *Women's mental health* (pp. 70–90). New York: Guilford.

34. O'Hara et al. (2000).

35. C. Zlotnick, S. L. Johnson, I. W. Miller, T. Pearlstein, & M. Howard. (2001). Postpartum depression in women receiving public assistance: Pilot study of an interpersonal-therapy-oriented group intervention. *American Journal of Psychiatry, 158*(4), 638–640.

36. *Postpartum depression and caring for your baby.* Retrieved February 6, 2006, from http://www.kidshealth.org/parent/pregnancy_newborn/home/ppd_baby_p7.html.

37. Swartz. (2007).

38. J. E. Gillham. (2003). Targeted preventive is not enough. *Prevention and Treatment*, 6. Retrieved March 7, 2006, from http://content.apa.org/journals/pre/6/1/17c.html.

39. A. L. Berman, D. A. Jobes, & M. M. Silverman. (2006). *Adolescent suicide: Assessment and intervention.* Washington, DC: American Psychological Association.

40. Depression and Bipolar Support Alliance. (2006). *The state of depression in America.* Retrieved January 15, 2007, from http://www.dbsalliance.org/pdfs/wpsearchable.pdf.

41. J. Prior. (1999). *Gender and mental health.* New York: New York University Press.

42. World Health Organization. (2000).

43. Depression and Bipolar Support Alliance. (2006).

Resources

During the course of researching the topics for this book, I came across many very valuable and helpful resources that I would like to share. Of course, anyone who wishes to get into a topic more thoroughly can review the materials in the notes. However, here is a short list of organizations, Web sites, articles, and books that were particularly helpful.

ORGANIZATIONS

American Association of Suicidology
5221 Wisconsin Avenue, NW
Washington, DC 20015
Ph: 202-237-2280
www.suicidology.org

American Psychiatric Association
1000 Wilson Blvd., Ste. 1825
Arlington, VA 22209-7300
Ph: 703-907-7300
www.psych.org

American Psychological Association
750 First St., NE
Washington, DC 20002-4242
Ph: 800-374-2721/202-336-5500
www.apa.org

Depression and Bipolar Support alliance
730 N. Franklin, Ste. 501

Chicago, IL 60610-0049
Ph: 800-826-3632/312-642-0049
www.dbsalliance.org

Depression and Related Affective Disorders Association
2330 West Joppa Road, Ste. 100
Lutherville, MD 21093
Ph: 410-583-2919
www.drada.org

MacArthur Initiative on Depression and Primary Care
www.depression-primarycare.org

National Alliance of the Mentally Ill
Colonial Place Three
2107 Wilson Blvd., Ste. 300
Arlington, VA 22201
Ph: 800-950-6264
www.nami.org

National Center on Caregiving
Ph: 800-445-8106
www.caregiver.org

National Institute of Mental Health
6001 Executive Blvd.
Bethesda, MD 20892-9663
Ph: 866-615-6464/301-443-4513
www.nimh.nih.gov

National Mental Health Association
2001 N. Beauregard St., 12th Floor
Alexandra, VA 22311
Ph: 800-969-NMHA/703-684-7722
www.nmha.org

Robert Woods Johnson Foundation
Depression in Primary Care
www.wpic.pitt.edu/dppc

WEB SITES

Depression. National Institute of Mental Health. (2000). Available: http://www.nimh.
    nih.gov/publicat/depression.cfm.
Depression among older adults. National Institutes of Health. (2007). Available: http://
    www.nihseniorhealth.gov/depression/toc.html.

Depression: A treatable illness. National Institute of Mental Health. (2003). Available: http://menanddepression.nimh.nih.gov/inforpage.asp?jd=15.

Depression during and after pregnancy. Womanshealth. (2005). Available: http://www.4women.gov/faq/postpartum.htm.

Depression in older adults and the elderly: Signs, symptoms, causes and treatments. Helpguide. (2006). Available: http://www.helpguide/org/mental/depression_elderly.htm.

Facts for families: Bipolar disorder in children and teens, No. 38, June, 2004. American Academy of Child & Adolescent Psychiatry. (2004). Available: http://www.aacap.org/cs/root/facts_for_families/bipolar_disorder_in_children_and_teens.

Gay male and lesbian suicide, by P. Gibson. (2006). Available: http://lambda.org/youth_suicide.htm.

Men and depression. National Institute of Mental Health. (2005). NIMH Publication No. 05-4972. Available: http://www.menanddepression.nimh.nih.gov/infopage.asp?id=10.

Mental health: Culture, race and ethnicity—Supplement. Mental Health: A Report of the Surgeon General. (1999). Available: http://mentalhealth.samhsa.gov/cre/toc.asp.

NIMH fact sheets on depression and other illnesses. National Institute of Mental Health (2002). Available: http://www.nimh.nih.gov/publicat/coocurmenu.cfm.

Postpartum depression, by K. A. Leopold, & L. B. Zoschnick. (2005). Available: http://www.obgyn.het/femalepatient/default.asp?page=leopold.

Postpartum depression and caring for your baby. Available: http://www.kidshealth.org/parent/pregnancy_newborn/home/ppd_baby_p7.html.

BOOKS AND ARTICLES

American Psychological Association. (2006). *Handbook of counseling and psychotherapy with lesbian, gay, bisexual, and transgender clients* (2nd ed.). Washington, DC: Author.

American Psychiatric Association. (1998). *Let's talk facts about depression.* Washington, DC: Author.

American Psychological Association. (1993). *Practice guideline for major depressive disorder in adults.* Washington, DC: Author.

Bell, A., & M. Weinberg. (1978). *Homosexualities: A study of diversity among men and women,* New York: Simon & Shuster.

Berman, A. L., D. A. Jobes, & M. M. Silverman. (2006). *Adolescent suicide: Assessment and intervention* (2nd ed.). Washington, DC: American Psychological Association.

Cochran, S. V., & F. Rabinowitz. (2000). *Men and depression: Clinical and empirical perspectives,* San Diego, CA: Academic Press.

Culbertson, F. M. (1997). Depression and gender: An international review. *American Psychologist, 52,* 25–31.

Dukakis, K., & L. Tye. (2006). *Shock: The healing power of electroconvulsive therapy,* New York: Penguin.

Emslie, G. C., B. Kratochvil, B. Vitello, S. Silva, T. Mayes, S. McNulty, et al. (2006). Treatment for adolescents with depression study (TADS): Safety results.

Journal of the American Academy of child and Adolescent Psychiatry, 45(12), 1440–1445.

Fouad, N. A., & P. Arredondo. (2007). *Becoming culturally oriented: Practical advice for psychologists and educators.* Washington, DC: American Psychological Association.

Freeman, C., & M. Powers (Eds.). (2007). *Handbook of evidence-based psychotherapies: A guide for research and practice.* West Sussex, England: John Wiley & Sons, Ltd.

Gotlib, I. H., & C. L. Hammer (Eds.). (2002). *Handbook of depression.* New York: Guilford Press.

Jay, K., & A. Young. (1977). *The gay report: Lesbians and gay men speak out about their sexual experiences and lifestyles.* New York: Summit.

Lickey, M. E., & B. Gordon. (1991). *Medicine and mental illness: The use of drugs in psychiatry.* New York: W. H. Freeman.

McGrath, E., G. P. Keita, B. Strickland, & N. F. Russo. (1990). *Women and depression: Risk factors and treatment issues,* Washington, DC: American Psychological Association.

McIntosh, J. L. (1991). *Lifespan perspectives of suicide.* New York: Plenum Press.

Nolen-Hoeksema, S. (1990). *Sex differences in depression,* Stanford, CA: Stanford University Press.

Nydegger, R. (2006). Postpartum depression: More than the "baby blues?" In T. G. Plante (Ed.), *Mental disorders of the new millennium* (vol. 3). Westport, CT: Praeger.

Papolos, D., & Papolos, J. (2006). *The bipolar child* (3rd ed.). New York: Broadway Books.

Pleck, J. (1981). *The myth of masculinity.* Cambridge, MA: MIT Press.

Power, M. (Ed.). (2004). *Mood disorders: A handbook of science and practice.* Chichester, UK: John Wiley and Sons, Ltd.

Prior, J. (1999). *Gender and mental health,* New York: New York University Press.

Real, T. (1997). *I don't want to talk about it: Overcoming the secret legacy of male depression.* New York: Fireside.

Rosenthal, N. E., & M. C. Blehar (Eds.). (1989). *Seasonal affective disorders and phototherapy.* New York: Guilford Press.

Shneidman, E. S. (2001). *Comprehending suicide: Landmarks in 20th century suicidology.* Washington, DC: American Psychological Association.

Swartz, K. L. (2006, 2007, 2008). *Depression and anxiety: Johns Hopkins white papers.* Baltimore, MD: Johns Hopkins Medicine.

Tiihonen, J., Lönnquist, J., Wahlbeck, K., Klaukka, T., Tanskanen, A., & Haukka, J. (2006). Antidepressants and the risk of suicide, attempted suicide and overall mortality in a nationwide cohort. *Archives of General Psychiatry, 63*(12), 1358–1367.

Torrey, E. F., & M. B. Knable. (2002). *Surviving manic depression: A manual on bipolar disorder for patients, families, and providers.* New York: Basic Books.

U.S. Department of Health and Human Services. (1993). *Depression in primary care: Detection, diagnosis, and treatment.* Alaska Federal Health Care Agreement. Rockville, MD: Author.

Index

About the Author

RUDY NYDEGGER is Chief of the Division of Psychology at Ellis Hospital in Schenectady, New York, and a Clinical and Consulting Psychologist in practice for more than 30 years. He is former President of the New York Psychological Association, and current Chair of the Legal and Legislative Committee for the organization. He is also Full Professor of Management and Psychology at Union Graduate College and Union College, and has also been involved in teaching for more than 30 years.